The Struggle for Amazon Town

THE STRUGGLE
FOR AMAZON TOWN

Gurupá Revisited

Richard Pace

LYNNE
RIENNER
PUBLISHERS

BOULDER
LONDON

Published in the United States of America in 1998 by
Lynne Rienner Publishers, Inc.
1800 30th Street, Boulder, Colorado 80301

and in the United Kingdom by
Lynne Rienner Publishers, Inc.
3 Henrietta Street, Covent Garden, London WC2E 8LU

Library of Congress Cataloging-in-Publication Data
Pace, Richard, 1956–
    The struggle for Amazon Town : Gurupá revisited / Richard Pace.
       p.   cm.
    Includes bibliographical references and index.
    ISBN 1-55587-339-1 (alk. paper).
    ISBN 1-55587-352-9 (pbk. alk. paper)
    1. Gurupá (Pará, Brazil)—Politics and government.   2. Gurupá
(Pará, Brazil)—Social conditions.   3. Gurupá (Pará, Brazil)—
Economic conditions.   4. Social conflict—Brazil—Gurupá (Pará)—
History—20th century.   5. Social movements—Brazil—Gurupá (Pará)—
History—20th century.   I. Title.
F2651.G98P3   1997
981'.15—DC21   97-242
                                                                    CIP

British Cataloguing in Publication Data
A Cataloguing in Publication record for this book
is available from the British Library.

Printed and bound in the United States of America

      The paper used in this publication meets the requirements
∞ of the American National Standard for Permanence of
      Paper for Printed Library Materials Z39.48-1984.

    5 4 3 2 1

To Olga

CONTENTS

Illustrations

Map

ACKNOWLEDGMENTS

There are many individuals and institutions to thank for assistance in the completion of this book. Foremost I wish to express my gratitude for the patience and guidance given me by the late Charles Wagley. One could not ask for a better teacher, scholar, researcher, and friend. I also thank Marianne Schmink of the University of Florida for her skillful assistance in the planning, development, and execution of this work. Additionally, Conrad Kottak of the University of Michigan offered much appreciated aid in the design of the television research, as well as generously providing financial assistance from his National Institution of Mental Health grant.

I thank the Federal University of Pará and the Nucleus for Advanced Studies of the Amazon for important support—in particular, I appreciate the personal attention I received from Samuel Sá. His insights into the workings of the Catholic Church in the Amazon region were very valuable. The Museu Goeldi also aided me at critical junctures of research. Arlene Kelly, formerly of the Museu, provided me with invaluable historical insight and helped me establish initial contacts in Gurupá.

I acknowledge the financial support given me by the University of Florida Amazon Research and Training Program, the University of Wyoming Anthropology Department, and the Fulbright Fellowship program. None of these organizations, of course, are responsible for the content or views expressed in this book.

I extend my gratitude to David Keeling, a cultural geographer from Western Kentucky University, for his valuable comments on the manuscript. I am also indebted to Olga Torres Pace, my wife, for her assistance and support throughout the process of creating this book.

Finally, the anthropological tradition of protecting the identity of consultants prevents me from directly acknowledging the many acquaintances and good friends I made in Gurupá. But I will always value my memories of them and the lessons they have taught me.

Richard Pace

1

INTRODUCTION:
STUDYING AMAZON TOWN AGAIN

During many trips between 1942 and 1961 Charles Wagley studied a small rural community located on the lower Amazon River in the state of Pará, Brazil. From this fieldwork, and from work undertaken by his colleague Eduardo Galvão, in 1953 Wagley produced a book that many today consider the classic statement about indigenous *camponês* (small-farm) life in Amazonia, *Amazon Town: A Study of Man in the Tropics* (1976). I remember reading the book as a graduate student of Wagley in the early 1980s and being fascinated by its descriptive detail of life set in such an exotic environment. I also remember a telling passage in the 1968 edition in which Wagley made the following observation about the community he called Itá—a pseudonym for the town and municipality of Gurupá:

> The lethargy and backwardness of Itá, and of all similar communities, is a threat to the world, not just to Brazil. People cannot continue to be illiterate, hungry, badly clothed, ill-informed, sick, and deprived of the minimum facilities of a modern community without seeking in desperation for some formula to provide them with rapid change during their lifetime. . . . *They will not remain passive for long.* (1968 ed.:311; emphasis added)

This passage stuck in my mind as I ventured to Gurupá in 1983 to initiate a new study of the community. Although almost twenty years had passed since Wagley's words were written, I felt very much forewarned about the political climate I encountered. Decades of struggle against hunger, poor health, scant education, and limited economic opportunity had erupted into social turmoil. Gurupá was no longer the serene little community of 1948 Wagley had described but one of many political hotbeds of conflict simmering along the Amazon as people struggled for land, resources, and livelihood.

During my stay in Gurupá, when I stood in the streets of the town and listened closely, I overheard ideological battles pitting small farmers and extractors of forest products against merchants and large landowners, poor

Amazonia and Gurupá

Lawrence Guy Perry, 1992

Atlantic Ocean

Caribbean Sea

Pacific Ocean

BRAZIL

Belém-Brasília Hwy.

Bragança

Belém

Marabá

PARÁ

Macapá

AMAPÁ

Santarém

Altamira

SURINAME

FRENCH
GUIANA

GUYANA

VENEZUELA

RORAIMA

Boa Vista

Pôrto Velho

RONDÔNIA

Guajará Mirim

BOLIVIA

COLOMBIA

AMAZONAS

Rio
Branco

ACRE

PERU

ECUADOR

PANAMA

Trans Amazon Hwy.

Madeira R.

Amazon R.

Branco R.

Negro R.

Japurá R.

Solimões R.

Purus R.

Juruá R.

Xingu R.

Tocantins R.

Araguaia R.

Tapajós R.

(Inset map)

Pucurui R.

Bacá R.

Gurupá

Great Island of Gurupá

Baquiá R.

Moju R.

Jocojó R.

Mayau R.

Gurupá

Maracoá

Amazon R.

Carrazedo

Macacos

against rich, and when the rhetoric became heated, communist against capitalist. The words, I was to learn, were backed by action. Mirroring political actions taken by other groups in Amazonia, people in Gurupá joined to challenge the local status quo. Some formed a variety of cooperatives to buy and sell goods, bypassing local merchants and their inevitable price markups. Many joined to organize a workers' political party (Partido dos Trabalhadores) and reorganize the local rural union to pursue land rights for the poor, to improve agricultural production, and to preserve the forest from destructive uses. Many participated in rallies to protest political irregularities by local leaders. Some even organized human blockades (called *empates*) to stop evictions of their neighbors from contested land or to thwart extraction of forest resources by outside interests. Conversely, there were reprisals against these activists. Retaliations ranged from slander on public-address systems to destruction of property and death threats (unlike many other places in Amazonia, to date there have been no political murders in Gurupá).

As I conducted my research in 1983, and again in 1984, 1985, 1986, 1990, and 1991, the economic and political changes sweeping the community fascinated me. The Amazon region during this period reverberated from the impact of two decades of massive economic development projects: highways through virgin forest, colonization settlements, timber extraction, hydroelectric dams, cattle ranches, and mines. Conflict, violence, and environmental destruction were integral parts of the process. Although Gurupá was not the site of any of these projects, it was still deeply affected by them.

As a result I became engrossed in the passions of development, political mobilization, and protest. I was drawn into a set of questions about the relationships among the local, regional, and national political economies. I wanted to find out how development—or underdevelopment—affects people, how Gurupaenses (people from Gurupá) perceive their social and economic plight, and how they unite to try to improve their living conditions.

To understand these questions I found myself paying special attention to certain aspects of social existence, most notably, social class, labor relations, wealth production and accumulation, resource use and depletion, political power, and social conflict. In Gurupá this meant analyzing the rise and fall of extractive industries, such as rubber, timber, and palmito; changes in agricultural production; trends in deforestation; patterns of migration; the impact of wage labor; the vicissitudes of local and national politics—including the church/state conflict and the rise of an opposition political party and rural union; and the local struggle over land and resources between the working and dominant classes. The result of my inquiries, presented here, is a story of struggle and change in Gurupá. It is an interpretation of economic transformation and political upheaval occurring within and beyond the community and the impact on the local human condition.

Why Gurupá?

By all accounts Gurupá is a poor and relatively unimportant place. Although it has a rich history and has experienced nearly every important trend in Amazonia's past, today it is only one of many small, seemingly sleepy river towns that dot the lower Amazon River. So why is Gurupá's story important? How does one benefit from reading about this strange place in a distant land?

Students, colleagues in other disciplines, and even people from Gurupá have often challenged me to answer these questions. There are several ways to respond: The most compelling reason to study Gurupá is that several social scientists have previously studied the community. A restudy, therefore, provides a detailed picture of change through time, something that few anthropologists have the opportunity to do. Besides Wagley's *Amazon Town,* there is Galvão's book on religion, *Santos e Visagens* (1955); a historical dissertation of the area including Gurupá (Kelly 1984); a short anthropological restudy of Wagley's work (Miller 1976); another short anthropological study of the community's health care delivery system and use of medicinal plants (Magee 1986); and a year-long study of economic and political processes in the community by an agricultural economist (Oliveira 1991). From this rich source of information I have fashioned an analysis of the community that stretches over 400 years.

Another response focuses on the value of native views of reality. This is pertinent when trying to explain group behavior that is not predictable from broad theoretical models. June Nash commented on this need in her critique of world systems theory, an approach to history that has typically overlooked native responses to Western capitalism (the problem of the passive periphery). She writes that too much emphasis on broad theoretical approaches leads to a real danger of losing sight of the "internal logico-integrative schema that provides the motivation and apprehension of what is happening in the world" (Nash 1981:408–409). In other words, to understand what people do throughout the world one must first understand how they perceive the world and how they think as groups. One must understand their culture as well as their opportunities and their restrictions. To understand the internal logico-integrative schema, anthropologists traditionally collect detailed information through ethnographies.

Finally, a study of Gurupá is relevant to the understanding of the total development process occurring in Amazonia. To date most research has concentrated on development hot spots, such as sites along the Transamazon Highway and surrounding areas, or on the impact of development upon Native American peoples. Studies covering the more isolated and less affected indigenous camponês communities are limited (Nugent 1993:17; Parker 1985:xxviii). Their exclusion from study is significant because they represent a very large proportion of the Amazon population.

Therefore, a study of Gurupá, a community on the margins of recent development, should add a needed dimension to understanding the overall pattern of Amazonian development.

Interestingly, it was this same lack of political and economic distinction that first attracted anthropological interest to the community. Wagley and Galvão describe Gurupá as a small, poor, underdeveloped peasant community. To Wagley these qualities made Gurupá representative of underlying problems of the Amazon at the time. He wrote, "Because Itá is a poor community without any special industry or natural gifts and without any special distinction, a study of Itá focuses a spotlight on the basic problems of the region" (1976:22).

Since Wagley's study the Amazon has erupted into a complex mosaic of social and environmental changes stemming from development programs, migration, deforestation, and social conflict. This complexity makes Gurupá less representative of regional processes than it might have been at one time. Still, as suggested above, a study of Gurupá can yet add in other ways to an understanding of local, regional, and historical processes that affect the human condition in the Amazon region.

The Study

There are many twists and turns along the path to completing a study such as this. Each will have some impact on a researcher's final interpretations and on the way in which the culture is presented to the reader. In this section I will lay out some of the parameters of the study. I pay special attention to the chain of events leading to my research, the types of assistance I received from consultants and colleagues, the process of establishing rapport in the community, and the general methodology used to collect data.

The beginning of this study dates to 1978. It was then, during a short trip to the port city of Belém, that I first became interested in studying the Brazilian Amazon. At the time I was an undergraduate exchange student in the middle of a year-long stay in the southern city of São Paulo. During the school break in January I toured Brazil, from north to south. The Amazon region intrigued me the most. The exotic beauty of the Amazon, the excitement of development and change, and the drama of social conflict made a lasting impression upon me. I decided on that trip to return someday to increase my understanding of the region.

Three years later I began to realize this goal when I returned to Belém to conduct several months of research for my master's degree in anthropology. I investigated self-help network formation among the poor of a Pentecostal church and a Catholic Christian base community in a large shantytown. During this research I learned firsthand about the urban component of social conflict in Amazonia: struggles for land, jobs, food, and political freedom. I also began researching liberation theology—a progressive social Christianity—which provides a politico-religious framework for mass popular mobilization and protest throughout Amazonia as well as much of Latin America.

Although this research proved eye-opening for me, particularly as it entailed living and working among people struggling against great odds to improve their lives in a shantytown, I decided that I would conduct my dissertation research in the countryside. The urban crowding, noise, and pollution had become too distractive— plus I still wanted to experience more of the beauty of the Amazon River and forest.

Fortunately, at this time I was a graduate student of Charles Wagley at the University of Florida. I approached him for advice on a good location to conduct rural research, and he suggested I do a restudy of Gurupá. I eagerly consented. Doing the restudy appealed to me not only because it would be conducted in the rain forest, but also because it would afford me the opportunity to work very closely with one of the top American Brazilianists of the time on a project he himself had undertaken some thirty years earlier.

I first traveled to Gurupá in May 1983. I had planned to investigate the impact of regional development policies on the local political economy and compare this to published accounts of events occurring in other parts of the Amazon. I had set up a research plan to examine the new industries being established in the area, the changes in agriculture production, the degree of deforestation, the scale of migration, the shifts in labor relations (such as the introduction of wage labor), the changes in local politics, and the rise of social conflict. These were important elements of social change affecting other parts of the Amazon.

After spending two months in Gurupá on this initial trip I realized that my research plan was inadequate to understand what was occurring. For example, there were few new industries operating in the community, there were no innovations in agricultural production, there was limited deforestation, migration into the community was slight, and wage labor was barely present. Yet local politics were explosive with much of the local *campesinato* (small farmers and forest resource extractors), the rural union, and the Catholic Church jointly engaged in an intense struggle with the local dominant class (merchants and large landowners) for control of the political economy. There were also other unanticipated sources of change affecting the community that caught my attention. One was the recent arrival of television, which had opened Gurupá to a new realm of global information.

For my second trip, which was to last eleven months (1984–1985), I prepared anew to study the evolving realities of Gurupá. This time I planned to focus on the unfolding political struggle, particularly the Catholic Church's role in political mobilization and activism. During this second stay in Gurupá, however, I was unexpectedly led back to the issues of economic change and environmental destruction that, although limited in scope in Gurupá compared to other parts of the Amazon, were nonetheless at the root of the political struggle. Again I had to reformulate my research agenda.

During this trip I also began to study in detail the arrival of television. Dr. Conrad Kottak of the University of Michigan had recruited me to be part of a multisite project examining the impact of television throughout Brazil. This collaboration greatly strengthened my understanding of the medium and the types of changes it was bringing to Gurupá. It also allowed me to better understand Gurupá's relation to other Brazilian communities as I compared and contrasted my ethnographic findings with those of other project anthropologists who were working in northeast and south Brazil.

I made three subsequent trips to Gurupá: one in 1986, another in 1990, and a final trip in 1991. These trips allowed me to add detail to my study and to follow the emergence of a strong opposition political movement, an event that was also being played out in many other parts of Amazonia as well as in much of Brazil.

I spent approximately sixteen months doing research in or near Gurupá over the course of my five visits. This included some thirteen months in the municipality of Gurupá, ten of which I spent in the town where I kept a permanent residence, and three months in the countryside with many hosts. Most of the time in the countryside was spent in five hamlets or neighborhoods (Bacá, Jocojó, Camutá, Mojú, and Mararú), while the remaining time was spent on five boat trips surveying approximately 75 percent of the 9,309 square kilometers that comprise the municipality (I did not visit the northwestern part of the municipality). Additionally, I spent one month traveling the Transamazon Highway and descending the Amazon River from Santarém to Gurupá. The remaining two months were spent in Belém and Rio de Janeiro, conducting interviews, meeting with colleagues, buying books, and eating heartily in restaurants to regain weight lost during the rigors of conducting research in a tropical environment.

Data Collection

Much of the information presented in this work is detailed, qualitative data provided by a small number of key consultants—individuals especially enlightened about some aspect of life in the community studied. For this study I singled out twelve key consultants and engaged in extensive dialogue with them. These people were knowledgeable about local events and/or were especially receptive to my presence in Gurupá. Through them I learned about the local culture and ongoing events. I spent long hours in conversation with them and intruded into many facets of their lives. These individuals had a high level of tolerance and patience with my undoubtedly bothersome persistence. I have concluded that their reasons for interacting with me included curiosity, diversion, wishing to be associated with a "high-status" foreigner (in terms of what they considered to be high educational and wealth levels), and simple friendship.

Among my key consultants were storekeepers, small farmers, timber extractors, fishers, day laborers, civil servants, local professionals, and church, union, and political leaders. Two-thirds of these individuals were men, one-third was women. I also found three of Wagley's previous consultants, who graciously consented to many hours of conversation. The names of these consultants, as well as all others, in this work are fictitious to protect their privacy.

Several others assisted my fieldwork. First was Olga Torres Pace, my wife, who accompanied me for seven and a half months. Particularly valuable was her ability to establish rapport for both of us in the community. Through her daily conversations with neighbors (she is a native speaker of Spanish, which enabled her to pick up Portuguese quickly) and through her free haircuts and English classes, Dona Olga (Mrs. Olga), as the people came to call her, became well known in town. The townsfolk, however, were always a little puzzled at her free services. The prevailing opinion was that they were part of a religious *promesa,* or promise, she had made to Saint Benedict—the town's most cherished saint—as repayment for some previous miracle or to protect her from some future harm.

Another important colleague who shared the field experience with me was Brazilian agricultural economist Paulo H. B. Oliveira. We were together in Gurupá for only two days, but our joint research time in the community totaled over two and a half years. I found his insider's, native interpretation of local culture and events extremely helpful as we compared research notes during a meeting in São Paulo in 1991.

I was also fortunate to be visited by anthropologist Conrad Kottak, his wife Betty Kottak, and their son, Nick Kottak, who are, respectively, Wagley's son-in-law, daughter, and grandson. They visited Gurupá for about a week in 1985 to help in the design of the television research and to experience Gurupá, about which they had heard many stories. It was a truly unique experience to introduce Wagley's family to Gurupá. The visit also afforded me the luxury of discussing my ongoing research with Dr. Kottak. We discussed theory and methods while paddling through flooded forests, dining on rice, beans, manioc, and Cokes, and swinging lazily in hammocks during the hot afternoons.

Rapport Building

With Olga's help—and with the good name of Charles Wagley, to whom I always referred whenever introducing myself—rapport building in town was easy. People liked the idea of talking to someone who was writing another book about Gurupá. Politicians, merchants, administrators, farmers, and even figures from the local underworld (smugglers, cattle rustlers) were willing to talk openly about community life. There was a simple charm and basic trust to these discussions that I relished, something that is far more difficult to find in urban settings and, as I later discovered, among the many settlements springing up around the development project areas to the south of Gurupá.

Often an ethnographer can identify an event that really breaks the ice with the local population and leads to the path toward rapport building. It is usually some event that reveals the humanness of the researcher, who, before that event, was perceived as an exotic being, a higher-status individual, a nuisance, or a threat. My event was a trip to the small hamlet of Jocojó. Reaching this destination required traveling several hours by boat followed by an hour's trek into the forest. During the journey I revealed my humanness by slipping and sliding in the mud, falling into a stream, and returning home a dirty, ragged, bruised mess.

As the story about me, the clumsy *americano,* spread throughout Gurupá, so did people's willingness to smile at me, talk to me, and be friendly. It seems that introduction to Amazonian life by baptism with mud created a symbolic tie to others who dealt with such hardships (or avoided them) on a routine basis. The talk of my clumsiness also brought forth tales from the past, when Wagley and Galvão had made a similar trip to Bacá with similar results. They had ventured into the forest with a questionable guide and had wandered through the middle of a swamp. They were forced to wade through knee-deep mud, returning home bedraggled and bruised just as I had. After hearing this story I felt relieved that history was simply repeating itself.

There were two instances in which rapport building was more problematic. One occurred in the countryside of Gurupá among the inhabitants of the many settlements scattered along the numerous waterways. Access to these people was by slow-moving canoe or by relatively expensive diesel motorboat. The motorboat had to be rented and food provided for the captain and assistant. The simple logistics of staying in these communities limited the amount of time I could dedicate to establishing rapport there.

In addition, the main dynamic of Gurupá's struggle for land, resources, and power was occurring in the countryside. This conflict created an uneasiness among the people about strangers, especially odd-looking foreigners who collected data that went to the heart of the local tensions: land tenure, resource use, political affiliation. I tried hard to overcome their suspicions by repeated visits to a few selected communities and frank, open discussions about local, national, and international political economies. General approval of my work by the local priest, who was very influential in the countryside, also aided in rapport building. So did the support I received in the latter stages of research from Paulo Oliveira, who was also active in the countryside.

Still, during the early parts of my research there was hesitation in conversation about politics, which in all honesty was necessary for the protection of various individuals. I did notice that the rural inhabitants conversed more freely about politics in the countryside than in town. As one rural resident commented, "There are too many ears in town that will get workers into trouble if they speak too freely."

The second problem in establishing rapport occurred with the local Catholic priest, Padre Chico, an Italian native who had been living in Gurupá for over a decade when I first met him. Since the Catholic church was an important part of the political struggle taking place I really wished to converse with him. However, in our initial encounters Padre Chico always seemed distracted and reluctant to talk. At first I speculated that the presence of an anthropologist in the community threatened or intimidated him in some way. I knew he had a brother in Italy who was an anthropologist and who conducted research in Africa. Perhaps the padre's knowledge of anthropology led him to reject the discipline on the basis of its relativist treatment of religious beliefs. I also knew he had read the parts of Wagley's book that criticized the church's negative view of local religious festivals in the 1950s (Wagley 1976:213). Although he had stated that he accepted the critique as accurate (see Miller 1976:317), maybe the priest nevertheless determined to shut off my inquiries because of past grievances. This latter assumption proved to be partly true, although the grievances were not with Wagley or Galvão.

As time passed during my fieldwork I realized that the key to the priest's guarded reception was his deep personal commitment to the issue of praxis—the union of theory and action. Padre Chico was very involved with liberation theology, which focuses not only on the spiritual well-being of the laity, but also on the human rights and political economic empowerment of disenfranchised groups. At the time of my stay in Gurupá he was part of a growing movement throughout Brazil that mobilized the poor to pursue their basic rights. Padre Chico had dedicated himself to this goal, and he expected all individuals similarly interested in the political plight of Native Americans, indigenous camponeses, and migrants in the Amazon to similarly use their abilities to empower the powerless. He was wary of outsiders who come to the Amazon to collect data for scientific pursuits or to conduct some business venture but then just leave and never aid the local population in its struggles. Before I left Gurupá he and other church members repeatedly told me, "Não leva seu estudo para os Estados Unidos" (do not take your study to the United States). By this they meant I should use my information to benefit the local people in their struggles and that I should publish in Portuguese.

The priest's concern with praxis had led to problems with an anthropologist who had preceded me in Gurupá. In 1973 another of Wagley's graduate students, named Darrel Miller, had spent the summer in Gurupá doing research for his mater's. On the basis of this research he wrote a final, updated chapter to Wagley's *Amazon Town* (1976:296–325). Padre Chico, who had spent time talking with Miller during his stay (see Miller 1976:317), was very critical of the work. In particular he felt Miller had neglected the entire political conflict unfolding there and did not grasp the church's role in the emerging struggle. He was also dismayed that Miller cut his ties to the community following the conclusion of his research.

The priest's critique of Miller's work—justified or not—unsettled me, for it raised serious questions about how an outsider like Miller, or me, with a less-than-fluent command of the language, could really understand another culture, let alone proceed to write authoritatively about it. Wagley's research had been conducted jointly with Brazilians Eduardo Galvão, Clara Galvão, and Cecília Wagley who provided invaluable insight into the local culture. For most of my research, however, I, like Miller, lacked such collegial insight. I was also uncomfortable about writing my ethnography and then abandoning the community to its fate while I enjoyed a comfortable middle-class lifestyle as a college professor.

I have never satisfactorily answered these concerns, but I am not alone in worrying about them: Many anthropologists have puzzled over adequately comprehending and writing about another culture, which has led to several recent experiments in ethnographic writings such as hermeneutic and postmodern anthropology (see Marcus and Fischer 1986). My approach to this dilemma, however, has been more moderate. I have tried to conduct careful fieldwork and to later review my written accounts with people from Gurupá. Their input changed some sections of the research and reaffirmed others, though we still disagree in places.

The work of Paulo Oliveira, who conducted his independent study of the community between 1988 and 1989, focused on political mobilization within the rural union. It was a unique study in that he stayed a year in the community, used the members from the rural union to carry out an extensive survey of the municipality, and then followed up the study with grant writing for developmental funds. I was fortunate to be able to compare my research with his, and I was relieved to find that our major conclusions about political and economic processes in Gurupá were the same. This diminished some of my fears of incorrectly interpreting local events, and I benefited from his insight into several other events in the local struggle about which I was not aware.

I have dealt with the dilemma of praxis less well. Although I have maintained contact with people in Gurupá over the years, I have not been as active as I might have been in their struggle for political empowerment and a better life. My involvement is limited to publishing a few articles, writing this book, and discussing the plight of Gurupá and the Amazon in countless anthropology classes in the United States. By comparison, Oliveira has remained active by helping to document and facilitate union organization and writing grants for funds to encourage greater agricultural production and distribution of food.

This difference between Paulo and me raises some serious questions that anthropologists must face: To what extent should researchers devote themselves to helping the people they study, particularly if they are poor, oppressed, and powerless? What steps should an anthropologist take to aid people—write forcefully about their cause, donate money, solicit funds for development projects, support opposition movements, support nongovernmental organizations, or support the government? In a politically fragmented community what side should an anthropologist take? Or should researchers remain detached, objective, and politically neutral, if that is possible? Also, what is the role of the anthropologist as a foreigner? Does too much interaction with a people lead to charges of imperialism, and does too little lead to claims of exploitation of a people to further the career of the anthropologist?

There are probably as many responses to these quandaries as there are anthropologists. Much depends on one's personal politics and the ability to engage or not engage oneself in the lives of ethnographic subjects over the long term. Also, much may depend on the specific community studied—whether it is seeking concrete results from research to help improve the local community, or whether it is simply asking for a sensitive and unbiased recording of life. I must admit that I have not found a satisfying answer to these dilemmas. Minimally, in this work I try to present an accurate view of Gurupá, the problems it faces, and the steps the local people are taking to improve their lives.

Methodology

The methodology I used for data collection in this study included participant observation, informal and semiformal interviewing of acquaintances and key consultants, and the application of two interview schedules.

Participation observation involved attendance at all town events including religious and secular festivals, weddings (upon invitation), birthday parties, funerals, sports events, Masses at the Catholic Church, neighborhood Bible meetings, religious processions, political events (rallies, speeches, elections), dances, nightly activities in bars and pool halls, social promenades around the town square, public viewing of television, and vaccination campaigns.

In addition, Olga and I participated in ceremonies to establish fictive kin (*compadresco*) ties. By passing over the bonfire during the Saint John festival in June we both acquired co-parents and a godson of the bonfire. Also, when infections struck, which was a common occurrence in the tropical environment, I attended curing sessions conducted by such folk healers as *benzedeiros* (blessers). I should mention that I did not go completely "native" in terms of folk healing. I always visited the town health post before my visits to blessers. In the countryside participation observation included trips to *roças* (gardens), to rubber trails, and to timber extraction sites. I also participated in conversations at trading posts and at religious meetings.

Informal and semiformal interviews were conducted with consultants whenever the opportunity arose. Interviews frequently took place on the streets, at the butcher's market, at the docks, in trading posts and stores, in bars, on boats, at the church, in roças, and in people's homes. Questions were always open-ended with dialogue taking whatever direction the consultant and I could navigate.

The final data-collecting method was the administration of two sets of interview schedules. Interview schedules are similar to questionnaires except that the interviewer reads the questions to the respondent aloud and then the interviewer records the answers. Dr. Kottak designed the interviews for use in the study on the impact of television in Brazil (see Kottak 1990; Pace 1992). I expanded these interview schedules to include significant questions about political-economic change.

The first interview schedule was a household survey given to five groups of people; my wife and I administered a total of 108 of these surveys. One group consisted of a 9 percent random sample of homes in the town of Gurupá (forty-nine homes), and the remaining four groups resided in the countryside (fifty-nine homes). Two were from rural farming hamlets on the terra firme (land never flooded by the river), Jocojó and Camutá; and two were from rural neighborhoods on the *várzea* (daily or seasonally inundated floodplain), Mojú and Mararú. This sample was selected to represent the major ecological zones in the municipality, and the selection process did not involve any other sampling technique.

The second interview schedule was an individual survey given to various members listed in the household surveys. A locally hired research assistant and I administered a total of eighty-nine individual interviews, sixty-one within the random sample in town, twenty-eight in the countryside.

As stated earlier, all of the personal names of community residents used in this work are fictitious. All of the geographic names, however, are authentic. Wagley and Galvão used the real geographic names for local rivers, streams, and places in their study, so I simply followed their precedent. I, however, chose not to use the pseudonym Itá for the town and municipality. Wagley and Galvão used the pseudonym to protect the identity of the community, but by the time I began writing several other researchers had already used Gurupá's real name in published accounts. There remained little benefit to continued use of the pseudonym.

Structure of the Book

The remainder of the book presents data on the human condition in Gurupá, the structure of the political economy, and the types of changes that have taken place over the last 400 years. Chapter 2 focuses on the setting and general problems besetting the community. Chapters 3 and 4 review the historical data on Gurupá to identify the roots of poverty and political-economic struggle. Chapter 5 addresses the impact of contemporary economic development plans for the region and Gurupá. Chapter 6 describes the changes taking place in labor relations and land tenure. Chapter 7 focuses on local adaptations to poverty and underdevelopment. Chapter 8 defines the local class structure, the traditional political process, and the struggles of the rural union and opposition political party. Chapter 9 describes the role of the Catholic Church in the political mobilization of the camponês class. Finally, Chapter 10 concludes the study with comments on the structural limitations of the political economy.

2

AN AMAZON COMMUNITY

To describe the setting of Gurupá I have chosen to focus on three principal themes: poverty, ecology, and sociocultural change. My attention to these themes, and downplaying of others, springs from my theoretical interests and training (political economy, cultural ecology), the contemporary interests of the academic community (environmental and social issues in the Amazon), and the concerns expressed by the local population. As shown in the following pages, each theme is an essential element in defining the human condition in Gurupá.

Discussion of poverty, ecology, and change in Gurupá, however, is not without certain problems. Each term carries with it several biases. "Poverty," for example, may be defined in a variety of ways. In the United States we like to quantify the notion in terms of salary earned, possessions owned, or access to food, education, and health care. But there is clearly a sliding scale. What is considered poverty in one country may not be poverty in another; few people in Gurupá would consider the poor of the United States to be in poverty. The Gurupaenses understand that poor Americans have more money (even if it is government subsidies), have more possessions, eat better, and have better access to health care (even if it is the emergency room at the hospital) than most Gurupaenses. At the same time many people in Gurupá do not see themselves living in desperate poverty, although in terms of the above criteria they are much poorer than poor Americans.

This does not mean that poverty is simply a state of mind. There are certain minimums for human survival, particularly in terms of nutrition and health, that researchers can use as a baseline for comparison. But beyond this poverty can be variously defined. When I say that most Gurupaenses live in poverty I am referring to data such as undernutrition rates, infant mortality rates, and disease rates. I am also referring to comparisons of life chances of Gurupaenses to those of the wealthy and middle classes of Brazil. In these terms nearly all of the people in Gurupá rate as poor or very

15

Gurupá's municipal trapiche (wharf) and commercial area

poor, with only a few families obtaining the national status of lower middle class.

There is another interesting measure of poverty that comes from physical anthropology and archaeology: Researchers in these disciplines have made comparisons between contemporary Amazon populations (indigenous camponeses) and prehistoric ones to reveal that stature seems to have declined since European contact. In fact, most measured individuals in prehistoric populations were relatively tall (males averaged 172 centimeters) and are comparable to the present-day Brazilian landowning, educated class and to the U.S. average (Roosevelt 1994:14). Each of these populations is taller than the indigenous camponeses of today. Here stature is likely a sign of nutritional status and general health. One interpretation of these data is that precontact Native Americans were in better health and suffered far less poverty than do contemporary Amazonians.

The theme of ecology is similarly problematic. One current debate over Amazonia centers on humanity's place in it. At one extreme is an ecocentric view that considers people's presence in the environment as destructive. Humans harm the intricately complex local ecology by destroying the forest and rivers for short-term gains (agriculture, cattle ranches, timber extraction, hydroelectric dams). At the other extreme is an anthropocentric view in which nature exists for human use. Humans must transform nature for it to be of value. In other words, the Amazon should be "developed" for human benefit. Recently there has been a third, mediating view of the human/nature relationship called *sustainable development*. In this view humans should use nature for their own benefit but in a way that does not cause serious long-term destruction to the ecosystem and, consequently, to the human populations dependent upon it.

Sustainable development is the contemporary catchphrase for the Amazon, but it too is a troublesome term. How does one define it precisely in ecological terms? What part of the ecosystem do we preserve, and what part do we alter? What species do we maintain or introduce and at what population density? Furthermore, who controls the development process and benefits from it? One of the great risks of sustainable development may not be its feasibility or its actual conservation qualities but its subversion of important social issues by seemingly cut-and-dry environmental issues. This occurs when discussions of Amazonia are dominated by the language of nature while the condition of the human occupants takes a backseat. When this happens, Amazonian society, particularly its indigenous camponeses, becomes invisible and therefore easily marginalized by more powerful and affluent interests who wish to remold the region for their benefit (see Nugent 1993). Thus the world argues over nature as the people of the Amazon suffer.

The third theme, sociocultural change, is more redundant than problematic. It is redundant because cultures always change no matter how simple or complex they may be. So why designate a special category to something that is integral to all aspects of culture? One reason to do so is the very nature of this study: It is primarily a comparison of two periods in Gurupá's history—the late 1940s to the early 1950s and the late 1980s to the early 1990s—although historical information dating back to Native American–European contact is also included. I compare and contrast these periods to comment on the direction that changes in the human condition are taking.

Another reason to highlight sociocultural change stems from the theoretical baggage of social science. For many years the dominant paradigm was an approach called *functionalism,* which viewed culture as a snapshot, a one-time view suspended in time. In other words, history and change were less important than how things work now. Why was so much emphasis placed on this view? Some suggest that it served an important political function. It allowed social scientists to ignore the consequences of European and American colonialism, particularly problems of human rights abuses created by destroying and rebuilding native economies and political systems to benefit the colonial powers. Only in the past few decades have anthropologists begun to contend with this issue, which is an uncomfortable endeavor steeped in self-criticism.

I have designed the present discussion of poverty, ecology, and change to describe what the human condition is like in Gurupá as seen through the eyes of one ethnographer. These elements all combine to form the backdrop for the contemporary struggle in the community.

First Impressions

I remember well the first trip I took to Gurupá in May 1983. The dry season had just begun, and the rains fell only once or twice a day for twenty minutes or so. Olga and I left the comforts and security of the port city of Belém (population one million) and traveled thirty-six hours (500 nautical miles) upstream on a large wooden riverboat. The boat carried some 300 people, about 100 more than the official posted capacity. To make matters worse, we left Belém on Friday the thirteenth. This was an ominous beginning for two novices venturing into the Amazon.

I learned two valuable lessons on that first trip. One was the importance of sleeping in a hammock in the tropics. The second was the folly of consuming boat beans. In both cases my inappropriate folk view—my cultural baggage—led me to great discomfort. My obsession for privacy, my desire for a bed, and my unjustified fear of theft led me to insist on a small cabin with bunk beds. The cabin did offer privacy and a very small measure of security, but it also turned out to be a furnace because of a lack of ventilation. I remember lying in my bunk at night, sweating profusely and developing an annoying case of prickly heat while I watched the wiser local people swaying peacefully in their hammocks strung along the covered deck. The gentle river breeze and the thin material of the hammock made for a comfortable sleep.

Boat beans were a second curse for me on that initial journey. Ironically, I thought I was well trained in the dos and don'ts of food consumption in foreign countries. I had lived in Brazil for a year and a half and had already paid my gastronomical dues after eating food from street vendors and unsavory restaurants. But the boat beans confused me. I carefully watched their preparation. The boat's gallery seemed sanitary. The cook boiled the water. Yet one hour after eating the beans I began making frequent trips to the toilet. Later I concluded that anything cooked in river water, whether boiled or not, was not for the stomach of a foreigner.

Besides the personal discomforts, the trip up the river proved generally relaxing, almost monotonous. Most people spent the time aboard talking, playing cards, or lazily swaying in their hammocks. I found the view disappointing. Except for a few narrow straits near the town of Breves, the forest shore was too far from the boat to distinguish much detail. For the most part the view consisted of the muddy brown river water, a distant unbroken green wall of forest, and a blue sky highlighted with swiftly moving clouds. The images I held of an Amazon teeming with life (monkeys swinging from trees, parrots flying overhead, or a river abounding with fish) or, conversely, an Amazon being destroyed (burning forest, polluted water, or small farmers battling against rich landowners) were nowhere to be seen from the boat. The only break in the constant sky, forest, and water motif occurred when the boat docked briefly in one of the small towns that dot the waterway.

I should mention that there was one other event of note on this first trip. It occurred when the boat passed by a community whose residents paddled small canoes out to the moving boat to beg for food or clothing. Passengers aboard the boat threw small gifts wrapped in plastic sacks into the water for them to retrieve. I found it interesting that many people on board, who were mostly the urbanized poor of the Amazon, patronized the "poor helpless river dwellers." Some even called them defenseless *índios* (Indians) while others scoffed at the "lazy, useless *caboclos*" (a pejorative term referring to rural inhabitants of the Amazon). What I witnessed here is the widespread feeling in Brazil that anything rural is inferior, anything urban is superior—not unlike some views in the United States. As a foreigner with a different worldview I wondered if the rural lifestyle was really that bad. I had witnessed the poverty, crime, and pollution of Brazilian cities in which most of my travel companions lived and could see little virtue in it. But what about life in the countryside?

On the second morning of travel the riverboat reached Gurupá. The river had widened in front of the town to some 2.5 kilometers across. Since

the river divides just before Gurupá, with one channel weaving northeast to
Macapá and the other east to Belém, the immense 2.5 kilometers I saw in
front of the town was only half the width of the river.

The Town

I vividly recall my first distant glimpse of Gurupá. It appeared to be little
more than a narrow white strip carved out of a dense green forest that nearly engulfed it. As the boat neared the town I strained to identify the salient
structures that I had memorized from Wagley's description and Miller's
update (Wagley 1976:22ff.; Miller 1976:297ff.). I expected some change
since I knew from census material that the town had grown from 500 people in 1948 to nearly 3,000 in 1983. The municipality of Gurupá that sur-
rounds the town had expanded from 6,094 to 9,309 square kilometers. I had
also learned of a landing strip for small planes built behind the town. No
roads, however, connect Gurupá to the outside world.

The first landmark I distinguished was a gleaming silver *brasilite* (cor-
rugated asbestos material) roof of a large abandoned sawmill. A dock that
had previously been used to load lumber onto foreign-bound cargo ships
protruded from the sawmill. Next to the sawmill stood another abandoned
building that once housed a palmito canning factory. Both industries prospered briefly and then closed, in part because of financial problems caused
by weak national and international markets for their products. On successive trips to Gurupá in the 1980s and 1990s I witnessed the dismantling and
eventual decay of the remains of these buildings. The gutted remains serve
as a harsh reminder of the promise of economic boom and the reality of
economic bust that has wreaked havoc upon the Amazon economy for centuries.

The next visible landmark I observed was a rocky outcropping rising
10 meters above the river where most of the town lies. On the eastern end
of the bluff I recognized the reconstructed fort that used to guard the
Amazon River against Dutch, English, and French intrusions in the seven-
teenth century. Near the fort stands the highly visible Catholic church with
its whitewashed walls and shiny zinc roof. As the boat passed the church a
dozen skyrockets hissed their way skyward, fired from aboard the boat.
This was the traditional salute to honor Saint Benedict, who is housed in
the church. The saint protects river travelers, rubber collectors, and the
poor. The skyrockets serve as a payment for a promesa to the saint as he
keeps the travelers safe on their journey.

Clustered next to the church were several parish buildings. One was a
long brick *barracão* (shelter) with large open arches in the walls. The barracão serves as the location for the celebration of Gurupá's patron saint's
festival—Saint Anthony—and for the larger festival for Saint Benedict. A

second building, a two-story, whitewashed structure originally meant to be a high school, serves as the nuns' residence and as a classroom for an occasional church-sponsored seminar. Down the street a block was the new headquarters for the parish and home for the priest. This building is the finest in town, making it both a source of pride to supporters and the envy of detractors of the Catholic Church. As I learned during my research, community sentiment toward the church was acutely polarized because of its activist stance against the social and political ills affecting Gurupá.

Following the church buildings were several rows of houses. In 1985 when I again traveled to Gurupá I noticed a bright new sign advertising the Bank of Itaú just to the side of the houses. This bank opened and closed within several years despite doing brisk business. Closure occurred because of the bank's nationwide financial problems and changes in government policy designed to support rural branches of banks. The closure eliminated Gurupá's only readily available source of finance capital and disrupted many local timber extraction initiatives, for better or worse.

As the riverboat continued to pass in front of the town the next visible landmark was the infamously extravagant town hall. Construction of the hall began in the early 1900s just as the collapse of the rubber boom hit Gurupá and sent the local economy into five decades of depression. Since that time maintenance costs have drained municipal coffers and periodically forced the local government to abandon the building. In 1984 the municipal government finally secured funds to make repairs. The town hall now overflows with a variety of government agencies. They administratively link communities such as Gurupá with the rest of the country.

In the distance behind the town hall I could see a high communications tower. The tower serves a public radio-telephone post with two outgoing lines to Belém. In 1986 this service was expanded to include a dozen private telephones in the homes of some of the more affluent residents. Just below the tower, although hidden from the view from the river, sat a large satellite dish for receiving television transmissions. State and local politicians had the dish installed in early 1986, just in time for the local population to view the World Cup soccer games—a politically expedient move timed to bolster the image of local politicians. By the 1990s the town boasted approximately 200 small, inexpensive, black-and-white television sets. Nightly glimpses of national and international events became commonplace and have had a powerful impact on the collective worldview of the community.

A kilometer after the riverboat passed the fort and church it pulled into a small inlet to dock at the municipal *trapiche* (wharf). The local government rebuilt the wharf after Wagley's study. It now extends 25 meters into the river. Typically there are many 5- to 10-meter diesel-powered boats tied up along it. People began buying or building these boats in the 1950s. For those who can afford them they create a superior alternative to traditional travel by canoe and sailboat. Although they are not the most comfortable way to travel—being cramped to ride in, hot, and outrageously noisy—they do cut travel time to the far reaches of the municipality by days.

I remember being impressed with the way the boat crew skillfully docked our vessel despite the swift current. As they performed this feat I stood on deck and surveyed the crowd of some 150 people who waited on the wharf. Their physical features nearly ran the gamut of human diversity—Native American, African, European, and many mixtures. Most were dressed in shorts, T-shirts, and sandals, while a few had on long pants, button-up shirts, and shoes. Parked alongside the people were two automobiles—a Volkswagen van and a Volkswagen hatchback, the latter being Gurupá's only taxi. The drivers stood by their vehicles patiently awaiting the disembarking of goods and people. In all, the town boasted four cars and three trucks that were in working condition. Also in the crowd, three men with pull carts waited to haul cargo or luggage into town for a fee.

Olga and I had gathered our belongings and were preparing to disembark along the narrow plank bridging the gap between boat and wharf. A member of the boat crew stopped us and insisted we were mistaken about our destination. To him we appeared as typical young tourists who were "roughing" a ride upriver for the sport of it. He knew that no tourists got off in Gurupá. After some persuasion I convinced the crew member of our destination, and he walked away shaking his head. We then awkwardly descended the gangplank into the crowd of Gurupaenses.

In the confusion of loading and unloading along the wharf I attempted to ask directions. I had the name of one of Gurupá's two public places to stay—Benedito's boarding house—given to me by Gurupá's ex-mayor, whom I had met in Belém. While we stood on the wharf looking bewildered, a man dressed in a baseball cap, shirt, shorts, and sandals came up to us and introduced himself as Benedito Carvalho, the proud proprietor of our intended accommodations. We were very relieved to make our first contact. In my excitement I grabbed my luggage and told Olga to do the same, resisting the requests from the cargo carriers for help. Off we went behind Benedito into town.

Wagley described a simple dirt path weaving through a swamp and then up a hill into town in 1948. What we walked upon, however, was a wide paved street lined with warehouses, stores, bars, restaurants, dance halls, a meat market, and even a large brick Pentecostal church. The former swamp had become the commercial center of the town. Lost among all the buildings was the once-prominent trading post, the Casa Gato (house of the cat), which Wagley often frequented while in Gurupá. It used to be the principal trading post for the community, where the merchant imported goods to exchange for locally produced goods. The descendants of the original owner of Casa Gato still reside in the house and still conduct business.

However, today they represent only one of many merchant families active in Gurupá.

In retrospect I imagine that we must have been a rare sight as we walked through town that first day—two tourists scurrying to keep up with Benedito, sweating in the rising heat of the day, and burdened by heavy loads of baggage, because I did not wish to pay for a cargo carrier. The situation got the better of us both and before we reached our destination our abilities to contain our boat beans dissipated. We both arrived with soiled clothes. What an introduction to the field.

Benedito's boarding house, or Seu Bena (Mr. Benedito's) as people referred to it, is an unpretentious, somewhat weathered, wooden and brick structure that serves as store, trading post, boarding house, restaurant, and home for Benedito and his family. In front is the store/trading post, followed by the small restaurant and kitchen, the boarding house with four rooms on top, the residence and bathrooms, and finally, a small backyard (*quintal*) complete with medicinal herbs, chickens, and occasionally a pig. The whole complex is only 10 meters wide, although 40 meters long (approximately 33-by-131 feet). Seu Bena was to be our home for nearly two-thirds of our stay in Gurupá. There we were well cared for by Benedito and his wife, Carmita.

The first night at Seu Bena, however, proved to be less than restful. Neither Olga nor I was prepared for the nightlife of Gurupá. It all started after we had finished our evening meal. Being tired, we decided to go to sleep early. We retired upstairs to our room and entered the hammocks with encompassing mosquito nets we had strung up earlier (no more beds). As we lay there we listened to several conversations around us. Benedito was talking to Carmita downstairs, the neighbors next door were discussing politics, and out in the street a group of young men were reliving the day's soccer match. Since the thin wooden walls muffled the conversations, I soon ignored them and they faded into a background hum as I drifted off to sleep.

The first surprise came at midnight. The state-run electric company turned off the energy for the whole town. Later I learned this was the usual practice, as the local government rations electricity. Six hours of power a day, from six in the evening until midnight, unless there is a shortage of diesel fuel. Electricity in Gurupá is supplied courtesy of the Brazilian government, which had been making great efforts to provide electricity at a low price to small Amazonian towns. The high price of imported oil, however, placed serious constraints on that goal. Benedito was prepared for the outage, and a small candle burned outside our door. The candle would light our way if we needed to use the bathroom downstairs, although that was problematic too since the pump supplying water to the town was routinely turned off at 8:00 P.M.

I remember gazing skyward in the darkness through a glassless window and seeing more stars than I ever had before. The Milky Way sparkled brilliantly, and the Southern Cross rode high in the sky. The air was cool, and I felt very comfortable swaying in my hammock. Everything seemed at peace. Then the rats came. Rats were to be our companions in all our residences in Gurupá. They were the large river variety that came out nightly in search of food. They scurried along the roofs, the rafters, and sometimes the floors. The sound of rat movement never bothered me too much. I always felt secure under my mosquito net, through which no rat, bat, tree-climbing frog, lizard, spider, scorpion, or snake could penetrate. The problem with rats, however, is that they fight among themselves, emitting high-pitched squeals. The squeals drove me to endless attempts to trap and poison them. One night I set a newly purchased rattrap and eliminated eight rodents in rapid succession before the rest caught on and avoided it. But the attack did not seem to make even a dent in the household population. In the end we had to learn to coexist.

In addition to the rats there were a couple of rooting pigs outside our window. Town residents turned their pigs loose at night to scavenge for food. Olga, being raised in the heavily industrialized city of East Chicago, Indiana, had no idea what type of beast was making the noise. I explained and she fell silent in her hammock.

Then around 1:00 A.M. the most eerie sound I have ever heard began. It started far in the distance, where we knew the cemetery was located. The sound was a hoarse, ghostly, haunting moan. Over the next fifteen minutes the sound crept steadily toward us, growing in intensity as it neared. By the time it reached Seu Bena it was a deafening roar, at least it sounded so to me. At this point I had identified the sound. It seems that every rooster in town was joining in a loud and annoying crow-in. I knew that roosters crow early in the morning, but Gurupá roosters start an hour after midnight and continue all through the morning. I estimated that well over 100 roosters were out there crowing in unison, stopping, and then commencing anew, repeatedly throughout the night. The noise was too much for Olga, whose urban mind-set had conjured up some sort of nightmarish beast. She pulled up my mosquito net and nimbly slid in beside me despite my protests. Cramped but safe, we both fell asleep exhausted.

The next day Olga and I went to formally introduce ourselves to the local authorities. Our first stop was the mayor's office, where I presented a letter of introduction from Charles Wagley. The mayor, known as Dona Cecília, received us warmly. Several older civil servants also responded affectionately upon hearing Wagley's name. They set aside their work and told a number of tales, some true, some exaggerated, about the tall American; his Brazilian wife, Cecília; his colleague and companion, Eduardo Galvão; and Galvão's wife, Clara—all of whom had lived among them many years ago.

Over the next few weeks I initiated a daily informal interview routine that took me to many places where people tend to congregate—trading posts, stores, bars, the wharf, the town hall, the market, the church, and the soccer field. In time I also established friendships with several people who served as key consultants—individuals who gave me detailed information on the history and current activities of the community—whom I visited regularly. Benedito Alves was the first consultant with whom I developed rapport. I spent many hours talking with him and the people that wandered into his establishment. It seemed the perfect place to conduct my informal interviews, and Benedito loved to talk. But I had some difficulty in those early days understanding his dialect, which is called Paraense (originating from the state of Pará).

Eventually I improved my comprehension of the local dialect, which became apparent three years later when the Kottaks visited. Conrad and Betty were fluent in Portuguese as it is spoken in the northeast and south of Brazil but somewhat at a loss to understand the variations used in Gurupá. So I assisted them in conversation. As I took pride in my linguistic accomplishment I realized that I now spoke Paraense, which non-Amazonians frequently identify as a low-status dialect. When I later traveled outside the Amazon, people found this situation hilarious. It never seemed to matter to them when I endlessly explained that all languages and dialects are equally complex and structured, that speaking a particular dialect does not make one more or less intelligent. To them the irony of an educated foreigner speaking "hick" was simply too humorous to ignore.

During the first few weeks in Gurupá I also began a systematic reconnaissance of the town and countryside. Part of this project was to map the town. I continued to update this map throughout my various visits. The town is laid out on a grid system wherein six streets run parallel to the river and ten are perpendicular to it. Only three of the streets were paved in 1983. This number increased to seven by 1991. Wooden signs with names of important people, saints, or historical events mark each street. Despite this convenience, people still refer to the streets by number—First, Second, Third, and so forth, as they had in days past (Wagley 1976:23).

I inventoried the buildings in town and came up with the following list: a small hospital, a medicine post, a pharmacy, a legal forum and house for a judge and prosecutor when working in town, an electrical plant with two large diesel-powered engines, a pump house that supplies approximately 60 percent of the town with filtered water, a post office, a public library, a police station and jail, a machine shop, an office for the rural union, and a state school encompassing six grade levels, as well as the previously mentioned church structures, bank, town hall, and airstrip. Within the town there are also some eighteen retail stores and/or trading posts, fourteen dance halls (most only function twice a year during festival times), seven bars, four restaurants, three bakeries, and a watch repair shop. All these establishments are small in scale, and all have limited provisions. My consultants told me about one house of prostitution, although no one would point it out. In addition, Gurupá has three cemeteries, a soccer field, and a lighted sports complex for indoor soccer, basketball, and volleyball.

Compared with Wagley's 1948 description the town has filled out and expanded (Wagley 1976:24). There are no vacant blocks. Most homes are closely spaced. Some are connected to one another. All are flush with the street. Behind the houses are the *quintais* (backyards), often surrounded by a wooden fence or brick wall. Atop the brick walls are assorted pieces of jagged glass fragments, fixed there to dissuade thieves from scaling the wall even though theft is not much of a problem. In the quintais people have fruit trees, raised herbal box gardens, chickens, ducks, pigs, laundry facilities (there was only one washing machine in the municipality), and outhouses. The condition of most houses appeared to be better than described by Wagley. Many houses I observed in the 1980s were only a few years old and well kept. Even many older houses—some over 100 years—had been renovated, especially the facades facing the street. The houses near the riverfront are kept brightly painted in pastel colors. The farther from the river, however, the more likely houses are to be unpainted.

The general upgrading in housing conditions suggested to me a new cycle of prosperity in Gurupá. During my research I learned that the prosperity, limited as it was, resulted from government development policies designed to stimulate extraction of timber and palmito and to search for oil deposits. Timber extraction most impacted Gurupá. It supplied many individuals with cash and inexpensive materials to improve homes. As a result the community's houses are overwhelmingly made of locally sawn wood (90 percent of the town's houses), whereas in 1948 a large portion were made of the less-valued palm thatch (Wagley 1976:25). I counted only 1 percent of houses made from palm thatch. There are also a few houses constructed of *taipa* (wattle work filled with clay, with a sand and lime plaster finish; 1 percent) and some made of highly prized brick covered in plaster or cement (8 percent). The houses are roofed with ceramic tile and brasilite (51 percent) or with palm thatching (49 percent). All have raised wooden floors (a precaution against insects, not against flooding) or concrete floors.

Another sign suggesting economic prosperity is people's increased ability to consume imported durable items. In the random sample survey administered in 1985–1986 I found that 67 percent of households owned gas (rather than charcoal or wood-burning) stoves, 43 percent owned refrigerators, 63 percent possessed radios, 57 percent had wristwatches, and 66 percent had beds—a status symbol regardless of its impracticality.

The urban ecology of Gurupá reflects levels of affluence, just as Wagley found in 1948 and Miller in 1974 (Miller 1976:308). The most highly prized land is located near the river. Wealthier families tend to live there; most of the prosperous businesspeople, civil servants, politicians, and the clergy live on the first two streets that run parallel to the river. On the remaining four streets the poor reside. Table 2.1 shows another aspect of this spatial distribution pattern: Houses lacking electricity and those with palm-thatch roofing—both features that local residents recognize as symbols of lower status—are more prevalent on streets farther from the river.

Table 2.1   Percentage of Homes Lacking Electricity and Possessing Palm Thatch Roofing in Gurupá, by Street

Street	% Lacking Electricity	% with Palm Roofing	No. of Houses
1st	10	13	60
2nd	38	16	141
3rd	58	57	124
4th	57	57	91
5th	79	69	85
6th	100	93	15

Note: 1st Street is closest to the river, and 6th Street is the most distant.

At first glance the changes I observed in the town suggest that Gurupá had prospered since the time Wagley and Galvão described it. The community has grown and boasts new businesses, new services, new buildings, and new consumption habits. But the physical appearances are deceptive. As my research progressed I learned of many serious problems in the community.

Two major problems are high unemployment and high underemployment. There are few jobs to be found in the urban sector, especially since the large sawmill and palmito factory closed down and the state oil company, Petrobrás, left the area. People frequently complain about the lack of employment opportunities. In the individual interviews given to the random sample in town, 39 percent of the respondents said that the lack of jobs is Gurupá's main problem.

Other primary problems identified included lack of food (8 percent), high cost of living (8 percent), political infighting (7 percent), and a combination of poor education, health, transportation, public administration of funds, and courtesy (13 percent). Twenty-five percent of those interviewed did not respond to the question.

The only widely available jobs are in subsistence agriculture and extraction of forest products. Many urban residents, however, dislike the agricultural work because prices for produce are so low that they provide for little more than bare survival. Extraction (of timber, rubber, palmito, cacao) is also not very desirable work to townspeople because it is a difficult job that does not compensate the physical labor involved. Even when people reluctantly extract, overharvesting of many products has led to resource depletion and eventual loss of jobs. Depletion of resources also creates a degraded environment and limited future use by the local population. As I will show later, resource depletion is a principal cause of social tension in Gurupá.

Since jobs, particularly wage labor jobs, are difficult to secure on a permanent basis and usually pay poorly, many households suffer persistent shortages of money, which of course makes it difficult to obtain food. If individuals in town lack cash and do not have access to a garden plot for food crops (which many do not), then the only "free" food is fish caught in the river.

Even with money, however, food may be hard to come by. Because of the structure of the rural economy, the volume of food produced locally and transported to town is often not enough to support the urban population. Much of Gurupá's food, therefore, is imported from distant municipalities. All imported commodities are expensive because of the substantial price markups entailed. A survey I conducted in 1985 compared the prices of twenty-one commonly used items sold in the major retail store in Gurupá to the prices for the same items in a Belém supermarket. The items were rice, beans, manioc, sugar, salt, powdered milk, condensed milk, crackers, coffee, corn flour, canned meat, bottled water, soft drinks, cigarettes, soap, razor blades, lightbulbs, pens, matches, steel wool, and toilet paper. The results of the survey showed that prices in Gurupá average 79 percent higher than in Belém (the markup was based on transportation costs, local taxes, and merchants' profits). In addition, there is a 17 percent price differential between costs at Gurupá's retail store and costs at its leading trading post, which sells goods on credit.

People continuously voice complaints about the persistent lack of food and employment. Conversations on the street inevitably turn to discussions of where fish, meat, or fruit might be obtained. When people walk down the street with food they are bombarded with questions about who is selling, where are they selling, and how high the price is. When a boatload of fish pulls along shore there are long lines of people vying to buy the limited supply, although the law requires fish to be sold at the market where all can have access to it. When cattle are slaughtered and the meat is sold in the market, chaos results from crowds of pushing and shouting people who hope to get a piece of meat before it's all gone. The only hint of order in the marketplace occurs when the elderly are present, for they get first choice of beef on the basis of a municipal decree.

Olga and I were generally spared the struggle to obtain food since we had sufficient money with us and since Benedito was assured access to food for his restaurant through his personal network. Occasionally, there were townwide shortages of beef, rice, and beans that no amount of money could overcome. Everyone had to subsist on manioc and fish during these times. Overall we ate satisfactorily, although we both experienced weight loss because of the climate and the general lack of sugar and fat in the local cuisine.

The children of Gurupá do not fare very well with food. Olga and I conducted a survey to assess the health and nutritional status of the school-age children in town. For two weeks we went to the federal school and took measurements on height, weight, upperarm circumference, and tricep skin folds. We used a nonrandom sample of 209 children between the ages of five and nine. Later, with the aid of physical anthropologist Ricardo Santos, we calculated the results using the Gomez scale (Pace and Santos 1988). The results show that 51.2 percent of the study population suffers from first degree undernutrition (i.e., individuals are only 90 percent to 75.1 percent of the normal measurements for their age and sex group based on international standards), 16.3 percent suffers from second degree undernutrition (75 percent to 60.1 percent of normal measurements), and 0.5 percent suffers from third degree undernutrition (less than 60 percent of normal measurements).

Health care delivery is another problem for the community. There is one doctor, one dentist, one nurse, one biochemist, and ten nurse aides working in one small hospital. This staff is responsible for the health of the entire urban and rural population of the municipality, which had grown to 17,011 by 1989 (in comparison to other rural municipalities in Pará, however, Gurupá's health care is much better than the average system). For serious ailments people have to go to Belém for treatment. This requires extra payments for transportation and room and board, which many people cannot afford.

Gurupá's hospital deals with high rates of disease and trauma with minimal facilities and supplies. In the period between 1981 and 1985 the hospital recorded the following number of cases: measles, 77; cholera, 4; tetanus, 2; infectious hepatitis, 41; intestinal parasitic infections, 1,530; malaria, 189 (180 occurred in 1985 alone); leishmania, 5; tuberculosis, 28; leprosy, 30; meningitis, 3; and gonorrhea, 1 (SESPA 1985). According to Gurupá's health officials, these numbers greatly undercount the disease rate in the municipality since many people do not or cannot come to the hospital. In the case of malaria, for instance, probably more than half the cases go unrecorded according to the local physician. The state health agency, the Secretária de Estado de Saúde Pública (SESPA), listed the infant mortality rate between 1980 and 1988 at forty-two per thousand (SESPA 1990; the U.S. rate ranges between twelve and fourteen per thousand). These disease and death rates, and the poorly equipped and staffed hospital, prompted one health official in Gurupá to comment that it is a myth that public health care really exists in Gurupá.

Because of the continuous problems concerning employment, food,

and health care, many town residents hold low opinions of Gurupá in relation to surrounding municipalities. Gurupá is considered an *atrasado*
(backward) place that has experienced little progress. People frequently
commented to me that Gurupá is one of the oldest towns in the Amazon
(founded around 1609), yet, unlike many of its younger neighbors, it has
failed to improve itself. For many residents there is an explicit hierarchy of
desirable places to live according to availability of food, jobs, health care,
and educational facilities. Belém usually tops the list, followed by smaller
towns such as Santarém, Macapá, Breves, Óbidos, Almerim, and Porto de
Moz. At the bottom of the list is Gurupá.

I frequently asked the people what they felt caused their poverty, as
this question elicited local perceptions of the political economy. The
answers indicate the internal logico-integrative schema within which their
motivations and apprehensions toward what is happening in the world are
based. They also helped me define and comprehend the different paths
taken by the opposing factions in the struggle for control of Gurupá. The
answers I received fell into four general categories, though many people
hold more than one view simultaneously.

One explanation of poverty blames character inadequacies of the population. According to this view, people in Gurupá are lazy, unintelligent, or
even racially inferior. They have underachieved and remained poor, while
other industrious, intelligent, or racially pure individuals (usually people of
European descent who live in the south or the First World) have over-
achieved and become rich. Although this view has no scientific validity, it
nevertheless is a popular folk belief in Gurupá, as in much of the world.

A second explanation for the community's backward state blames poor
resources and poor location. Gurupá has no precious metals, no oil, and little agricultural potential: Lacking these resources the community has not
developed any industry and therefore cannot generate wealth. In addition,
the community is located far from urban and industrial centers and has had
to depend on river transportation for trade. Many Gurupaenses see river
transportation as slow and costly. Quite a few people feel that Gurupá's
poverty is a direct result of high prices paid for imports.

A third explanation places the blame for low quality of life on the local
dominant class, which is seen as continuously exploiting the poor.
According to this viewpoint, Gurupá has had ample chances to develop and
prosper. But a corrupt dominant class has repeatedly embezzled municipal
funds and discouraged economic development to preserve its privileged
position and power.

The final explanation for impoverishment in Gurupá blames structural
inequalities inherent in the capitalist system. To people holding this view,
capitalism rewards greed, exploitation of fellow humans, and political
repression of dissenters with great concentrations of wealth in the hands of

a few. The system is unjust and is at the root of poverty. It must therefore be transformed.

The Interior

Like the town of Gurupá the countryside of Gurupá has changed since 1948. In fact, the main dynamic of economic and political change in the municipality is occurring there; recognizing this, I attempted to spend as much time as possible in the countryside, although this was fraught with logistical problems.

People in Gurupá define the countryside, or simply "the interior," as all land outside the town limits. It includes the vast majority of the population and of the land area of the municipality. In the years since Wagley's study the rural and urban population of the municipality has grown only modestly in comparison to other Amazonian municipalities—from 11,700 in 1950 to 17,011 in 1989 (IBGE 1956; IDESP 1989). A small part of this increase is due to an expansion in the municipality from 6,094 to 9,309 square kilometers.

Gurupá's interior forms only a tiny portion of the vast Amazon ecosystem. This system stretches 3,000 kilometers (1,860 miles) from the Atlantic Ocean to the Andes Mountains and 2,500 kilometers north to south. Although 80 percent of the Amazon lies in Brazil, it does extend into Guyana, Surinam, French Guiana, Venezuela, Colombia, Ecuador, Peru, and Bolivia. Altogether the Amazon's drainage basin is some 6,000,000 square kilometers, roughly the size of the continental United States (Moran 1993:2–3).

The mighty Amazon River drains the Amazon forest. The river has over 1,000 tributaries that feed into it from its origin in the Andes Mountains to its mouth in the Atlantic Ocean. One-fifth of the earth's freshwater flows through it daily, which is more freshwater than the earth's next eight largest rivers combined.

Amazonia consists of many types of forests, savannas, mangroves, and floodplains. It is not a solid, undifferentiated ecosystem but a very complex, and not yet understood, ecological mosaic. Emilio Moran (1993) listed no less than twenty-five major vegetation types in Amazonia, with the disclaimer that the list is hardly exhaustive. There is also great diversity in the region's soil, river types, and rainfall patterns. The region is well known for its diverse flora and fauna; various scientists have estimated that anywhere from one-fourth to one-half of the world's species of plants and animals live here. This includes an estimated 80,000 species of plants; up to 30 million species of animals, which include one-half of the world's species of insects; one-fifth of the world's bird species; and some 2,000–

3,000 species of fish (Miller and Tangley 1991:53-86). Of course, scientists often contest these estimates since no one can be certain of the total number of species existing in Amazonia.

The Várzea

The largest part of Gurupá's interior, approximately 75 percent, consists of an ecological zone called the *várzea*. The várzea is the floodplain of the river that is seasonally or daily inundated. Throughout the Amazon region the várzea accounts for only 2 percent of the total land area that, nevertheless, equals somewhere between 64,000 and 80,000 square kilometers, or nearly twice the size of the Netherlands (Sternberg 1975; Moran 1993:86). There are three broad types of várzea found in Amazonia: the upper floodplain located upstream from Manaus, the lower floodplain located between Manaus and Santarém, and the estuary located roughly from Santarém to the Atlantic Ocean.

Gurupá is located in the estuary. The distinctive feature of this várzea type is diurnal flooding caused by the ocean tides. Although Gurupá is 500 nautical miles inland from the ocean, the tidal action raises and lowers water levels more than 1 meter twice a day. A second, smaller part of Gurupá's várzea floods only with seasonal rises in the river caused by heavy rains that fall between January and June.

The várzea is a complex ecozone. Structurally, it consists of the high várzea (the banks and natural levees located next to the river channel) followed by the low várzea (the permanently, seasonally, or daily flooded shallow lakes or *igapós* [forest/swamps] that stretch inland). *Paranás,* or riverside channels, may border the igapós. *Furos,* or natural channels, connect the low várzea to the river, although during the dry season such channels may dry up and isolate the shallow lakes and swamps.

Soils on the high várzea tend to be relatively rich in nutrients, which is not the common pattern for most Amazon soils. This anomaly results from the deposit of silt carried by the Amazon River and its tributaries from the distant Andes Mountains. Gallery forests and some grasslands are found here. Intensive agriculture is also possible, the only constraint being the short growing season (three to four months) when the water levels are low enough to plant.

Soils in the low várzea tend to have diminished fertility, particularly at the end of the floodplain where floodwaters deposit only fine-grain sediment (Parker 1981:57–58). Igapó forests made up of palms and other inundation-tolerant species dominate the vegetation in this area (Moran 1993:27; Parker 1981:58), and biodiversity is generally reduced here (Anderson 1990). In areas of daily inundation the constant rise and fall of water eliminates agricultural activity.

The várzea area has always been of primary importance to the economy of Gurupá. People have extracted many resources here, including hardwoods, softwoods, oleaginous (oil-bearing) seeds, palms, cacao, and rubber. Cattle ranchers have also used the natural grasslands found here for pasture. Additionally, the várzea is a rich source of edible riverine fauna including many species of fish and an occasional water turtle, caiman, otter, capybara, or manatee. Of secondary importance to the local economy are the small várzea garden plots dedicated to the production of such quick-growing crops as corn, beans, and rice.

Transportation throughout the várzea is by boat. During the period I conducted research the most effective way to reach the remote areas was by small diesel-powered boat. Travelers can rent them for about U.S. $15 a day, plus fuel and food for the pilot and assistant. Alternatively, one can hitch a ride from boat owners making daily runs to most parts of the municipality. The most arduous method of transportation is by canoe, for paddling to distant settlements could take a day or two, though such travelers can harness some wind power by stringing up a hammock for a sail.

Most of Gurupá's várzea lies across the Amazon River on the Great Island of Gurupá. Here people have lived for generations in communities strung out along the high várzea. My surveys of the area revealed that people typically build their houses several hundred meters from one another. This arrangement is both an ecological and an economic adjustment to the ubiquitous extractive activities in the area, as it allows each household direct access to the waterway for transportation. The constant rise and fall of the water level in the tidal várzea also means that residents must build their houses and walkways on stilts. Fewer wooden walkways are required when people build houses directly on the bank.

Spatial separation is also an economic adjustment to the extractive economy. People on the várzea make their living by collecting rubber, cacao, and açaí (*Eutrepe oleracea,* which produces a palm seed used to make a traditional drink); by cutting timber and palmito (among the trees used to produce palmito is the same tree that produces açaí); and by planting subsistence garden plots where the land permits. In the case of rubber and cacao extraction, which have historically been the mainstays of economic activity in Gurupá, people tend to live close to the trees to save time in daily transportation. Although people have planted some trees to increase densities, the constant threat of disease and pests means that most trees are still widely scattered to escape attack. In turn, maintaining easy access to the scattered trees has meant that people build their houses fairly distant from their nearest neighbor.

Despite the distance between individual households on the várzea there are community clusters, or "neighborhoods" as Wagley described them (1976:29). These neighborhoods organize themselves in two ways, although these ways are not mutually exclusive. First, neighborhoods organize around a trading post maintained by a local landowner or merchant.

The landowner or merchant supplies basic necessities and some consumer items while buying the produce of the neighborhood residents. Often the trading post is the social, as well as the commercial, center of the community. Here people stop by to chat, hear the latest news, and, particularly for the men, get a shot of *cachaça* (a type of rum).

Second, the Catholic Church organizes the neighborhoods into political-religious sectors. Before the 1970s many neighborhoods organized themselves into religious brotherhoods to celebrate the festival of the community's patron saint or saints. The church had little actual control over these organizations. Since the 1970s, however, the resident priest has made a tremendous effort to organize and build upon these brotherhoods. As a result many várzea neighborhoods have become cohesive social-religious groups known as *comunidades eclesiais de base* (ecclesiastic base communities), or simply *comunidades*. Some of these comunidades have communally run trading posts (bypassing the high prices charged at the traditional trading post) and medicine posts. Nearly all coordinate labor exchanges among members. In addition, these comunidades organize themselves into grassroots political organizations active in an incipient rural union movement and in support of the local opposition political party (Partido dos Trabalhadores, or the Workers' Party).

The seasonal rains set the rhythm of life on the várzea. In the rainy season (January through June) the river rises and turns the area into one great lake dotted with small islands of land. Human movement anywhere is by boat. For the novice boater, such as myself, this can lead to difficult and usually humorous consequences. More than once I was responsible for sinking a canoe. I never quite understood if it was my clumsiness or my weight that submerged the low, shallow-constructed wooden canoes.

During the dry season (July through December) the waters recede and all this changes. I remember walking once on the same spot where six months earlier, a meter above my head, I had helped paddle a canoe. Of course, during this time of year the inexperienced forest trekker is challenged by twisted roots, mud, and assorted brush that make movement difficult. I was always in awe of the ease and swiftness with which the várzea dwellers traversed land and water.

Ecological diversity is immense in the várzea. Mammals, birds, fish, insects, aquatic plants, and flood-resistant plants abound. I saw untold numbers of fish and waterfowl, parrots, macaws, monkeys, capybaras, turtles, and even some caiman. What impressed me the most, however, was the insect life. There are many places I stayed where mosquitoes and biting insects were so numerous they made life intolerable. The várzea dwellers deal with these plagues during peak seasons by burning various barks and woods that act as repellents, by covering their bodies with forest oils that have repellent properties, and by developing a strong resistance to the irritation of the bites. These measures, however, do not always protect the people from malaria-carrying mosquitoes.

The Terra Firme

The second ecological zone, constituting approximately 25 percent of the municipality of Gurupá, is known as the terra firme. It is the upland area that is never inundated by water. Throughout the Amazon region this ecozone makes up 98 percent of the total land area—some 4,000,000 square kilometers. The terra firme is incredibly diverse in terms of soil types, climate variations, and plant and animal communities that are little understood by science. Moran (1993:29) distinguishes a minimum of four very broad habitats: lowland savannas, blackwater ecosystems, upland forests, and montane forests. Gurupá's terra firme is upland tropical moist forest (true rain forest begins farther west).

Despite the diversity of the terra firme, there are a few constants. One is the general poor quality of soils—a striking paradox given the lush rain forest that exists upon them. According to Pedro Sánchez (1981:347), the humid tropics contain some of the best and worst soils in the world. Moran (1993:11–14) emphasizes the patchiness of Amazon soils, which makes site-specific generalizations about the quality of soils difficult. Still, as a general rule of thumb, Amazon soils are poor.

Many soils are part of pre-Cambrian geological formations known as the Guiana and Brazilian Shields. These are some of the oldest land surfaces on earth. Over the millennia the combination of warm temperatures and torrential rainfall, often more than 3 meters (120 inches) a year, has leached most of the nutrients from these soils, leaving them acidic and unfertile. Approximately 93 percent of Amazonian soils are in this state, leaving a mere 7 percent suitable for conventional agricultural production as practiced in temperate climates (Cochrane and Sánchez 1982).

The immediate question that arises from this state of poor-quality soils, then, is how the forest continues to grow. The answer is rapid nutrient cycling. The forest grows, dies, decomposes, and then recycles its nutrients to the living plants with only minimal use of the soils. In fact, nearly all nutrients used in plant growth are stored in the biomass, not in the soil. Researchers have estimated that for tropical rain forests in general, 75 percent of the ecosystem's nutrients are stored in trunks and branches of plants, 15–20 percent in roots, 4–6 percent in leaves, and 2 percent in the litter on the forest floor (see Moran 1981:24–25).

The nutrient cycling, somewhat simplified, proceeds as follows: Each year up to 20 percent of the total biomass dies and falls to the ground. There it rapidly decomposes and mineralizes through the physical and biological actions of warm temperature, rainfall, bacteria, and mycorrhizae fungi. Only ten to twelve weeks are needed to mineralize 50 percent of the litterfall at any one time (see Moran 1981:25). The root system of the forest, the bulk of which extends only 30 centimeters (1 foot) into the soil, then quickly absorbs the nutrients and sends them back into the biomass.

The condition of most Amazonian soils limits agricultural activity. Clear-cutting of land for planting, which is a common practice in temperate climates, is usually ineffective since it removes the nutrients from the system. Plowing likewise does little good since subsoils are nutrient poor. To deal with these limitations indigenous populations have developed a form of agriculture known as *slash-and-burn*. In this system the farmer cuts the vegetation on a small plot of land, allows the debris to dry, and then burns it. The farmer spreads the ash upon the ground to act as a natural fertilizer. This method effectively releases the nutrients from the biomass onto the ground where planted crops can use them. The farmer uses the plot for approximately two years, until the nutrients are used up, and then abandons it (leaves it fallow). The forest then reclaims the area. In ten to twenty years the same plot will be refarmed after the nutrients in the biomass have been restored. When farmers practice slash-and-burn agriculture with a low population density it is a sustainable use of the tropical forest.

In Gurupá the local farmers report that the terra firme soils are of varying quality for slash-and-burn agriculture. Many told me that some land will produce fair yields of corn, bananas, beans, and rice. However, a good portion of land is reported to be adequate only for the growing of manioc (cassava), a hardy, starchy root crop that is a staple food of Amazonia.

To the present, farmers have used the terra firme of Gurupá for limited production of staple crops, mainly manioc, which will not grow on the wet várzea. Since there has been little in the way of a developed transportation system through the terra firme, agriculture is confined to the areas immediately surrounding one of the many *igarapés* (streams that are navigable by canoe at least part of the year). People do regularly travel to the more distant terra firme to hunt and, more recently, to extract timber for export. However, extracting timber on the terra firme is an expensive endeavor, and few people can afford the capital investment needed to build logging roads and obtain a truck to transport logs.

I observed that most of Gurupá's terra firme settlements are accessible only by boat or by foot. There is one dirt road in the community, a 12-kilometer stretch linking the town to the interior on which trucks and bicycles can pass. The road was built in the 1970s with the hope of eventually connecting it to the Transamazon Highway, which is approximately 200 kilometers to the south (on some governmental planning maps of the area there is a road shown that extends to Gurupá). Financial problems with road construction throughout the region and a general lack of interest for the project among regional planners led to its cancellation. Local people use the road to haul some timber and agricultural produce and to transport people to and from Gurupá. In the 1980s the municipal government sent a truck to the end of the road twice a week, if the small bridges had not washed out or if the mud was not too deep to keep the truck from passing.

I used the road extensively to reach several terra firme settlements. As with the outings to the várzea, trips along the road usually resulted in some form of adventure. The few trips I took by truck seemed to always end with a flat tire or a wheel sunk in the mud. So I tried bicycling. I purchased a heavy-framed, balloon-tire bicycle with a rack for carrying goods—or, more commonly, passengers—on back. The added weight of cargo or a passenger, plus the assorted problems of navigating deeply eroded ruts, avoiding the forest overgrowth, and maintaining balance in mud and sand, always left me exhausted upon arrival. My final alternative was to walk. I began to prefer this method once I built up my stamina. By walking I observed more of the forest flora and fauna. I was also able to engage in prolonged and interesting conversations with people who accompanied me. As an added bonus, whenever I began to feel overheated, there was always a nearby stream to plunge into.

The communities established on the terra firme arranged themselves into hamlets ranging in size from five to eighty households. Since there are few ecological restrictions, houses in the terra firme hamlets tend to be more closely clustered than those in várzea neighborhoods. I calculated that an average of 10 to 20 meters separate most houses, which allows some privacy but still facilitates visual contact with neighbors. Residents often arrange the houses in an elongated oval around a central path.

Residents of all terra firme hamlets engage in agriculture, and many also seasonally migrate to participate in extractive activities on the várzea. In these agricultural hamlets there is a greater need for communal labor in food production. Individuals meet these needs with the help of extended family and by the temporary formation of labor exchange groups. My consultants told me that labor exchange groups are sometimes known as *puxirão* or *convite,* although more frequently they call them *troca dias* (exchange days) and *mutirão*. In mutirão participating members give a day or two of work to another individual in exchange for future claims to labor. Usually no money is involved, although the individual asking for labor sometimes supplies coffee or food to workers. I did not observe the more elaborate labor exchanges described by Wagley (1976:69) that involved much food and drink.

Since the mid-1980s the rural interior has shared in the limited economic prosperity that was described for the town of Gurupá. The timber boom has provided wages and cheap building supplies. Consequently, almost all interior houses (100 percent of the 59 sample homes located in two terra firme hamlets and two várzea neighborhoods) are made of sawn wood, and all are raised on stilts and have wooden floors. Formerly, most houses were made of palm thatching. I also observed prosperity in terms of roofing materials used. Within the rural survey sample, 34 percent of households have imported ceramic tiles, brasilite, or zinc for roofs in place of the formerly ubiquitous palm thatching. In addition, the possession of durable consumer items suggests prosperity. Within the sample 51 percent of the households have gas stoves, 68 percent radios, 24 percent wristwatches, 29 percent beds (instead of hammocks), and 5 percent kerosene refrigerators.

Many interior communities have benefited from the expansion of government services. Education is one of the more visible services offered. In 1948 only one rural community had a school. By the beginning of the 1990s, however, over ninety interior hamlets and neighborhoods had schools. These schools are usually one-room affairs (classes are often held in someone's home), with one teacher handling first through fifth grade. Books and equipment are chronically scarce, but the mere presence of a teacher is a welcomed change for the residents. Another service offered to the interior is a vaccination campaign by Gurupá's hospital. Several times a year the hospital staff, teachers, civil servants, and other volunteers venture into the far reaches of the interior to give vaccinations against childhood diseases. This campaign is coordinated with the national campaign. Although there are many problems with transportation, finding interior residents, shortages of vaccines, and keeping a supply of ice to preserve vaccines, the campaign is very important to the health of people in the interior.

Despite these signs of prosperity there are persistent problems that lowered the general living standards in the interior. For one, electricity is virtually nonexistent. More debilitating is the lack of access to medical treatment (beyond the vaccination campaign) because of the long distance to be traveled to the town's hospital (which can take days by canoe to traverse) and the deficiencies of the town's health care delivery system. Also, interior residents do not treat their drinking water, which is taken from the same rivers and streams in which they dump most of their waste. Outhouses, which would help correct part of the problem, tend to be few on the terra firme, and on the tidal várzea the high water tables and daily flooding make them all but useless. Furthermore, few people have the luxury of mosquito netting and therefore sleep exposed to insects. Consequently, a resurgence of malaria in Gurupá (probably transported from Pará's gold mines) has spread quickly within the population. Between 1984 and 1985 the reported number of malaria cases jumped from 7 to 180 (SESPA 1985).

Problems of availability of food in the interior, however, are not so severe as they are in town. People told me that for the most part food is available year-round for all but the tidal várzea areas. Interior residents always have access to gardens for crops, rivers for fish, and the forest for fruits and game. Interior inhabitants often comment about this virtue. When I asked in the individual interview schedule whether life is better in the

interior or in town, half of those who preferred the interior said their preference was based on food availability and the fact that one does not need
money to obtain it. Twenty-nine percent chose the interior because it is
calmer and safer, 7 percent because there are more jobs, 3.5 percent
because community aid exists, and 3.5 percent because external appearance, such as clothing, is not important. Of the 50 percent who responded
that town life is better, three-fourths said this is so because there are more
consumer items available.

Employment, also, is less of a problem in the interior than it is in town.
One can always tend a garden and work in extraction of rubber, cacao, timber, or palmito. The major drawback, however, is a low return for labor.
Most interior inhabitants, especially those who do not own land, tend to
only eke out a living. These hardships, and the attractions of town life
(more people, consumer goods, electricity, entertainment, and so on), draw
large numbers of people from the interior.

Conclusion

The description of the setting of Gurupá's town and interior shows in part
how the municipality has changed since the time of Wagley's and Galvão's
initial studies. Standards of living, measured in terms of housing and consumer items, have improved somewhat. Yet problems of employment, food
availability, health care, and education remain. Other changes have been
modest, particularly in comparison to other parts of the Amazon. For example, in Gurupá there has been no rapid urbanization such as that which
occurred in cities like Belém, Santarém, Macapá, or those along the
Transamazon Highway. Nor has Gurupá experienced massive economic
development such as that seen in places like Jarí, Carajás, or Macapá. At
the time of my research Gurupá had not suffered a high level of violence
over land and resources, as had southern Pará. Nonetheless, Gurupá shares
in some of the basic changes that are remolding the Amazon today. To better understand these changes, the next two chapters will review the historical background of Gurupá to identify certain ecological, economic, and
political structures that have both limited and guided contemporary
processes.

3

THE DEMISE
OF THE NATIVE AMERICAN

I remember walking the dirt streets of Gurupá and along the eroding river-banks with my father, who visited me for two weeks in 1986. Trained as an archaeologist, he continuously picked at bits of rock and broken pottery lying on the ground or protruding from the steep banks. From our short excursions we speculated endlessly on what might lie buried below the surface and what stories these materials might tell—thousands of years of Native American habitation followed by colonial war, slave raids, colonial subordination, and poverty? I knew as an ethnographer that Gurupá's past was an essential part of understanding Gurupá's present condition. So I began searching the existing literature for archaeological and historical studies to see what had been written about Gurupá.

What I found were only bits and pieces of research on prehistoric cultures in areas distant from Gurupá. It appears that archaeological study in Amazonia had been limited until recently because of intellectual provincialism and infighting in the academic community (see Roosevelt 1991). In terms of historical data I was very fortunate to locate the doctoral research of Dr. Arlene Kelly. Her work, which entailed the patient retrieval, translation, and interpretation of historical documents scattered about the small towns of the lower Xingu and Amazon Rivers, provided me with a solid database for nearly 400 years of Gurupá's history.

Once I had read the available literature on the prehistoric and historic periods I understood a great deal about the roots of the present-day human condition in Gurupá. Much of what exists today derives from European conquest and the incorporation of the region into the emerging world economic system. For Gurupá this process began around 1590. Over the following 400 years the varying tugs and pulls of the world system, combined with regional and local initiatives and resistance, created a complex, ever-changing lifestyle. As we shall see, this lifestyle was rarely sustainable, always steeped in inequality, and continuously impoverishing the surviving population.

I divide the history of Gurupá into seven periods. Each is marked by some political or economic event of major significance for the entire Amazon valley. The first is the Native American period that lasted thousands of years, although it is poorly documented. Second is the European conquest and religious mission period, 1590–1758; and then the Directorate period, 1759–1799. The fourth period, 1800–1850, is the era of economic decadence and political turmoil, followed by the rubber boom, 1850–1910; the rubber bust and subsequent depression, 1910–1963; and the final period—the development and integration era—starting in 1964 and proceeding to the present. In this chapter, I examine the first three periods. Chapter 4 covers the fourth through sixth periods, and the final period is addressed throughout the remainder of the book.

The Native American Period

Archaeologists have not determined when human occupation of the area surrounding Gurupá began. To date there has been no archaeological excavation very close to the municipality. What I have pieced together about the area comes from archaeological research in nearby locales, records left by the first European chroniclers, comparisons to contemporary populations, and a certain amount of logical deduction about what might have been. This leaves much room for debate, and scholars of Amazonia have long argued over the nature of human occupation of the region (see, e.g., Lathrap 1970; Meggers 1971).

Recent research in Amazonia, however, suggests a general developmental sequence (see Roosevelt 1991:111–115, 1994:4–11). It is likely that the first humans to visit Gurupá came sometime after 10,000 B.C. At this point nomadic foragers occupied the Amazon basin. They lived in small and widely scattered groups. Some subsisted by hunting large, now-extinct fauna, while others focused on small game, fish, shellfish, palm seeds, and tree fruits. Sometime between 6000 and 4000 B.C. a population residing at Gurupá might have developed a sedentary village. Archaeological remains show that várzea peoples in the region were living on fairly permanent sites, subsisting by fishing, plant gathering, and broad-spectrum, small-game hunting (Lopes, Silveira, and Magalhães 1989:186). They also produced pottery, which makes this group the earliest known pottery-making population in the Americas (Roosevelt 1994:5). By 2000 B.C. it is possible that the inhabitants of Gurupá developed horticulture as their population grew. Throughout the region the staple crop was manioc. Additional crops included corn, rice, beans, sweet potatoes, peanuts, fruits, cotton, and tobacco.

As an alternative scenario, the people of Gurupá might have preferred inhabiting the terra firme area. Throughout Amazonia less populous societies existed in the terra firme. They organized themselves into small (100–400 individuals), mobile, and highly dispersed groups and subsisted by horticulture, gathering, and hunting. They possessed a very basic division of labor based on age and sex. Kinship ties (marriage, descent) provided the organizational structure for economic activity. This system produced little surplus, but at the same time people rarely suffered food shortages. They lived in extended family groups in communal houses; they were basically egalitarian, having equal access to power, prestige, and resources; and they lacked any centralized political leadership. Instead, leadership was temporary, situational, and lacked much coercive force.

If the population at Gurupá, however, developed várzea horticulture, they may have developed into a densely populated, complex society (Lathrap 1974:149–151). In surrounding areas of Amazonia, such groups as the Omagua, the Tapajós, and the Marajoara developed into chiefdoms. These societies organized thousands of people, possibly tens of thousands. Their subsistence was based on horticulture, gathering, fishing, and hunting in a finely balanced adaptation to the várzea and terra firme ecosystems (Bunker 1985:60).

Archaeological research shows that these groups possessed large public works (mound building), differentiated settlements, elaborate ceremonial art, long-distance trade, and elitist symbolism (Roosevelt 1994:7). They had a complex division of labor, coordinated by specialists directing seasonal use of resources and collection of surpluses. Kinship ties still formed the basic structure for economic activities, although social ranking altered social relationships. An elite group that held more status and power than others developed, yet there was no major differential access to resources needed for survival.

The elite likely consisted of members of high-ranking lineages thought to be descendant from deified human ancestors. The lineages produced a paramount leader or chief who acted "on behalf of a social whole in coordinating specialized activities, planning and supervising public works, managing redistribution, and leading in war" (Wolf 1982:96–97). The chief held political power—the ability to use coercion against members of the group—but this power was constantly restrained by kinship obligations. In other words, if chiefs abused their power, then their kin groups would withdraw support and another person could assume the chiefly position. The chiefdom engaged in large-scale warfare and diplomacy and created large tribute systems.

Gurupá is located midway between the sites of two of the complex várzea societies that developed at different times during this period: the Tapajós culture (at the intersection of the Tapajós and Amazon Rivers near the present-day city of Santarém) and the Marajoara culture (on Marajó Island at the mouth of the Amazon River). It is logical to assume that these societies influenced the populations of Gurupá. In order to speculate on what kind of society might have developed in Gurupá, a short discussion of the Tapajós and the Marajoara follows.

The Tapajós

Three chroniclers described the Tapajós chiefdom: Friar Carvajal (1934) in 1542, Cristóbal de Acuña (1942) in 1639, and Maurício de Heriarte (1874) in 1692. Carvajal reported that Tapajós settlements stretched 150 miles and were densely populated. They built their villages on rises in the floodplain that were above the seasonal flood line. John Hemming (1978:497) estimates their population to have numbered at least 25,000, although the population may have been several times that size.

Tapajós subsistence relied on many resources from both the várzea and terra firme. The Tapajós grew manioc, maize, rice, and fruit. They captured and corralled large numbers of river turtles, they fished, and they hunted manatees. Additionally, they hunted forest animals and waterfowl and collected a variety of plants. Betty Meggers (1971:141) speculates that specialists were present to coordinate these activities. They had to cope with the cycle of high and low water on the várzea, which could lead to potentially dangerous variations of food availability. Through careful organization the Tapajós developed a sustainable system of local resource management that supported a high population—a feat that contemporary populations in the area cannot match without the aid of food importation.

Political organization centered on a paramount chief and subordinate village chiefs. They also had religious specialists who undoubtedly consulted or controlled the supernatural realm. In particular, the religious specialists dealt with aspects of the agricultural cycle, such as when the floods would come and recede or when to plant.

The Tapajós had a well-organized military and were known for their fierceness and willingness to fight. Heriarte states that the population could assemble 60,000 warriors (see Meggers 1971:133). When fighting on water they could gather hundreds of canoes, each holding twenty to thirty men. Carvajal's report of one battle notes that the warriors dressed in feather decorations, shouted, and played trumpets, drums, pipes, and rebecs (three-stringed musical instruments) while engaging the enemy (Hemming 1978:194). The most feared weapon of the Tapajós was the arrow tipped with deadly curare poison.

Despite such bellicosity, Meggers (1971:145) speculates that most warfare among várzea groups was directed toward the terra firme groups rather than other várzea groups. Continuous warfare among the neighboring várzea groups would have been mutually destructive. Warfare with terra firme groups, however, was less detrimental while allowing for the capture of slaves. Slaves may have played an important role as expendable labor for várzea chiefdoms. The slaves could increase production during times of abundance but be discarded during times of scarcity without disrupting the social structure (Meggers 1971:144).

The Marajoara

Since the culture of Marajoara had disappeared before European contact, information on it comes entirely from archaeological excavations. Roosevelt (1991) has summarized the current data. It appears that at its height the Marajoara population numbered well over 100,000 (Roosevelt 1991:404). The group lived on the várzea of Marajó Island, a large flat area about the size of Switzerland. To escape the seasonal flooding of the várzea the people constructed mounds of earth. Large sites, containing twenty to forty mounds, might have been inhabited by more than 10,000 people at a time (Roosevelt 1991:404).

Subsistence was based on seed crops, wild plant collection, and intensive seasonal fishing (Roosevelt 1991:405). Since the area shows signs of 1,000 years of continual occupation, it is reasonable to conclude that the population had devised a sustainable use of the environment.

Fishing and agriculture were labor-intensive activities, as was the construction of massive earthworks and mounds found on the island. Additionally, there appears to have been considerable craft specialization—particularly, pottery, lithic tools, and ornament production. Organization of these activities required some sort of centralized power and probably led to the development of a ruling elite and a subordinate underclass.

Other evidence of social inequality comes from the osteology studies of Marajoara people. Skeletal remains show disparity between two classes of people in terms of health and nutritional status, although the data are not entirely conclusive (Roosevelt 1991:405). If more data were found to support this analysis, then it would suggest that the Marajoara were on the verge of forming a class system, or an early form of the state. The skeletal remains also suggest a warrior group that underwent physical training. Males were tall and well muscled in such a way that suggests systematic preparation and participation in warfare activities (Roosevelt 1991:407).

The Gurupaenses

Because of Gurupá's location on the várzea and its proximity to the Tapajós and Marajoara societies, it is logical to assume that the populations of these societies interacted with and influenced the people of Gurupá. What form this influence took is uncertain. Trade and warfare might have led to some type of populous and complex society in Gurupá, even if it were not a full-fledged chiefdom. The records of the first Europeans in the vicinity of Gurupá were very brief in their reference to the local population. The Dutch called the group "the Mariocai" and reported trading with them for forest products (Kelly 1984:25). I would argue that the people of Gurupá lived a life of economic self-sufficiency, environmental sustainability, egalitarian or rank social relations, internal peace, and external militarism, though I can speculate little else about Gurupá's prehistory.

The European Conquest and Religious Mission Period, 1590–1758

The arrival of the Europeans, accompanied by their deadly diseases, wars of conquest and enslavement, environmental destruction, and colonial exploitation, shattered the world of the Native Americans living in Gurupá. Throughout the Amazon region, the results of European contact were massive population decline and a concomitant collapse of social and cultural life. What emerged from the ashes of Native American life were new cultures with vastly different patterns of economic production, social interaction, and environmental use.

Motivations for the European Arrival

Such Europeans as the Portuguese, the Spanish, the Dutch, the French, and the English came to the New World for a number of reasons. Two very important ones were the desire to accumulate wealth and the drive to use this wealth to build and consolidate states in home countries. The European peninsula at the time of contact consisted of a number of militaristic states intent on expanding their domains, capturing booty wealth, and establishing and maintaining trade routes. During the last two centuries preceding overseas expansion most of these states were confronting the limits of such activities. In what historians call the "crises of feudalism," a combination of worsening climate, food shortages, widespread epidemics, depopulation, excessive exploitation of peasants to pay for war, and the corresponding rise in peasant rebellions—all occurring from A.D. 1300 onward—led Europe to the brink of collapse (Wolf 1982:108–109).

According to Wolf (1982:109) the way out of the crises was additional militarism to capture more booty wealth and trade routes in areas removed from Europe. Contact with the Americas, an event predicated on the closure of the overland trade route to Asia and the desire to find an alternative sea route, proved to be very important in overcoming the crises. By forcefully acquiring the resources of the Americas, as well as those of Africa and Asia, Europe could continue to consolidate politically, accumulate wealth, and basically live beyond its means (Wolf 1982:109).

By the sixteenth century European state building and struggles for domination took on a global character. European trade, conquest, and colonization were increasingly linking the world into one system. This system was larger and more tightly integrated than any political economic system before it. The keys to the rise of this system were the powerful tributary system the Europeans devised and the technological innovations in transport (shipping) and warfare (firearms). The spread of epidemic disease, particularly in the New World, also played an important role as it greatly decreased the numbers of resistant populations.

The tributary system of the Europeans was not totally unlike other systems that developed around the world with the rise of primary and secondary states. It was a system in which the ruling class (royalty, oligarchies) extracted surplus wealth from dominated classes by means of political or military coercion. In the process of wealth extraction the dominated primary producer retained direct access to resources, usually land for agricultural production. The local overlords, merchants, or the central state bureaucracy required the primary producer to pay tribute (Wolf 1982:79–80). The tribute financed the states' military forces and war campaigns, it compensated state bureaucrats and church officials, it enriched merchants and nobles, and it paid for conspicuous consumption by the royal courts.

Military conquest effectively increased the types and amount of wealth that were collected. Through conquest the wealth of other populations was plundered and transported to Europe. The Spanish and Portuguese, in particular, benefited from their previous wartime experience expelling the Moors from the European continent, using superior military technology (metal weapons, armor, firearms, horses, navies) and the spread of disease to conquer and pillage vast areas. Following conquest the Europeans forced direct payments of tribute from dominated peoples—either as taxation, wage labor, labor drafts, or slavery.

Trade also brought new types of wealth into the tributary sphere of exchange. Merchants and even missionaries (especially in Latin America) successfully expanded this realm of wealth by setting up markets throughout the world. The merchants bought up surplus tribute, transported it elsewhere, and then sold it for a sizable profit. Missionaries, too, collected the production of their missioners and sent it to be sold elsewhere for a profit. With their innovations in shipping the Europeans quickly capitalized on acquiring and marketing a wide range of commodities found worldwide. Their success enabled them to reinvest profits to acquire even more commodities for the market.

As the merchant class and missions flourished they challenged the limits of tributary systems by establishing decentralized markets. In previous empires a single centralized state political authority forced subjects to pay tribute. The availability of coercive force limited the amount of wealth gained through tribute taking. But decentralized markets operated very differently. They were based on impersonal exchanges using prices ideally set by supply and demand. Merchants and missionaries entered into exchange arrangements with primary producers and encouraged increased production of export commodities in exchange for imports. Over time a group of primary producers might intensify commodity production to the neglect of other activities and come to depend on the merchants and missionaries for tools, prestige goods, and even food (Wolf 1982:86). As this occurred it enabled merchants and missionaries to manipulate and change existing productive systems and even to underwrite coercive systems of commodity production (Wolf 1982:86). Through this process they expanded and strengthened their hold on the world system even further.

The search for wealth and the drive to consolidate states sent European armies, merchants, missionaries, and colonists to the corners of the earth. Their successes and failures, however, meant great suffering for multitudes of contacted and conquered peoples. Establishing tributary systems was a violent process. Warfare, slavery, and alterations of production systems for commodity export destroyed millions. Millions more died from Old World diseases. In terms of Amazonia, European expansion released such horrendous destructiveness and restructured life so completely there that its effects are still resounding in the lives of contemporary populations.

European Expansion and Domination Struggles

The first European expedition to travel the Amazon River and pass by Gurupá occurred in 1500, led by the Spanish explorer Vicente Yáñez Pinzón. It was not until the 1590s, however, that Europeans succeeded in systematic penetration and settlement of the region. At this early date the Dutch, French, English, and Portuguese all ventured into the region in hopes of finding booty wealth to appropriate, lucrative trade networks to develop, and colonial footholds to build. Not much booty was found—no gold or silver—so they traded tools and various trinkets for forest goods and fish. From the start Amazonia proved to be a poor place to generate large amounts of wealth for the Europeans.

The first Europeans to settle near Gurupá were Dutch mariners and traders. They established a series of three small wooden fortifications along the lower Amazon and Xingu Rivers. Gurupá—or Mariocai, as the Dutch called the site after the population living there—was the third in this series, built in 1609. The Dutch traded for dye, timber, and mother-of-pearl. They were also interested in sugarcane cultivation along the Xingu River to the south of Gurupá (Kelly 1984:25). Although the returns for these endeavors were low, the settlements did serve to support Dutch claims to the area. Gurupá was particularly important since it was located in a strategic position that the Dutch believed guarded the passage to the entire upper stretch of the Amazon River (Kelly 1984:31). The settlement retained this strategic importance until the 1760s when Europeans discovered a second, northern entrance to the Amazon at Macapá.

Almost immediately upon their arrival the Dutch, English, French, and Portuguese embroiled themselves in warfare over colonial territorial claims. This conflict continued sporadically over the next 100 years. Many Native Americans participated in these wars, allying themselves with different European states and serving as soldiers in the hopes of defeating rival indigenous groups and obtaining European trade goods. In the end the Portuguese were successful in establishing claim to the Amazon valley by expelling the French from Maranhão in 1615, the Dutch from the lower Amazon by 1640, and a final French intrusion into the area of Macapá in 1697.

Gurupá was the site of several colonial battles during this period. The first occurred in 1623 when a contingent of Portuguese soldiers and Native American archers attacked the Dutch trading post (Kelly 1984:27; Oliveira 1983:172). The Portuguese won the battle, although the surviving Dutch fled to a nearby island. Following this victory a Dutch warship with an English captain appeared in Gurupá, and in the ensuing battle the Portuguese killed all but one of the crew members on board (Kelly 1984:27).

After the victories the Portuguese captain-general, Bento Maciel Parente, built the fort of Saint Anthony of Gurupá. A garrison of fifty soldiers and an unspecified number of Native Americans were left there under the command of Captain Jeronimo do Albuquerque to prevent foreign powers from entering and trading in the region (Kelly 1984:28). Although the garrison was never completely successful in stopping foreign trading, especially for manatee and timber, it successfully prevented foreign colonization attempts (Kelly 1984:48, 65).

One foiled colonization attempt involved an Irish and Dutch settlement called Mandiutuba, which was built in 1625 several kilometers to the west of Gurupá (Oliveira 1983:172). Some of the Dutch were survivors of the earlier trading post of Mariocai. Gurupá's garrison, reinforced by 50 soldiers and 300 native archers sent from the costal town of Belém, attacked and killed between 100 and 114 of the settlers (Kelly 1984:29). Later, in 1639, the garrison surprised and captured a second Dutch warship near Gurupá (Kelly 1984:29; Hemming 1978:580, 583–584). Finally, in 1697 the garrison at Gurupá helped repel the French intrusion into the Amazon at Macapá (Kelly 1984:69).

Primarily because of its military importance, the Portuguese Crown designated Gurupá as a captaincy—a geopolitical division designed for settlement and development that is entrusted to an individual or the state—one of only five in the entire Amazon region at the time, and it was under the control of the state (Kelly 1984:72).

Destruction of Amazonian Societies

As the Portuguese were securing the territory around Gurupá and much of the lower Amazon region from competing European powers, they were also developing a colonial political economy to extract wealth for transfer back to Portugal. To set up their tributary system, the Portuguese began appropriating indigenous land, resources, and even labor. John Bodley (1990:24–41) has labeled this appropriation "the frontier process." Essential to its functioning was the ideology that all land, resources, and labor were freely available to the newcomer. Colonialists ignored or deemed irrelevant the rights and interests of the indigenous inhabitants. This ideology inevitably led to lawlessness and violence as the newcomers used any means possible, particularly "force or deception, to ruthlessly and profitably obtain the land, labor, minerals, and other resources they sought" (Bodley 1990:25). The societies they encountered in warfare or in peace were coerced into labor drafts, enslaved, forced out, or simply exterminated.

In Amazonia the Portuguese attacked and destroyed all indigenous societies within their reach that resisted the appropriation process. They also attacked and destroyed those indigenous groups who submitted peacefully. Even those societies who allied themselves with the Portuguese and took part in campaigns of conquest alongside them suffered the same fate. Assimilating Amazonian economies into the evolving world economy was brutal. Hemming (1978:217–237) has described this process as "anarchy on the Amazon."

The Portuguese wars of conquest against the native populations were usually one-sided affairs. The Portuguese were well equipped with metal swords and firearms against the natives' wooden clubs and arrows. The Portuguese wore quilted and leather armor or metal cuirasses and helmets, effective against arrows, while the natives went into battle naked (Hemming 1978:222). Most important, the Portuguese recruited thousands of native warriors eager to defeat their Amazon rivals and gain European trade goods. The battles were bloody and decisive. There were reports that some were so cruel that rivers ran red with blood (Hemming 1978:221). A Capuchin priest, Cristóvão de Lisboa, described the horrors of conquest: Besides killing and enslaving,

> they razed and burned entire villages, which are generally made of dry palm-leaves, roasting alive in them those who refused to surrender as slaves. They overcame and subjected others peacefully, but by execrable deceit. They would promise them alliance and friendship in the name and good faith of the King. But once they had them off guard and unarmed, they seized and bound them all, dividing them among themselves as slaves or selling them with the greatest cruelty. (Hemming 1978:221)

The Europeans had another great weapon against the Native Americans: Old World diseases. For millennia the New World populations were isolated from the various plagues that ravished Europe, Africa, and Asia. As a result they had developed no immunities to a long list of contagions that the Portuguese, and later the Africans, brought with them. Diseases such as smallpox, measles, malaria, tuberculosis, and even the common cold spread rapidly through the region, often decades ahead of the European contact. The level of depopulation was great. Coupled with warfare and the abuses of slavery and other forms of coerced labor, death by disease was so rampant that no várzea civilization was left intact after only 150 years of contact with the Europeans (Meggers 1971:121). Sicknesses, which still ravage today, have eliminated an estimated 99 percent of the lowland Native American population—truly part of humanity's worst holocaust.

How did the groups at Gurupá and the surrounding areas fare during conquest? European chroniclers reported that the Tapajós at first resisted Portuguese attempts to control them since they were numerous and well organized for war. Exposure to disease and persistent raiding by the Portuguese, however, eventually weakened them. In 1637 Bento Maciel Parente, the son of the man by the same name who had built the fort in Gurupá, led a brutal attack against them. Acuña recorded the events of the war, stating that Parente sailed "in a launch mounting a piece of artillery and other smaller vessels, with as many troops [Native American allies] as he could get, and fell upon the Indians with harsh war, when they desired peace" (cited in Hemming 1978:237). The Tapajós surrendered and were disarmed. The Portuguese then herded the warriors into an enclosure while the native allies of the Portuguese sacked the village, pillaging all objects and raping women. After these events the population continued to suffer from disease and slaving raids until it existed no more.

What about the Mariocai of Gurupá? Although there are no reports of the events, it is likely that the group was attacked and defeated, or that it submitted peacefully to Portuguese rule. Next, disease undoubtedly took a heavy toll on the people. The surviving population probably worked for the Portuguese, possibly as slaves, producing commodities for export, providing labor for transportation (paddling canoes), serving as warriors for conquest campaigns, or as guides and soldiers for slaving raids. Eventually, they assimilated into a growing ethnic mix of natives brought to Gurupá.

Reordering of Amazonian Societies

By the time the chaos of conquest had ended the Portuguese in Gurupá and elsewhere in Amazonia were well under way in establishing their colonial economy. For this economy to function over the long term, the Portuguese needed to replace the acquisition of booty wealth—mainly in the form of "red gold," or indigenous slaves—and simple trade with indigenous populations with the production of export commodities. In the northeast of Brazil the commodity of choice was sugarcane, produced on plantations worked first by Native American slaves and then by African slaves. The Portuguese had obtained fantastic wealth from its production, thus it is little wonder that they wished to duplicate this system by establishing sugar plantations in the Amazon. Although there are no records from Gurupá during this time, the Portuguese presumably grew some sugarcane, employing native labor. Modest quantities of tobacco, cotton, and manioc may also have been grown. Profits were likely low for these crops since the colonists did not develop plantation production. Part of the reason for low profitability was the ecological inappropriateness of monoculture in Gurupá and most parts of the Amazon, as previously discussed.

Faced with the improbability of developing a productive plantation economy, the Amazon colonists turned to the extraction of forest and river products. They deployed labor to gather a variety of products and to sell them on the world market. Collectively, the products were known as *drogas do sertão* (backland drugs). Among the drogas extracted, many of which came from Gurupá at one time or another, were cacao (chocolate beans, which were also cultivated), cloves, oleaginous seeds, vanilla, annatto fruit (the pulp of which is used to make a yellowish red dye), cinnamon, sarsaparilla, anil, senna (dried leaves used for medicinal purposes, especially as purgatives), pixurim (a substitute for nutmeg), carajuru (a bark used to make red dye), timber, aromatic bark, and tree cotton (Reis 1974:34; Sweet 1974:57; Parker 1985:7). The colonists also took riverine fauna (fish, turtles, manatees) and animal skins.

Although extraction of drogas do sertão and other resources did not generate as much wealth as agriculture did in other parts of Brazil, the colonists saw it as a more cost-efficient form of exploitation for the region. Extraction did not require large investments to clear land, tend crops, or buy machinery. Nor did it require a large labor force, at least in the early years of colonialism. All that the colonists needed to do was to pay for a small crew of collectors, numbering as few as three or four, and to gather a convoy of canoes (Weinstein 1983:12; MacLachlan 1973:206). There was also flexibility in what they collected. If a particular resource was not earning sufficient profit in an overseas market, or if extractors had depleted it during earlier treks, there were always other commodities to fall back upon (Weinstein 1983:12). This latter condition—depletion of extracted resources—however, led to serious ecological consequences for the colonial economy.

Resource Depletion and Environmental Destruction

From the beginning of the colonial period the Portuguese in Gurupá and elsewhere in Amazonia engaged in reckless pursuit of profit in extractive activities. Since their economic fortune did not depend on the sustainable use of the local environment—they imported food and supplies and could always move on when needed—they did not attempt to manage extracted flora or fauna. The colonists viewed forest and river management as uneconomical and unnecessary for wealth accumulation. The usual practice was to simply exploit resources beyond their capacity for natural regeneration, then seek other resources elsewhere. The colonists established this pattern in Gurupá by the late 1700s, as suggested by the census data (see page 61). The result in Gurupá and much of Amazonia was serious environmental impoverishment that, along with labor shortages, led to the ultimate downfall of the colonial economic system (Bunker 1985:60–61).

The overharvesting of river fauna, particularly turtles and manatees, was one example of environmental catastrophe that likely affected Gurupá. These animals were important sources of meat and oils in the indigenous diet. The Portuguese also wanted the meat and oils for local consumption and export, but they resorted to nonsustainable levels of hunting to yield a short-term profit (Bunker 1985:64). They devastated the animal populations, depriving the indigenous people of an important food source. This was one event in the series that led to the declining nutritional status of indigenous populations, as evidenced by the declining stature between precontact and contemporary peoples mentioned earlier.

Additionally, the rapid reduction in numbers of river fauna seriously disrupted the river ecosystem. Manatees, through their grazing, were crucial to clearing lakes, oxbows, and river channels of excessive water vegetation. This enabled the penetration of light and the production of complex organic molecules essential for life throughout the food chain. Small turtles were an important source of food for large fish. Both turtle and manatee wastes were necessary to stabilize nutrient cycles required for fish survival (Fittkau 1973). The depletion of manatees and turtles inevitably led to a decline in the fish populations throughout Amazonia, diminishing a staple of the regional diet.

Labor Recruitment

From the beginning the Native Americans were essential to the functioning of Gurupá's extractive economy. The Portuguese were few in number and not willing to labor manually in the New World, even when they came from peasant origins. Throughout Amazonia, Native Americans provided the human power to collect resources, paddle canoes, grow food, salt fish, produce turtle butter, and build houses and churches. The indigenous populations also possessed the knowledge of the diverse Amazonian ecozones that enabled them to journey into the forest for months at a time and retrieve the scattered forest products. In addition, they possessed the knowledge to hunt, fish, and produce food crops in small subsistence gardens to feed the colonists. Perhaps most important, the Native Americans were a locally available, cheap source of labor. Unlike other parts of Brazil the sites of the Amazonian colony were too poor to import large numbers of African slaves, so they relied almost exclusively on indigenous labor.

I should note that Gurupá is an anomaly in this context. Because of the presence of a military garrison, officials who worked at a prison built there, and various personnel involved with monitoring river traffic and trade, the town supported a number of individuals with the financial resources to import African slaves. Gurupá's African contingent grew to represent 31 percent of the town's population at the time of the first population census in 1783 (Kelly 1984:143). The African slaves worked as household servants and in agriculture. Extraction was likely left to Native Americans.

As world demand for extractive products grew so did the need for native labor. Most natives, however, did not wish to dedicate as much labor to the extractive economy as the Portuguese demanded. As Bodley wrote, "Undisturbed tribal cultures really are well-integrated, self-contained, satisfying systems, and their members cannot be expected to suddenly begin working for the material rewards of an alien culture without some form of compulsion" (1990:115–116). Although the cultures of Native Americans were not "undisturbed," they had few incentives to labor for the Portuguese.

Labor recruitment became the critical factor in the colonial economy. The Europeans had to gain control over labor to force it into commodity production in order for the tributary system and/or decentralized markets to function. During the conquest and mission period the Portuguese accomplished this in two ways. One was the brazen enslavement of Native Americans. The second was placement of natives in religious missions where the Europeans enticed or forced them into commodity production for both the Catholic Church and the colonists. Both forms of labor recruitment occurred in Gurupá.

Slavery and wage labor became the principal features of the new labor relations linking European and Native American societies. In both cases there was great human suffering as the new labor relations ripped apart the fundamental fabric of Native American society and replaced it with stratification, nonsustainability, and cultural disintegration.

Slavery

Both the Native Americans and the Europeans had long traditions of slavery. What was different about slavery in seventeenth-century Amazonia, however, were the massive numbers of people enslaved and their use in the production of export commodities for the world market. At first the Portuguese sought workers through the purchase of slaves whom the várzea populations already possessed. As the demand for labor grew, they encouraged the Native Americans to increase raids on rival groups to capture more slaves. When these increased efforts could not meet the demand, the Portuguese conducted slaving raids themselves.

Gurupá played an infamous role in Amazonian slavery. It served as a major staging ground for raids conducted both upriver and downriver

(Kelly 1984:66). The colonists brought many of the captured to Gurupá and forced them into extraction and food production. The Portuguese were very proficient in obtaining slave labor. Their country was the major global trafficker in human chattel, particularly from Africa, in the fifteenth and sixteenth centuries. As early as 1560 they were already using as many as 40,000 Native American slaves in the northeast of Brazil (Hemming 1978:143).

The slaving raids leaving Gurupá were deadly ventures, often killing many people during capture and transport. The raids quickly depopulated the surrounding areas. Franciscan missionary Friar Cristóvão de Lisboa criticized the scandalous nature of the raids and noted that by 1647 there were only "domesticated" Native Americans (individuals working for the Portuguese) for 100 leagues west of Belém (Kiemen 1954:56), an area that approaches the vicinity of Gurupá.

The Portuguese justified the raids in several ways: They were capturing souls for Christianity, conducting "just wars" in self-defense or retaliation against hostiles, and even rescuing (resgatado) native captives from cannibalism (Hemming 1978:150). Regarding the latter, Portuguese law allowed the purchase or ransom of a prisoner who was about to be eaten by an indigenous group. The only problem with this edict was that few Amazonian groups practiced ritualistic cannibalism (it was more a custom of costal Tupinambá populations to the south of the Amazon). The Portuguese took little heed of this detail and conducted persistent "ransom" expeditions.

Occasionally, the colonial government reacted to what it considered excessively cruel treatment of Native Americans and illegal raids by arresting and incarcerating individuals, including military officers. To house these and other criminals, the government established a regional prison at Gurupá because it considered the settlement sufficiently isolated for a prison, being Portugal's most advanced Amazonian frontier settlement until 1638 (Kelly 1986:69–70).

Life under slavery was brutal. The colonists took people from societies organized by social equality or rank and thrust them into unimaginable positions of inferiority at the hands of an alien culture. Many died simply from the psychological shock of such treatment. Countless others died from exposure to disease, from physical torture, and from the harsh work routines of commodity production. Food shortages and starvation became major problems. In part this occurred because of the disruption of indigenous systems of resource management and food production in such ecozones as the várzea. It also occurred because the colonists used the coerced labor force for the production of export commodities, not subsistence products. The limited food that was grown had to first feed the colonists.

The life of native forest extractors or natives sent to enslave other Native Americans was sometimes less enfeebling. These individuals experienced greater measures of freedom and even prestige from military engagements. But the physical rigors of extraction and the dangers of combat usually led to early deaths for these slaves.

Religious Missions

The uncontrolled slave raids and spread of disease in and beyond Gurupá ravaged the Native American populations and threatened the profitability of the colonial economy. The Portuguese Crown repeatedly tried to reduce the chaos and increase export by regulating labor recruitment. One attempt occurred in 1647 when all Native American slaves were freed and colonists required to pay "fair" wages to those employed (Kiemen 1954:65–67). Of course, this policy was heavily steeped in ethnocentrism. Wages could hardly be fair since they were culturally inappropriate and, as we shall see, were set well below basic levels of subsistence. Laboring for the colonists clearly led to a severe decline in the standard of living, for it would offer no advantage unless the native subsistence base was so destroyed that there was no other alternative.

The 1647 attempt failed to control the Europeans' abuse of the natives. As an alternative the Portuguese Crown decided to install the Jesuit religious order in the Amazon to oversee Native American populations. The Crown's intention was to have the Jesuits secure labor through a program of pacification (Kiemen 1954:98). With the Jesuits in charge of all Native Americans in Brazil by 1655, the Crown also hoped to temper the settlers' ruthless treatment of slaves and halt the decimation of indigenous populations (several years earlier the Franciscans had made a similar, but failed, attempt; see Kiemen 1954:42, 98; Sweet 1974:78).

In 1652 the Portuguese Crown allowed the Jesuits to establish a mission in the captaincy of Gurupá. The Jesuits were anxious to control the area since they felt Gurupá was the gateway to the Amazon (Kelly 1984:38). In 1655 two Jesuit missionaries arrived in Gurupá with a reported 100 freed Native Americans (Kelly 1984:40). Their arrival, however, aroused hostility among the colonists, who were unwilling to allow Jesuit interference in their use of native workers. The colonists soon expelled the two priests from Gurupá with a warning not to return. When word of this action reached the governor of the colony, reprisal quickly followed. The governor sent two perpetrators of the incident to Portugal for trial and exiled two others to the southern colony in Brazil. After the incident one of the missionaries returned and resumed work in the general area (Kiemen 1954:103; Kelly 1984:40–41).

By 1656 the Jesuits had established a mission named after Saint Peter close to the fort in Gurupá (Kelly 1984:42). They populated the mission through pacification efforts and slave raids. The former involved offering European trade goods to natives in exchange for relocation. For the latter, missionaries would accompany slavers on their raids. One such raid took place in 1658. Gurupá's captain-major, accompanied by a missionary, led an expedition of 45 Portuguese soldiers and 450 Native Americans to the Tocantins River (Kelly 1984:66). There they attacked and enslaved members of the Inheyguaras as punishment for unspecified past deeds. Such punitive raids on Native Americans originating from Gurupá continued until the beginning of the nineteenth century.

Once the Native Americans were in the missions the Jesuits grouped them by ethnicity, converted them to Christianity, and obligated them to become commodity producers of extractive and agricultural goods for both the religious orders and the colonists. Although many natives retained direct access to land and resources, their growing dependence on European goods and coercion within the mission eroded their economic autonomy. In the end they had little option but to produce commodities for export (Parker 1985:21). The natives were being integrated into the decentralized markets of the world system.

The mission became the essential link to the world system. In the missions indigenous groups organized themselves into communal work groups and produced goods in exchange for minuscule wages. Types of wages differed over time but could be as valueless as "trifling lengths of coarse cotton cloth," for which the workers had little use (Hemming 1978:219). The colonists established a rigid class system, bolstered by racial prejudice, to control production. The natives produced commodities, and the Europeans appropriated the surplus by means of underpaying wages. This was the principal form of tribute taking. Through this process the colonists transformed the Native Americans into a group of wage earners who supplied a demand for manufactured and imported goods, two basic ingredients for the expansion of the world system (Ross 1978:202).

Why did the Native Americans who avoided slavery accept this system? Some did so to avoid being the target of horrendous slave raids, as the religious missions offered some protection against the persistent raids (Ross 1978). Others did so because death from disease had depopulated their villages to the point that they could no longer survive autonomously. Many others, however, did not accept these conditions and fled into the forest after relocation. This was a common occurrence since the colonists could not easily supervise extraction activities and even subsistence agriculture in scattered garden plots. This allowed the worker considerable freedom of movement.

There was one other fundamental problem in retaining labor in the mission. Groups residing there were highly susceptible to diseases. Not infrequently, entire mission populations died in a matter of a few days from an infectious outbreak.

Despite the problems of labor retention, control over native labor in the missions gave the Jesuits a stranglehold over the colonial economy.

Colonists often had to obtain workers from the missions, especially when they depleted their supply of slaves or the government periodically outlawed slavery. Transportation, which was mainly in the form of canoes, also depended on native labor. This allowed the Jesuits to monopolize regional trade. In addition, the Jesuits extended their control beyond the mission by speaking and diffusing a pidgin of Tupi-Guarani languages, called *lingua geral* (general language), which became the trade language of Amazonia.

Jesuit control over the economy created constant tension with the colonists. In 1661 the colonists revolted in a regional uprising against Jesuit hegemony. The Jesuit hierarchy ordered Gurupá's priest at the time, a German named Betendorf, into hiding to escape the colonists (Hemming 1978:342). He hid in the forest with sixteen Native Americans for several months until they ran out of food. When he returned to Gurupá several settlers attempted to arrest him. The captain-major of the fort, however, was pro-Jesuit and protected the priest. He arrested the principal anti-Jesuit agitators and hung them after they confessed their sins to Betendorf (Kelly 1984:46; Hemming 1978:342). But in the following year Belém's town council sent a large task force to arrest Betendorf and two other Jesuits who had taken refuge at Gurupá. The captain-major was unable to intervene, although some colonists tried and failed to defend the Jesuits. One colonist died in the confrontation (Kelly 1984:67). With the arrest of Gurupá's missionaries all Jesuit missionaries in the Amazon valley were in the custody of the colonists.

Responding to the regional turmoil, the Crown rescinded Jesuit control over Native Americans in 1663. Town councils and governors assumed control. The colonial government gave the mission of Saint Peter to the colonists. The Jesuits of Gurupá eventually established another mission farther into the interior sometime around 1670 (Kelly 1984:47). They probably made this move to minimize the colonists' interference with mission activities.

With the colonists back in control of native labor the economy plummeted to a state of near collapse by 1680. This downturn happened at a critical time for the Portuguese Crown. The Crown had grown desperate for colonial revenues since it had used much of its wealth for military ventures and political demands of the state, as well as for conspicuous consumption by the royalty (Wolf 1982:119). The Crown had also lost much of its tribute-generating territories in Asia and Africa because of Dutch expansionism.

To boost revenues from the Amazon region the Crown decided to promote export agriculture instead of faltering extraction (Parker 1985:16). To force the colonists into agriculture (particularly sugarcane cultivation) the Crown outlawed all pretenses for Native American slavery and returned control over indigenous populations again to the religious orders (Kiemen 1954:141, 143). The Crown then set up a trading company to import African slaves. By limiting access to indigenous slaves the Crown hoped to compel the settlers to abandon extraction and use the African slaves for agriculture. Although the plan failed, because of labor and ecological problems, and extraction continued to dominate Amazonian exports, the new laws did reestablish the religious orders to their former prominence. The Jesuits in particular benefited since they maintained the greatest number of missions in the region (Parker 1985:14).

The laws of 1680, however, left the colonists without a sufficient supply of workers. Conflict in Gurupá again mounted when the Jesuits returned. A rivalry spanning two decades developed between the religious order and the captain-major of the fort, Manuel Guedes Aranha. One of the first signs of this rivalry occurred in the 1680s when the Jesuits refused to send priests to minister to the local garrison and residents of Gurupá or to the mission of Saint Peter (Kiemen 1954:174). Later, in 1687 or 1688, Aranha raided a Jesuit mission in an adjoining captaincy and apparently confiscated the native workers (Kelly 1984:67).

The tensions created by these actions continued until 1693 when political decisions made in Portugal forced the Jesuits to surrender the mission at Gurupá to the Franciscans of Piety (Kelly 1984:53), an event that lessened the conflicts among Gurupá's colonists, the government, and the mission. However, over the next sixty years the mission system of Gurupá deteriorated greatly. By 1743 the French naturalist Charles de la Condamine passed through Gurupá and commented that the only Native Americans there were the slaves of the colonists. Six years later Gonçalves da Fonseca reported that successive epidemics of smallpox and measles had eliminated the Native Americans at Saint Peter (Hemming 1978:445). Other correspondence from this time reported that a second mission established upstream from Gurupá, Saint Joseph of Arapijo, received little attention (Kelly 1984:101).

To the south of the Amazon in the state of Maranhão the colonists vented their frustrations over the return of Jesuit control in a rebellion known as the Beckman Revolt. The rebellion, which occurred in 1684, persuaded the Crown to divide Jesuit control more evenly among the other religious orders. The colonists regained the right to conduct slave raids, although only under Jesuit supervision (Parker 1985:16). Still frustrated by these arrangements the colonists mounted slave raids deep in the Amazon interior beyond Jesuit control. By 1691 the colonists had to travel upriver for two months to find Native Americans (Hemming 1978:411). Ironically, the colonists' slave raids forced more Native Americans to seek refuge in the religious missions (Parker 1985:20). This pattern continued until 1757 when the Crown expelled the Jesuits from all Portuguese territories.

The Directorate Period, 1759–1799

In the first half of the eighteenth century Portuguese possessions in Asia continued to shrink, placing increased pressure on the Amazon colony to produce more wealth. But export production in Gurupá and the rest of the colony severely lagged behind the Crown's aspirations. Export agriculture was weak (sugar and tobacco) and extraction faltered as depletion of resources continued and Native American workers became more scarce.

At this point tensions between the Jesuits and the Crown escalated to new levels. The Jesuits controlled much of the colonial economy (both production and labor) through their missions and were accumulating wealth that was not taxable by the state because of a royal exemption granted in 1686 (Sweet 1974:95, 467; Parker 1985:22). Jesuit economic domination also kept tensions high with the colonists, as described in terms of Gurupá. The Portuguese Crown, desperate for revenue and spurred on by allegations of Jesuit political conspiracy against the Crown, finally acted to end the Jesuit stronghold in the region and the rest of Brazil. In 1755 the colonial government secularized the religious missions, and in 1759 it expelled the Jesuits from Amazonia.

Jesuit expulsion came under the rule of the Marquis de Pombal (Sebastião José de Carvalho e Melo). To reorder the mission system the marquis implemented a plan called the "Directorate," designed by his brother and governor of the colony, Francis Xavier de Mendoça Furtado. The Directorate mandated that there be no special laws to protect Native Americans and that they should share legal equality with the settlers (MacLachlan 1972:358). The colonial government appropriated control over the mission system. In each mission it assigned a Native American village chief to oversee social and economic activities. To aid the chief and rationalize economic activities—that is, increase profit—Governor Furtado appointed colonial directors. He placed them in the missions along with a secular parish priest (Parker 1985:25; Kelly 1984:113). The directors organized forest extraction, supervised agriculture, provided various labor levies, and generally assured that each mission became an integral part of the regional economy (Anderson 1985:52).

Through the Directorate the Portuguese Crown intended to create an agricultural economy modeled on the plantation economy of the northeast (Parker 1985:28). It gave tax relief and grants of indigenous labor to the colonists as incentives for agriculture. It arranged to once again import African slaves and also formed and subsidized a regional trading company to aid in transportation and trade of produce. These measures greatly favored Furtado, who obtained unrestricted access to native labor for his cacao production. He also became the director of the trading company.

During this period Gurupá served as an administrative center, a check-

THE DEMISE OF THE NATIVE AMERICAN

THE DEMISE OF THE NATIVE AMERICAN

point for river trade, and the site of a prison and fort. The town grew slowly, as indicated in the first population censuses taken in the colony (see Table 3.1). The 1783 census classified Gurupá as one of twenty-five *branco* (white) towns in the colony of Grão Pará (Kelly 1984:141). A branco town classification meant the settlement consisted of people of European descent and mixed descent but lacked many Native Americans. The classification made no reference to African slaves. The population figures for the missions of Saint Peter and Saint Joseph of Arapijo, renamed Saint Joseph of Carrazedo, are listed in Table 3.2. The census classified Saint Peter's as a Native American place without Europeans or brancos, one of nineteen in the colony. A captain-major and a sergeant-major (both colonists) directed the mission. The census also classified the mission of Carrazedo as a Native American place without Europeans or brancos. Two officials were in control, a principal and a captain. The 1784 census described the mission as possessing a church that was about to fall down, although the residents' homes were in good condition (Kelly 1984:146).

Table 3.1   Population Census for Gurupá, 1783–1797

Year	Free Luso-Brazilians	African Slaves	Other	Total
1783	269	124		393
1789	295	147	94[a]	536
1797	299	131	38[b]	468

Source: Adapted from Kelly (1984:142, 151–152, 179).
Notes: a. Listed as *agregados,* boarders or tenant farmers connected with a Luso-Brazilian family.
b. Listed as fifteen tenants and servants of European descent, eighteen salaried Native Americans, and five salaried mestizos (descendants of both Europeans and Native Americans).

Table 3.2   Population Census for Gurupá Missions, 1783–1797

Year	Saint Peter	Saint Joseph of Carrazedo
1783	86	194
1789	35[a]	164
1797	43	127

Source: Adapted from Kelly (1984:142, 146, 154, 181, 183).
Note: a. Of these, eleven were under the age of fifteen. In addition, fourteen whites, four African slaves, and one agregado had moved into the mission by this time (Kelly 1984:152).

Despite the reorganization of the missions and incentives for agriculture production in Gurupá and the rest of the colony, only the production of cacao improved. The major problems continued to be ecological constraints and labor shortages, as well as a lack of sufficient incentive to risk the less cost-effective agriculture over extraction.

The 1789 census reported that the town of Gurupá produced modest amounts of the following commodities: raw cotton, rice, cacao, coffee, manioc, oleaginous oils, molasses, cloth, manatee, piracuí (fish meal), and *aguardente* (liquor distilled from sugarcane) (Kelly 1984:167). The aguardente came from one distiller in 1789 and four distillers by 1795 (Kelly 1984:162, 166). African slaves probably produced most of the above commodities.

The mission of Carrazedo was more active in extraction. Between 1764 and 1767 it appears that Carrazedo played a major role in the regional production of the following commodities: 100 percent of pirarucu, (a type of fish), 19.44 percent of andiroba oil (used in making soap), and 19.33 percent of Brazil nuts, as well as smaller amounts of cacao, fine clove, estopa (a fibrous bark used for caulking), tobacco, and manioc, the latter being exported to Belém beginning in the late 1760s (Kelly 1984:116–121, 174). Table 3.3 shows the commodities produced in Carrazedo between 1764 and 1782. Of particular note, the elimination of some commodities extracted by 1782 likely resulted from overextraction leading to depletion.

Table 3.3   Reported Production in Carrezedo, 1764–1782

Products	1764	1765	1766	1767	1769	1782
Cacao	X	X	X		X	X
Fine clove		X				
Piracuí		X			X	
Brazil nuts		X		X	X	
Manioc flour		X	X		X	
Andiroba oil		X	X	X	X	
Tobacco			X		X	
Estopa				X		

Source: Adapted from Kelly (1984:169).

The structure of the secularized missions exacerbated the labor and incentive difficulties in Gurupá and the rest of the colony. Ubiquitous corruption enabled the colonial directors to establish dictatorial power over the village and to appropriate more labor than legally permitted (Parker 1985:30; Oliveira 1994:102–103). The directors allocated workers for extraction, where they earned the highest profits, rather than taking risks with agriculture. Further limits to agricultural endeavors occurred as the colonial government took its share of Native American workers for its own projects. Such was the case in Gurupá, where many missioners worked for the commander of Gurupá's fort on gathering expeditions and as fishers and hunters for other colonists (Kelly 1984:130). The 1784 census suggests this practice; it listed the distribution of nineteen individuals to business canoes and to the residents of Gurupá (Kelly 1984:145).

The Directorate did not succeed in improving the colonial economy. By 1790 the labor shortage became so severe that no sector of the economy, public or private, could secure its labor needs (MacLachlan 1973:222). In Gurupá there were periodic shortages of food and other commodities, as documented by a priest, Father Queiros, who spent Holy Week in Gurupá sometime in the early 1760s and noted that all construction work on the fort of Saint Anthony had stopped due to a lack of manioc flour (Kelly 1984:130). The missions of Saint Peter and Saint Joseph of Carrazedo also suffered. By the end of the Directorate period the populations and production of both missions declined sharply.

Epidemics of smallpox and measles, as well as high rates of defection from the mission, also aggravated the labor shortage (Kelly 1984:115). The colonial government mounted military campaigns to recapture runaway Native Americans and African slaves. The soldiers stationed at Gurupá (100 Luso-Brazilian soldiers and 150 racially mixed soldiers) were active in these seek-and-destroy missions (Kelly 1984:162, 164). However, the raids did little to remedy the situation.

By the end of the eighteenth century the Portuguese Crown faced the inevitable collapse of the colonial economy. In another reverse of policy it abandoned the Directorate in 1799. Although the Directorate lasted only forty-two years and had failed to remedy the colony's economic problems, it did create long-lasting changes for Amazonian society. These changes came as the Directorate ended the semiprotective segregation of the Native American cultures in the mission system. For example, the Portuguese replaced the use of lingua geral; Native Americans were encouraged to wear European clothes instead of traditional clothing; and houses were modeled after the small European cottage, with room partitions installed to discourage communal living. This last alteration was an attempt to impose the European idea of the nuclear family upon the indigenous cultures (Parker 1985:26; MacLachlan 1972:361). To encourage racial intermarriage, the colonial government offered material incentives in the form of land grants, free tools, tax exemptions, and even political posts to Portuguese men who married Native American women (Ross 1978:203–204; Wagley 1976:38; MacLachlan 1973:363).

Most destructive to the Native American cultures, however, were the new arrangements to maximize the availability of labor. The Directorate broke up the communally structured production units and replaced them with more "efficient" small family units. The idea behind this was to gain access to more wage workers and force more individuals into full-time commodity production. This practice had a devastating impact on the population since wages were not appreciably increased and groups could no longer pool resources and aid one another. Some families suffered greatly while others eked by. The demise of communal production also remixed ethnic groups formerly segregated under the religious mission system. This change led to the loss of much of the remaining cultural knowledge amassed during the millennia of cultural development in Amazonia.

Throughout the Directorate period the missioners worked on canoes (for transportation and trade), extracted forest products, produced fats and oils, dried and salted fish, and planted crops (Kelly 1984:116). They gradually scattered out along rivers and streams in their small family units to conduct the economic activities now unabatedly dictated by the market system and world demand (Ross 1978:206; Parker 1985:35). This system required geographic mobility and a loose social organization to function. Isolation and increasing dependence on the market economy were the results. The Native American survivors were evolving into an indigenous camponês class.

Conclusion

By 1800 the people of the Amazon had endured 200 years of colonial rule. The legacy of this rule was the establishment of three key patterns that were to shape and limit future events in Amazonia. The first was depopulation. The decimation of Native American societies was a fundamental factor impeding wealth accumulation in the colonial economy. Without indigenous labor the colonists had no one to extract, no one to farm, and no one to profitably exploit. This deficiency was to have a long-term effect on the economy in the following centuries. Each time there was an upswing in the regional economy with the promise of some type of intensified economy activity, labor shortages would severely limit growth potential. Disease and European greed for labor clearly led to underdevelopment in the region.

The second pattern was environmental destruction. Predatory extraction depleted many resources beyond their capacity to regenerate. Intricate ecological cycles were disrupted. In addition, the indigenous knowledge to manage complex ecosystems was lost as depopulation occurred. To date Luso-Brazilian culture and Western science have been able to replicate neither these management systems, nor the population levels of precontact groups without imported subsidies of food. Researchers will probably never know the full extent of these disruptions, but they clearly limited future use of the ecosystem by humanity.

Commodity production for export was the third pattern. This was a requirement of integration into the evolving world system. To implement it required the forcible appropriation of indigenous land, resources, and labor. This transformed Native American societies from self-sufficient and basically egalitarian or rank groups to an exploited and nonautonomous class of commodity producers (Ross 1978:193). Wage labor and slavery reduced the populations to an unprecedented level of poverty. Stratification further degraded human existence. A class system evolved consisting of the dominant Portuguese and the subservient Native Americans and mestizos. Still the Portuguese Crown was unhappy with the wealth it extracted from the system and continuously tried to make the Native Americans and colonists produce more wealth, which in turn led to more depopulation and environmental destruction. The result was great impoverishment so that a few could profit modestly. By the end of the eighteenth century the Directorate dismantled the last vestiges of Native American society. An exploited indigenous campesinato emerged.

Front counter of Seu Oscar's trading post, Gurupá

4

THE RISE OF THE
INDIGENOUS *CAMPESINATO*

During my time in Gurupá I made a habit of lending or giving away Charles Wagley's Portuguese version of *Amazon Town* and then soliciting comments. The book fascinated people. It showed them they had a history, that they were distinctive, and that other people valued their story. But it also raised many questions for the readers. I remember two very common responses: "I did not know we were descendants of the Indians"; and, "Why have we been exploited for so long?"

I found the first response interesting since many people in Gurupá have physical features that outsiders would classify as Native American. That the Gurupaenses did not recognize this raises important questions about the way people, even scientists, classify ethnicity and race (see Shanklin 1994). On another level the comment went deeper. The culture of Gurupá has antecedents of Native American culture, but it is most assuredly not Native American. So what is the actual link between Native American and contemporary Gurupá culture, and how has the culture evolved over the last 200 years?

The second response, in which people puzzled over exploitation, arises within a context of social conflict and intense politicizing taking place in Gurupá, as throughout much of Brazil. Many people desire better explanations of how and why they are in their contemporary condition. How has history shaped their current struggles? This chapter deals with these questions.

As shown in Chapter 3, the first 200 years of European contact in Amazonia resulted in environmental degradation, colonial exploitation, and depopulation that transformed the indigenous population into an underclass entrapped in dependence and poverty. The population was evolving into a class of *camponeses* (small-scale farmers and extractors) linked by asymmetrical ties to the emerging world system. The indigenous campesinato, however, did not emerge full blown in 1800. Instead, it evolved with the fate and fortune of the regional political economy over the following 200 years. This time span includes three historic periods: the era of depression and revolution, 1800–1850; the rubber boom, 1850–1910; and the rubber bust and subsequent depression, 1910–1963.

The Depression and Revolution Period, 1800–1850

Violence in the form of warfare, slavery, and rebellions dominate the colonial history of Gurupá and Amazonia. It should be of little surprise that the rise of the indigenous campesinato was also born in violence, namely, in the Cabanagem Revolt. The revolt was a product of economic depression, environmental destruction, political turmoil, and a troublesome transformation in labor relations in the region.

Overexploitation of extractive resources and a drop in the international market for tropical products triggered an economic depression in the first half of the nineteenth century. The depression deeply affected the extraction and production of cacao—the leading export of the time (Santos 1980:28; Ross 1978:209). In addition, labor shortages severely limited productive capabilities. As the depression spread, members of the rural underclass, now freed of the Directorate, found themselves barely subsisting on devalued extraction or agricultural production and increasingly controlled by a newly evolving system of debt-peonage. Near the end of this period the combination of depression, exploitation, and frustration led to a brutal revolt by rural *cabanos,* a political and ethnic term for mestizos, Native Americans, and escaped African slaves who were forming the campesinato. They revolted against the urban-based elite in a struggle that crippled the region both politically and economically.

Part of the turmoil of this period was resistance to the evolving labor relations. With the end of the Directorate a new system of labor control, centered on the commercial trading post, replaced the mission system. The trading post became the main reference point for the emergent campesinato, who were scattered about geographically by the demands of extraction and subsistence agriculture (Parker 1985:35–36). The cabanos, or camponeses, depended on the trading post and the world system to supply them with certain foods, tools, medicines, and industrial goods. This was a legacy of the mission system. In exchange for these goods the camponeses provided extracted and agricultural products. Since currency was scarce in the region throughout the nineteenth century, exchange occurred through a system of credit and debt known as *aviamento* (Santos 1980:156). The trading post usually maintained a trade monopoly with workers that enabled the merchants to manipulate prices. This combination of price manipulation and credit control often left the camponeses in perpetual debt. In some cases the exploitative system resulted in debt-peonage and conditions of bare survival for the workers (Sawyer 1979:14; Wagley 1976:38).

The aviamento system not only tied the camponeses to the trading post, but it also tied the trading post to merchants located in Belém and beyond. Unequal exchanges between the trading post and these merchants or *aviadores* (suppliers) led to indebtedness for the trading post owner (Ross 1978:194). The aviador firms, which were often import/export firms as well, derived the largest share of wealth from the aviamento system. In general peninsular Portuguese owned these firms. They established themselves as intermediaries during the Directorate period (Anderson 1985:52). The aviador or import/export firms traded primarily with Europe. At this point in history the Amazon was more closely integrated socially, economically, and politically with Europe than with the rest of Brazil. This was because trade winds made sea travel to southern Brazil difficult and because of the lack of easily traversed overland connections southward.

The aviamento system and the local trading post now replaced the mission as the principal link to the world system. Aviamento siphoned wealth from the Amazon interior to the coast and then on to Europe. This system, however, did not function smoothly, nor did it generate massive amounts of wealth. The Amazon region remained a poor place.

Polarization of wealth occurred during depression years. Portuguese merchants, in particular, accumulated more wealth than most. Around Belém large landowners (*latifundiários*) prospered modestly by producing cacao, rice, coffee, sugar, and cotton with slave labor. Small landholders (*minifundiários*) and camponeses, by contrast, did poorly (Anderson 1985:54). The combination of polarization of wealth, the control of the economy by the Portuguese, and the intolerable debt-peonage relations experienced by the camponeses sparked the political turmoil leading to the Cabanagem Revolt.

The political turmoil began among urban elite circles when Brazil declared its independence in 1822. A sizable portion of the local urban elite refused to accept independence since the Amazon retained important commercial ties to Portugal (Anderson 1985:55). This elite faction generally consisted of peninsular-born individuals who were merchants and large landowners. They formed a political party called the Caramurus. A second faction consisted of Brazilian-born individuals who were principally small-scale shopkeepers, artisans, entrepreneurs, and small landholders (Anderson 1985:56). This faction formed the Filantrópico Party, which favored regional autonomy or independence for the Amazon (Kelly 1984:202). Political violence between the Caramurus and Filantrópico factions began in 1824 in Belém. Gradually, violence escalated, and by 1835 it had spread throughout the Amazon region.

The cabanos/camponeses initially participated in the political violence as recruits of warring elite factions. However, by 1835 the struggle took on class and racial overtones. Cabanos vented their frustrations against subjugation and impoverishment by attacking the landowning rich and occasionally people of European descent in general (Anderson 1985:70–71). Cabano forces attacked and seized Belém—the economic and political capital of the region. Several successions of cabano regimes governed the area. In the following year most towns along the Amazon River were involved in local cabano uprisings (Anderson 1985:73). Gurupá, however, was not very active in the turmoil of the Cabanagem, possibly because of the presence of the fort, although the militia undoubtedly engaged in conflict. Rather, Gurupá served primarily as a refuge from the war-stricken area (Kelly 1984:475).

Despite this widespread conflict, the Cabanagem did not develop into a coherent revolution. Instead, the Cabanagem played itself out as a series of localized rebellions (Santos 1980:34; Anderson 1985:70). By 1836 the Brazilian government subdued the uprising. Forces under General Francisco Soares de Andreia recaptured Belém from the cabanos, and six months later the army had pacified the remaining insurrections (Anderson 1985:76, 78). The toll taken by the revolt, however, was great. An estimated 30,000 people out of a total population of 130,000 for the entire region died from warfare or epidemics (Anderson 1985:80). In addition, the major plantations, sugar mills, and cattle ranches in the region were all damaged or destroyed.

Following the Cabanagem the region began a slow recovery period lasting until the 1850s. Many camponeses returned to extraction and agriculture activities, submitting themselves again to the labor relations organized through the trading post. They still retained direct access to land and resources. This created problems for the elite, who, as always, wished to force the population into higher levels of export commodity production. Most camponeses avoided excessive demands by relying on their own subsistence agriculture and on gathering and hunting. They produced commodities when in need of imported goods. They had this limited liberty because control over the campesinato in the extractive sector was always precarious at best. The isolation and mobility required for the production of extracted commodities tended to create a relatively autonomous population of quasi-independent producers. In many cases the producers were not subject to direct control or coercion by elites (Weinstein 1983:42).

Some camponeses, however, were not so lucky and were forced to join a draft labor program called Corpo de Trabalhadores (the Workers' Corp). The government created this program in 1839, and the military maintained it. It required individuals who were landless or without continuous employment to work in state-sponsored public works projects or private enterprises (Kelly 1984:252–253; Weinstein 1983:42). Gurupá served as one of the nine regional centers for the Workers' Corps. It employed 608 men in 1848 (Kelly 1984:276). With the Workers' Corps the regional elite hoped to gain greater control over labor. The elite designed the corps to help develop agriculture. Through agriculture the upper class wished to closely supervise workers and regulate their production. The elite also hoped to suppress any future revolt with this type of control. But the system did not function as envisioned. As with previous forced labor programs the Workers' Corps often broke down into pseudoslavery with military commanders abusing it for their own personal benefit (Kelly 1984:176). This was the case in Gurupá. The census of 1842 mentioned that the captain of the Police Guard and other military personnel retained a near monopoly on the use of the corps. They used the workers for private pursuits such as rowing, building canoes, or extracting forest products.

In terms of making a sizable labor force available to elites, the Workers' Corps was a failure. There were never enough competent soldiers to patrol the immense region and gather the high number of resisters (Weinstein 1983:43). Because of these failures the government abolished the Workers' Corps in the 1860s.

Hints of what life was like in Gurupá during the revolt and depression period come from various census materials and diaries of travelers. Both sources mention the community's undeveloped state. For example, in 1828 an English sailor named Henry Maw reported that Gurupá was an important town, although he observed that it was not flourishing (Kelly 1984:135). In 1842 a Portuguese lieutenant colonel, Antonio Ladilau Monteiro Beana, noted the poor state of repair of the church, the shortage of manioc that had to be imported, the degenerate state of the military in which 436 men out of 574 had no uniforms or arms, and the misery people lived in despite the abundance their surroundings offered (Kelly 1984:262–265). In 1846 the French naturalist Francis de Castelnau described Gurupá's houses as poorly constructed, the church as very old, and the fort as having some obsolete cannons. Castelnau was most impressed by the lack of food in Gurupá. He reported that local inhabitants begging for food continuously followed his group (Kelly 1984:272).

Another sign of difficulties during this period was the report of frequent epidemics in the town. For example, in 1823 and 1842 Gurupá reported violent fevers, possibly malaria, typhus, tuberculosis, yellow fever, colds, or dysentery. In 1844, 107 people died in Gurupá from fever (Gurupá had 900–1,000 people at the time). More outbreaks continued in 1845 and 1848 (Kelly 1984:427–429).

During the depression period Gurupá continued to serve as a site of the fort and prison. The town also continued as a river checkpoint. In 1849 the government established an inspection station to collect taxes on merchandise leaving the area (Kelly 1984:278). The population of the community grew throughout this period. However, Gurupá's growth did not keep pace with that of other surrounding towns. This led to a change in boundaries and the loss of control over one small town to a neighboring district (Kelly 1984:275).

Table 4.1 lists the population of Gurupá during this period. The census

Table 4.1   Population Census for Gurupá and Carrazedo, 1823–1848

Gurupá			
Year	Population	Slaves	Military
1823	826	248	154
1842	715	233	574
1848	1019	238	—

Carrazedo		
Year	Population	Native Americans
1823	210	148
1846	157	—

Source: Adapted from Kelly (1984:206, 211, 259, 273–274).

records also record that Gurupá had one primary schoolteacher and one priest to oversee the town, Carrazedo, and one other small town (Kelly 1984:207, 209). In 1828 Maw described Gurupá as one street running parallel to the river with some houses shaded by orange trees (Kelly 1984:234). By 1842 the town had expanded to two streets running parallel to the river with two grassy cross streets. The mission was in ruins. The church was described as made of mud and plaster with a tile roof. It lacked a belfry and was in need of repair. Most of the houses in Gurupá were roofed with thatch except for four with tile roofs.

The 1823 census recorded that Gurupá produced manioc, coffee, cacao, tobacco, rice, cotton, beans, and *breu* (a blue dye). There was one cattle ranch on the Majarí River that contained sixteen cattle and twenty-two pigs. People harpooned manatee and caught fish by line, net, and timbo poison (timbo is a poison taken from the branches and vines of *timbo vermelho* [*Derris urucu*]). When placed in a stream blocked by a barrier, the timbo stuns fish, which then float to the surface where they are collected by fishers. In addition, the census reported that local inhabitants hunted game with guns and dogs. It identified eleven types of timber harvested for export. The district also manufactured andiroba oil, aguardente, and hammocks.

According to the 1823 census there were six men using slave labor to produce agricultural goods. The remaining agriculture population consisted of small farmers not employing much slave labor. Gurupá also had six men distinguished in trade and business, who established a trade network with the Xingu valley and elsewhere to export sarsaparilla, clove, coffee, cacao, pirarucu, and manioc to Belém (Kelly 1984:208–210). These men were likely trading post owners and/or aviadores and among the first individuals to set up the aviamento system in Gurupá.

Three medium-sized landowners in Gurupá each possessed a square league (5-by-5 kilometer area) in the surrounding area. They produced manioc and coffee with slave labor. Manioc production, however, did not meet consumption needs, and Gurupá had to import manioc flour from the Xingu River settlements. Interestingly, Carrazedo, which was exporting manioc to Belém at the time, did not appear to supply Gurupá with manioc.

The census also reported that fishing and hunting in the area were good and that the area contained ample timber resources. Castelnau, cited above, reported cattle around the town. The census recorded the presence of a few artisans, including one tailor and his apprentice, one shoemaker, one iron-worker, one carpenter, and two stoneworkers. The school had eighty-four boys and seven girls enrolled (Kelly 1984:262–271).

The Rubber Boom Period, 1850–1910

By the 1850s Gurupá and the rest of Amazonia continued to recover from depression and political turmoil. The traditional landed elite reestablished itself politically and, through programs like the Workers' Corps, attempted to regain control over the regional labor force and develop a plantation economy. Developments in the extractive sector, however, preempted the course of events that might have led to a more agricultural-oriented economy. The discovery of a method to vulcanize rubber (treating rubber chemically to increase its elasticity and strength) and the development of innovative industrial uses for the material led to a boom in rubber extraction. The Amazon was the principal producer of raw rubber until the twentieth century and stood poised to gain great profits from rubber extraction (Barham and Coomes 1994a:40).

By the 1850s extracted rubber surpassed cacao as the Amazon's primary export. Between 1850 and 1880 the volume of rubber export increased by 500 percent and the value of rubber increased by 800 percent (Weinstein 1983:56, 70). With the development of the rubber tire industry, first for bicycles and then for automobiles, rubber extraction boomed into its "golden years" between 1880 and 1910. During this time the Amazon produced at least 50 percent of the rubber on the world market, with prices for the premium grade 50 percent higher than alternative supplies from Central America or Africa (Coomes and Barham 1994:241). Despite several crisis years in the international market (1889–1889, 1900–1901, 1906–1907), the rubber boom increasingly provided the Amazon with affluence never before experienced.

The rubber boom profoundly affected Gurupá. With rich concentrations of rubber trees on the várzea, the people of Gurupá were drawn into extraction as the price of rubber rose. In the early years of the boom Gurupá was one of four municipalities that produced most of the rubber for the entire Amazon region (Weinstein 1983:52). Gurupá's share of regional rubber production declined as tappers and merchants opened new rubber fields farther west in the Xingu and Tapajós River valleys. But the municipality continued producing significant quantities of rubber throughout the period. Even by the 1900s when overproduction had reduced the output of most trees by one-half to one-third (Weinstein 1983:169), Gurupá still received considerable revenue from extraction.

In the early years of the rubber boom Gurupá began to show some signs of rejuvenation from the previous years of stagnation. For example, in 1854 a postal agency served by a newly formed steamship line was opened (Kelly 1984:298). The town also grew to a total of 2,207 inhabitants (1,870 free people, 320 slaves, and 17 foreigners) in 1856, then increased again to 2,794 people (2,563 free people, 216 slaves, 15 foreigners), in 1872 (Kelly 1984:308, 346). In 1857 Gurupá became one of seven independent judicial *comarcas* (judicial divisions) in Pará and one of twelve districts with a municipal judge (Kelly 1984:312). The community also maintained its school and parish priest (Kelly 1984:301).

Despite these various developments, Gurupá's appearance remained one of neglect. A description of the town in 1852 by two American naval officers characterized Gurupá as a village of one street in which there was a great demand for salted fish (Kelly 1984:296). Records of the collections from the inspection station (1852–1853) showed diminishing revenues (Kelly 1984:299). The town council, lacking a public building, had to rent a private home in which to hold meetings (Kelly 1984:303). In 1859 the town council sent a report to Belém that stated, "In this municipality, all that exists made by the hand of man is a small chapel serving as the main church which is nearly annihilated, and the foundations of a ruined fort" (Kelly 1984:313).

By 1860 things had not improved much. In that year Pará's provincial president, Dr. Antonio Coelho de Sá e Albuquerque, visited Gurupá and confirmed the decay of the fort and noted the deteriorated condition of Gurupá's military garrison's arms (the garrison consisted of 4 companies, 535 soldiers, and 25 reserves in 1855 [Kelly 1984:303, 319–320]). The president reported that the once-important regional prison of Gurupá had decayed into a filthy lean-to lacking facilities or security. He also criticized the neglected state of agriculture, commenting that only the abundance of naturally growing products along the riverbanks kept the province from abject poverty (Kelly 1984:317).

Many of these above reports describing Gurupá's "backward" state also mentioned the growing importance of rubber extraction. As early as 1852 rubber dominated the town's commerce (Kelly 1984:297). In 1860, when President Sá visited Gurupá, he noticed that residents had abandoned whole blocks of houses and gone to the interior to collect rubber (Kelly 1984:317). President Sá, like many traditional elites, was critical of rubber extraction. He felt extraction blocked economic progress by scattering the population and drawing labor away from agriculture.

Despite criticism of rubber extraction by elites, the rising price of rubber attracted most able-bodied workers in Gurupá. A pattern of seasonal migration to extract rubber in the dry season (when rainwater did not interfere with latex collection) on Gurupá's island and várzea left the town all but deserted for six months a year. The labor drain affected nearly every occupation. For example, the five animal-powered aguardente factories/mills operating in 1862 experienced frequent shutdown periods due to a lack of workers (Kelly 1984:326). Even salaried professionals, like schoolteachers, were drawn to the quick returns of rubber collection and would abandon their posts (Kelly 1984:321). Agriculturalists, in particular, neglected their gardens to participate in the rubber boom. This created food shortages and forced the community to become even more dependent on expensive imported foods.

Between 1865 and 1900 Gurupá's rubber export increased by more than seventeen-fold—from 23,140 kilograms to 408,124 kilograms (Kelly 1984:342; Weinstein 1983:190). During the same time Gurupá exported animal pelts, tanned hides, cacao, nuts, *capaibla* oil, sarsaparilla, and tobacco (Kelly 1984:3342), although these commodities took on increasingly minor roles in the economy as the rubber boom progressed. In 1862 there were also twelve cattle ranches with a total of 6,548 head of cattle and horses. The ranches employed thirty-nine free workers and seven slaves (Kelly 1984:326).

The golden years (1880–1910) of the rubber boom brought additional changes to Gurupá. Immigrants from the drought-stricken northeast of Brazil swelled the urban and rural populations. Landowners and merchants from Gurupá and throughout Amazonia recruited the northeasterners to tap the rubber trees in an attempt to remedy the historical shortage of workers. This immigration increased the Amazon's population by 400 percent (from 323,000 to 1,217,000) between 1870 and 1910. This increase effectively occupied vast areas of the region (Santos 1980:109, 115).

In Gurupá's rural interior successful and powerful merchants arose with the rubber trade. Many of these merchants were of Portuguese descent, while at the turn of the century a large population of Moroccan and Spanish Jews came to dominate much of Gurupá's commerce (Kelly 1984:378; Wagley 1976:48; Barham and Coomes 1994a:49). In fact, a Jewish cemetery can still be found on the outskirts of town; it contains some twenty-three graves, most inscribed in Hebrew, dating between 1905 and 1915.

The Portuguese and Jewish merchants organized production through the trading post and export through the aviadores. Aviamento dominated labor relations, although rubber traders made some alterations in the system to handle the volume of export. In particular, since the local trading firms lacked the wealth needed to increase production to supply world demand, they devised a novel division of labor with international firms to obtain these funds. The foreign firms, largely of American, German, and English origins, specialized in exporting and arranging credit backed by international banks while the national aviador firms continued buying and financing rubber in the interior (Santos 1980:125–126). This union tied foreign capital, now produced under an industrial capitalist system, to a local, non-capitalist system capable of securing labor and logistical support to expand production. The Amazon economy, as a result, was articulated with European and North American industrial interests.

The large aviador firms, now with foreign capital, began recruiting large numbers of workers by extending credit and goods in exchange for rubber. As extraction expanded, the firms extended aviamento relations to agriculture and fishing (Santos 1980:158). Various intermediaries or agents of the aviador houses appeared in the aviamento chain to help organize trade. In all there could be six different levels through which goods and credit passed between the extractor and the rubber manufacturer (Weinstein 1983:16).

The aviamento chain was maintained by a pyramid of debt relations. At the top export firms and international banks controlled the large aviador houses through the threat of withdrawing credit. Without credit in the currency-starved economy a business would collapse. In the middle of the aviamento chain urban merchants controlled trading post owners and landowners (*seringalistas*) (Weinstein 1983:23). They used the threat of foreclosure on debts owed to keep the trading posts and seringalistas subservient to the aviador houses. Yet the aviador houses did not achieve a monopoly on the rubber trade. Throughout the rubber boom there were many opportunities for other traders of various sizes to successfully enter the market (Barham and Coomes 1994a:62).

The trading posts and seringalistas, in turn, usually kept the lowly rubber extractors in perpetual debt. Among the mechanisms the seringalistas and trading post merchants used to maintain debt were charging rent on land used (paid with a percentage of the rubber produced), charging transportation costs and sales commission for the service of selling the rubber in Belém or Manaus (often 50 percent of the market value of rubber), charging a commission for payment in cash (20 percent) or goods (10 percent) received by the extractor, setting local prices (inflating imported goods up to ten times over prices in Rio de Janeiro and in the more isolated portions of the Amazon, thus devaluing the rubber exports), controlling credit sources, and outright cheating of illiterate collectors on their accounts (Weinstein 1983:16, 18, 22, 49; Santos 1980:170).

In most cases when a trading post or seringalista advanced credit to a particular extractor, a patron-client bond was created. The bond was an unequal, paternalistic, dyadic social relationship that carried certain duties and responsibilities for the *patrão* (client) and subordinated *freguês* (client). For example, ideally the patrão would maintain personal ties to the *fregueses* (plural of freguês) and protect and intervene for them in dealing with the outside world. *Patrões* (plural of patrão) also advised the family on social and economic matters, helped obtain health care in times of need, and made loans. Fictive kin ties (compadresco) could reinforce the bonds. In this situation a patrão would serve as a godparent (*padrinho*) to a freguês's children, usually at baptism. As a godparent the patrão was responsible for overseeing a child's development, possibly helping with the education, and supporting the child if the parents died.

In return for these responsibilities, the patrão expected a monopoly on the sale of the fregueses' rubber as long as they had debts or resided on the patrão's land. The patrão also expected the fregueses to accept the inevitable price manipulations of the trading post and, if eligible to vote, to give political support to the candidate of the patrão's choice. With fictive kin ties these responsibilities were strengthened further. Although the patron-client relationship could appear quite personal and benevolent at times, especially when enhanced by fictive kin ties, it was still based on an unequal allocation of debt that led to economic exploitation and even violence (Weinstein 1983:181).

The extent to which the trading post or landowner could use this debt to control workers, however, varied by region and time. In general, the farther the rubber extractors were from Belém, and the closer the period was to its end in 1910, the greater was the control and exploitation of the campesinato. At worst, exploitation consisted of debt-slavery in which the landowner/merchant controlled the rubber tappers' mobility and their right to grow their own food. In these circumstances there was extreme sociopolitical subservience, hunger, and widespread disease. High worker mortality occurred.

This, however, was not the case in Gurupá. It was not the norm for the region, either. The very nature of gathering, which required a highly dispersed and mobile population, mitigated against extreme forms of regimentation and control (Barham and Coomes 1994a:50–54). Rubber tappers often had control over their working conditions (when and how hard to work), had access to the means of subsistence (land, game, forest products), and their mobility allowed them opportunities to evade intolerable demands (Weinstein 1983:14). Also, in all but a few cases, rubber extractors could mitigate the extremes of the aviamento system by secretly selling rubber to "pirate traders" (*regatões,* who were itinerate riverboat traders), hiding rocks or other items in rubber *pelles* (balls) to increase the weight and price received, engaging in forbidden subsistence activities, refusing to stay in the rubber field during the rainy season, and ultimately, breaking debt relations by fleeing the area (Weinstein 1983:102; Barham and Coomes 1994a:53).

In the lower Amazon a history of small landownership even enabled many tappers to work their own rubber trails and produce food. This allowed them to stay out of permanent debt to merchants. In Gurupá, for example, a *latifundiário,* or large landholding class, did not develop as it did in many neighboring municipalities. Gurupá's merchants did acquire large tracts of land (by purchase, foreclosure, intimidation, or invasion) on the várzea where the rubber trees were concentrated, but much land remained in the possession of small landowners. As indicated by the 625 land title registrations recorded between 1880 and 1910, most landholdings were a quarter or a half league in dimension (between 1 and 4 kilometers). In terms of rubber trails possessed, only 1.5 percent of land registrations recorded over 100 trails, while 61 percent reported 10 or under. One rubber trail on the average contained between 80 and 150 individual trees and covered a 3–5 square kilometer area (Barham and Coomes 1994a:45). In Amazonian terms, a large estate consisted of 100 trails or more, while a small holding, usually owned by a family of humble origins, consisted of 10 trails or less (Weinstein 1983:172). The reason Gurupá did not develop a latifundiário pattern was because of the early entry into rubber extraction by many small- and medium-sized landowners before the large aviador houses gained sufficient power to appropriate land (Weinstein 1983:47).

One consequence of Gurupá's land tenure structure was the general absence of debt-slavery abuses reported in other areas. Nevertheless, landowners did exploit workers by prohibiting them to plant crops. They also expelled individuals from land when caught trading rubber to regatões or spending too much time on subsistence activities. Almost ubiquitously, merchants manipulated trade that left the rubber tappers in persistent poverty. As in all of Amazonia, rubber profits seldom trickled down to the lowly extractor (Weinstein 183:70). Yet a combination of Gurupá's history of small landownership, its proximity to Belém for trade, and the availability of unclaimed terra firme for agricultural production insured that many Gurupaenses had access to land, food, and alternative trade that aviadores and seringalistas could not monopolize as they did in more remote areas of the Amazon.

Although Gurupá remained poor throughout the early part of the rubber boom, by the golden years of the boom the community finally prospered. By the turn of the century twenty general stores opened in town to handle the increased commerce (Wagley 1976:46). Warehouses for rubber lined the riverfront. Several gambling houses and a house of prostitution were opened. Rubber wealth was also lavished on the construction of a huge town hall, on a gas (carbide) lighting system for the streets, on stairs down to the river faced with imported marble slabs, on extravagant ironwork cemeteries, and even on shirts sent to be starched in Portugal (Wagley 1976:49, 51). According to a weekly newspaper printed between 1909 and 1910 (*Correio de Gurupá*), Gurupá became an active social center. There were banquets, balls, and birthday parties complete with champagne, wine, fine foods, and orchestra music (Wagley 1976:47).

Belém similarly experienced prosperity. The city initiated several cost- ly urban service projects (a water system, street lighting, trolley lines, and a telephone system). A lucrative urban real estate business also developed, complete with elaborate homes and public buildings financed by rubber fortunes (Weinstein 1983:87). There were even a few attempts to diversify the economy by developing industry in the city (factories producing choco- late, soap, bread meal, rope, paper, and so forth). But because of the Amazon's chronic shortage of labor, capital, and skilled technicians, and the way the elite invested capital (some in transportation infrastructure, much in conspicuous consumption), the economy experienced little sus- tained industrial growth (Weinstein 1983:9). Concerning transportation infrastructure, state governments and rubber traders constructed many docks and warehouses for the boom. The number of steamships also multi- plied as the number of major aviador houses employing them increased from eight in 1869 to forty-two in 1890 (Weinstein 1983:72).

During the golden years of the rubber boom the dominant class of Gurupá (merchants, large landowners, and some government officials) took on the airs of an aristocracy. People referred to them as *gente de primeira clase* (people of the first class). Socially subservient to the upper class was the working class (*gente de segunda,* or second-class people), which con- sisted of poor town dwellers, farmers, and extractors. They showed defer- ence to the elite by never sitting in their presence and always using the for- mal terms *Seu* (short for senhor or mister) or *Senhora* and *Dona* (mistress) when addressing or referring to them. The elite segregated parties, with the aristocracy in one room and the lower classes in another (Wagley 1976:103).

During Gurupá's rubber boom period several cultural traditions that originated in earlier years became firmly institutionalized. One major tradi- tion was the religious festival cycle. This cycle revolved around the two major festivals for Saint Anthony (in June) and Saint Benedict (in December). Saint Anthony is the town's patron saint and the favorite saint of the upper class. Saint Benedict is the protector of river travelers and rub- ber tappers, and guardian of the poor. Religious brotherhoods (*irmandades*) organized the festivals, and a resident priest (if Gurupá had one at the time) or a visiting priest performed the religious rites.

The saints' festivals lasted nine days during which there were nightly novenas that culminated with a religious procession on the final day. During the procession the brotherhoods carried a statue of the saint through the streets of town, often accompanied by fireworks and waving banners. In the interior the brotherhoods carried another statue of the saint as they went door-to-door to ask for donations (Wagley 1976:198–199). For Saint Benedict there was also a procession by boats in front of town (called *meia lua*, or half moon).

Commensurate with the religious celebrations were nine days of parties, dancing, music, and drinking. To take advantage of the concentration of people and the flow of money, many small-scale merchants from Belém set up stalls to sell wares. With the onset of the boom period the Saint Benedict festival became the most important in Gurupá because the local people recognized the saint as the protector of the rubber tapper and because the festival coincided with the end of the rubber harvest (just before the rains began) when a year's profits were at hand. By the peak of the rubber boom the festival of Saint Benedict had overshadowed the celebration of the town's patron saint, as well as the other summer festivals for Saint Peter and Saint John.

By the close of the rubber boom in 1910 the camponês lifestyle that first appeared in the late eighteenth century was firmly established (Parker 1985:37). Even the northeasterners that entered the region during the boom adopted it. The semi-independent, semi-market-oriented camponeses, enmeshed in a rigid class system structured around exchange and debt, became the dominant actors in the region. The campesinato syncretized Native American and Iberian knowledge for a unique worldview that became the basis for the evolving *Amazônida* (non–Native American Amazonian) culture.

The Rubber Bust and Depression Period, 1910–1963

In 1910 the rubber prices were high, and Amazonia enjoyed a near monopoly on the world's rubber supply. Because of their success the people of Gurupá and elsewhere in Amazonia took little notice of the fragile nature of their system. But the extraction system that had evolved was destructive to the trees, costly in terms of productivity, and not capable of keeping up with world demand. As early as the 1890s these limitations motivated foreign nations reliant on Amazon rubber to experiment with more cost-efficient systems of production.

The English, for example, began to experiment with rubber plantations in Ceylon using rubber seeds taken from Brazil by Henry Wickham Steed (Santos 1980:230–233, 256). After twenty years of effort they successfully established rubber plantations in Malaya, Ceylon, India, Burma, Borneo, Siam, and the Dutch West Indies. By 1910 the plantations produced the first sizable quantity of rubber, 8 percent of the world market (Santos 1980:236; Weinstein 1983:215). The Asian plantations soon outproduced the amount and undercut the price of rubber from the Amazon. In Asia labor was cheap and productivity higher as trees were concentrated in one area.

Until this point the Brazilians had done little to develop a plantation system for rubber. Landowners and merchants remedied reductions in rubber tree productivity, created by excesses in extraction, by simply expanding extraction to areas previously unexploited, such as the Xingu and Tapajós River valleys in Pará and, eventually, Amazônas, Acre, and beyond (Weinstein 1983:116). There were persistent warnings noted by elites, including several by provincial presidents of Pará, that a failure to plant rubber trees would lead to eventual collapse of the rubber economy. Yet, even as the English began to experiment in Asia, there was no change in the extractive economy.

Merchants and landowners resisted plantation rubber for four reasons. First, the Amazon's monopoly on world rubber production and the vast stretches of still-untapped rubber trees did little to instill a sense of urgency to convert to a plantation system.

Second, merchants/landowners and even international firms had a difficult time enticing or forcing workers to cultivate trees. Extraction paid better, and rubber tappers had enough freedom in the labor-starved, geographically dispersed, and decentralized rubber economy to avoid plantation work (Barham and Coomes 1994b:100)

Third, the opportunity costs of capital investment in plantations were very high. To successfully develop a plantation, a large amount of capital had to be invested over a considerable amount of time. Few merchants and landowners were willing to invest in such a venture given that much higher returns on investments were available from aviamento and wild rubber extraction (Coomes and Barham 1994:254).

Fourth, the huge profits gained through rubber production enabled the merchants, not the landowning class, to dominate the regional political economy. The merchants' rise to power occurred gradually as resistance to rubber extraction was strong throughout the 1850s, 1860s, and 1870s (Weinstein 1983:34). By the 1880s, however, the growing rubber wealth weakened the political power of the traditional landowning agricultural class. It eventually became subordinate to the politicians sympathetic to rubber merchant elites. Along with this change the importance of landownership as a source of wealth decreased as control of exchange relations became the key to the system (Weinstein 1983:49; Bunker 1985:67–68). With such a unique elevation to dominance it is little wonder why the merchant class was not enthusiastic about investing in rubber plantations that would likely diminish its privileged position (Weinstein 1983:224).

By the second decade of the nineteenth century the weakness of the extraction system became obvious. In 1913 the Asian rubber production equaled the Amazon's production, and by 1919 the Asian plantations controlled 90 percent of the market (Santos 1980:236). As the Asian plantations began producing, the price of rubber plummeted from U.S.$3.00 per pound in 1910 to $0.60 per pound in 1915 and then to $0.19–0.23 per pound by 1923 (Ross 1978:215). The effects of the price collapse had a devastating impact on Amazonian commercial establishments. By 1913 forty-seven aviador houses had gone bankrupt along with a host of other businesses associated with trade (Weinstein 1983:232). The speed with which so many companies failed was a sign of the very fragile nature of the aviamento system. Most of the assets of aviador houses consisted of uncollectible debts, which during the boom assured the company of a sizable clientele, but during the bust amounted to nothing (Weinstein 1983:234). As the rubber bust destroyed the commercial community, it also devastated local banks, the urban real estate market, and the public utilities of the major cities (Santos 1980:239).

The rubber bust hit Gurupá hard. The community had grown to depend almost exclusively on rubber revenues, and once these revenues disappeared the town quickly deteriorated. The population of the town dwindled to 300 people by 1920 (Wagley 1976:51). Many commercial families moved out of the town. They sold their lands at very low prices or simply left them to their fregueses to tend. People left warehouses and houses to decay. The extravagances of the town hall, gas lighting system, and marble steps were left unfinished, were broken down, or were simply removed. A writer for Belém's *Folha do Norte* newspaper who visited Gurupá in 1929 labeled the town an "ex-city" because of its degenerated state (Wagley 1976:52).

In the interior many rubber extractors left the seringais (rubber fields) for other areas. Many small landholders lost their land and moved away. Like the seringalistas they sold out at extremely low prices to the few merchants who weathered the bust. The people of Gurupá tell of others who lost their land to unscrupulous Portuguese traders through a process known as *apinhoar* (meaning to agglomerate or pile up). The traders would pressure clients to accept essential and nonessential goods on credit and use their land as collateral for later payment. Because of the depressed economy, the client rarely came up with the inflated payment, so the trader would take a piece of land instead. Many Portuguese merchants secured huge tracts of land this way.

By 1915 the bust had become a generalized economic depression. The merchant elite began to disperse. Some merchants returned to Portugal while others migrated south. The majority, however, stayed in the region, lowered their standards of living, and engaged in local trade on a much-reduced scale (Weinstein 1983:236). The foreign export houses began to disappear. Their functions were picked up by independent regional firms that bought reduced amounts of rubber in addition to Brazil nuts, cacao, timber, and rosewood. The rise of these regional firms also spelled an end to the aviador house that specialized only in commerce in the interior.

These operators became redundant as the native export houses were quite capable of running the exchange networks in the interior (Weinstein 1983:238). Interestingly, the new regional firms continued using the old aviamento system, allowing it to persist throughout the decline years (Santos 1980:243).

Return to Depression

The Amazonian economy struggled along after the rubber bust. With low rubber prices, merchants redirected extraction efforts toward the collection of a mixture of Brazil nuts, rubber, oleaginous seeds, and other forest commodities. In 1921 Brazil nuts overtook rubber as the region's most valuable export (Weinstein 1983:258). Cultivation of manioc, rice, and bananas and extraction of fish, turtles, and manatees took on greater importance in local trade. There was also a growing market for such animal hides as those of caiman and jaguar, which peaked during the 1950s (Bunker 1985:73). A few sectors, such as ranching, importing, and manufacturing, even expanded. This growth occurred as labor and small amounts of capital were freed from the rubber trade and as international competition declined (Weinstein 1983:255). There were also further attempts at agricultural development in the Bragantina area east of Belém between 1914 and 1916. As with earlier efforts the traditional problems of soil depletion after five to ten years of crop production limited these attempts (Weinstein 1983:252, 255).

Two other economic innovations occurred during this period. First, in 1924 the Ford Motor company attempted to develop rubber plantations in the Amazon region. Second, in the 1930s Japanese migrants introduced jute (a fibrous plant used to make rope), which became an important commodity until synthetic substitutes lowered its price. Later the Japanese introduced black pepper, which also became an important export crop (Bunker 1985:73).

As Gurupá's economy entered the depression it continued exporting rubber at very low prices. In addition, individuals extracted and traded cacao, andiroba and acuuba oil and seeds, fruit, some wood, and hides. The aviadores continued to come in both steamships and sailboats. However, there were fewer of them, and they made less frequent trips. The trading posts in the town and interior continued also, although they were reduced in number and their stocks limited. Because of this breakdown in the aviamento system, food shortages became more common in town. People I talked with remembered those years as ones of misery and hunger. Food scarcity persisted despite an increase in subsistence agriculture. The problem was the lack of an internal market to distribute food produced in the interior. Nearly all commerce passed through the aviamento chain, which diverted goods to Belém. It was rare for merchants to take and sell manioc produced on Gurupá's terra firme to Gurupá's islands. Manioc for the island camponeses most frequently came from Belém or the Xingu River valley, when it arrived at all.

In the interior the economic decline led to abandonment of many rubber trails and to the migration of workers. Many northeasterners recruited to work in the Amazon region returned home (Santos 1980:261). Those who remained joined with the indigenous campesinato in diversifying their economic activities. More time was spent in such food-producing activities as gardening, hunting, fishing, and collecting. The possession of land after the bust (land per se had little value at this point) cushioned the decline of rubber tappers. Massive starvation, epidemics, or insurrections did not occur in the Amazon region (Santos 1980:278). Rather, the tappers' standard of living slipped incrementally. While more time was spent in subsistence production most individuals also continued extracting forest goods for the market. Although the prices for rubber and other commodities were low, most individuals needed some income source to pay for industrial goods they had grown accustomed to (firearms, cloth, housewares, medicines) and for supplementary food (Weinstein 1983:246).

The economic decline generally affected the seringalistas and trading post owners more seriously. Many degenerated to conditions bordering on poverty indistinguishable from that of the extractors. Many landowners sold their land at low prices and moved on. Many trading posts closed down as they lost access to aviador houses (which had also closed down), had aviadores foreclose on debts owed, or simply lost the ability to extend credit to fregueses. For the seringalistas and trading posts that managed to survive, their ability to do business and generate credit for fregueses greatly declined. Without sufficient credit, landowners and merchants could not manipulate debt and patron-client relations. This diminished their ability to control the campesinato. As a result worker mobility increased. Most patrões were forced to endure this loss of fregueses while relying on strengthened paternalistic relationships to secure the labor of those workers who remained (Weinstein 1983:245). By the 1920s and 1930s patron-client ties and the aviamento system stabilized, although in a much weaker form, and the system continued to struggle along.

Because of the depressed times and lack of work in Gurupá throughout the 1920s and 1930s, many people began permanent, temporary, or even seasonal migrations in search of employment. River transportation was fast and cheap, so many traveled far. Those migrating permanently sought out more prosperous rural areas and larger urban centers within and outside the region. The effects of this migration on some interior communities were overwhelming. One example is the village of Paraíso (Paradise), located several kilometers downstream from Gurupá. Between 1920 and 1940 Paraíso was an active settlement. There were over 200 families located around a trading post. One family, the Mendoça Lemes, owned over 88,000 hectares upon which there were supposedly 1,800 rubber trails, or approximately 180,000 rubber trees. Contracted steamships from Belém stopped there and spent days loading rubber, cacao, hides, fruit, and wood for fuel. Only the strongest trading posts could arrange to have a ship stop to trade. This level of prosperity even earned Paraíso a place on most regional maps. However, as the depression years wore on and hardship for both the trading post and the camponeses took its toll, people slowly deserted the settlement. By the 1980s when I visited it, the once-active settlement of 200 families contained only a small trading post with few houses in the immediate vicinity.

Temporary and seasonal migration attracted many young men from Gurupá. Among the jobs people told me they held during this time were ranch hands for cattle ranches in Victoria on the Xingu River, agricultural laborers for the Japanese colonies in Monte Alegre, rubber tappers for the plantation system attempted at Fordlândia and Belterra on the Tapajós, Brazil nut collectors on the Trombetas River, jute cutters in Almerim, and subsistence agriculture and rubber workers in Oriximina. Many men returned after only a few months of work. They stayed in Gurupá until they found suitable employment, subsistence activity, or until their money ran out. In the latter case they would travel to find wage labor anew.

This migratory nature of the labor force had a negative impact on one attempt to establish plantation rubber during the depression years. In 1924, as mentioned before, the Ford Motor company established large rubber plantations on the Tapajós River at Fordlândia and Belterra. Despite planting several million trees and investing in substantial infrastructure, the venture failed. Ford's problems were twofold. First, concentrating trees increased the likelihood of disease and pests destroying large stretches of the plantation. A possible solution to this problem was to develop a pest-resistant variety of tree, but this proved too costly.

The second problem was the inability to fix labor to the land. Despite relatively high wages, there were persistent problems with labor turnover. Why? The Amazon camponeses, such as those from Gurupá, retained direct access to land and resources—their subsistence gardens and lands held in common for extraction, fishing, and hunting. This base allowed them to labor on the plantation for short periods of time, collect wages, then return home with the funds to buy needed commodities from the world market. After their money ran out, they returned to work for more wages. Most camponeses saw this as a superior alternative to working permanently for wages. It allowed greater freedom of action, more security for food production and diet, and the maintenance of patron-client relationships for long-term security. Without coercion there was no way of forcing the camponeses to accept the long-term wage labor relations. As discussed in the following chapter, the Amazon labor force was resisting integration into full-fledged capitalist labor relations.

The Miniboom

The depression period continued uninterrupted until 1942 when world events briefly created a demand for Amazonian rubber. World War II was raging, and one of the casualties was the rubber plantations of Malaya. The Japanese had overrun the plantations and had halted the export of rubber to the West. In desperate need of rubber for the wartime effort, the United States turned to the Amazon region. In an agreement with the Brazilian government known as the "Washington Accords," the United States began financing the revival of rubber extraction. Under the program the Brazilian government gave incentives to attract migrants from the northeast to reopen rubber trails in the Amazon. The Washington Accords also established the Serviço Especial de Saúde Pública or the Special Service for Public Health (SESP), the region's first program to oversee the health of workers. With this increased activity and the rising price for rubber, the Amazon experienced a miniboom during the next few years.

Gurupá experienced a reversal of fortunes with the miniboom. There was an influx of people to work the abandoned rubber trails. This immigration increased the municipality's population by 75 percent in ten years (7,081 in 1940 to 12,419 in 1950 [IBGE 1940, 1956]). The town of Gurupá grew slightly to nearly 500 people in 1948 and reached more than 600 in 1950 (Wagley 1976:58). People tell of boatloads of Ceareneses and Maranhenses (people from the states of Ceará and Maranhão) arriving in Gurupá. Some ships unloaded passengers while others continued upstream. Many people in Gurupá considered these northeasterners to be wild and dangerous people, quick to anger and to pull a knife in a fight.

Higher prices for rubber and other extracted goods during the war years led to modest levels of prosperity. The several solvent trading posts expanded business. Local consumption of imported manufactured goods increased. The municipality taxed rubber and oleaginous seed exports, which allowed it to continue work on the town hall begun in 1910, repair the public dock, build several public houses, and pay workers to weed the streets of the town from time to time (Wagley 1976:57). The municipal government, however, overextended its funding and left the municipality in debt for years to come. The federal government's increased interest in the Amazon during this time also led to the establishment of a SESP health post in town and the building of seven schools in the municipality (Wagley 1976:57). Charles Wagley's first visit to Gurupá in 1942 was in association with the health post he helped establish as part of the wartime Washington Accords. There was even a telegraph station that served the town for a while and a PBY seaplane of Panair do Brasil that stopped once a week on its route between Belém and Manaus. And finally, from gifts accumulated from rubber extractors and other devotees of Saint Benedict, the town repaired the church (Wagley 1976:57–58).

Rubber production throughout the Amazon during the miniboom relied on the remnants of the old aviamento system since it was a preestablished financial and logistical system. But the limitations of aviamento (wastefulness and cost), as well as the limitations of natural extraction (low productivity), constrained wartime production to an increase of only 32 percent between 1940 and 1944 (Wagley 1976:54). This failure led the United States to abandon the Washington Accords by 1945 when the Allied forces liberated the Malayan plantations from the Japanese and cheap Asian rubber reentered the world market. Without U.S. financing, Amazonian rubber production slipped back into its former depressed state. The miniboom was over. The only lasting influence of the boom was the establishment of SESP. The Brazilian government took over the program in 1945 and has continued it to this day.

With the end of the miniboom Gurupá returned to its depressed state. The town lost its telegraph station, and the number of riverboats visiting the community dwindled. In a three-month period in 1948 only twelve river steamers stopped to deliver mail, merchandise, and to load extracted commodities (Wagley 1976:58). Some people left the municipality, while those remaining returned to a mix of subsistence and extractive activities. The economy continued to revolve around rubber, despite the drop in prices. According to the 1950 census, rubber was Gurupá's primary export by volume—904 tons extracted—followed by 223 tons of acuuba seeds, 37 tons of cacao, 21 tons of the palm murumuru (*Astrocaryum murumuru*), and less than 1 ton of timbo. Also exported were 10,548 cubic meters of wood (IBGE 1956). In the 1950s and 1960s there was a modest market for alligator skins, followed by demand for spotted cats' furs and some experimentation with jute planting.

Despite the return of the depression the Brazilian state did not ignore the Amazon region as it had previously. There were public and private interests stirring to integrate the area with the rest of Brazil for national security reasons and to tap the rich resources of the region. For example, in 1940 Brazilian president Getúlio Vargas called for a "March to the West" to populate and develop Brazil's vast interior regions, including Amazonia. By 1946 the federal government proposed and approved funds for a long-term development policy for the Amazon. By 1953, after planning and bureaucratic delays, the program was ready for implementation (Mahar 1979:6). At that point the Brazilian national assembly created a state agency, the Superintendência do Plano de Valorização Econômica da Amazônia (Amazon Economic Valorization Plan Superintendency), or the SPVEA, and gave it responsibility for regional development. Among the SPVEA's lofty goals were to make the region self-sufficient in agriculture foodstuffs, to expand the production of raw materials for export and internal use, and to improve transportation, communication, and energy production (Mahar 1979:8).

The SPVEA never completed these ambitious plans, as the government diverted much of its funding to the industrializing south and to the building of the new federal capital in Brasília. Bureaucratic restrictions and corruption also hampered the agency (Hecht and Cockburn 1990:112). Because of these problems the SPVEA's impact on the region from 1953 to 1964 was largely limited to the building of the Belém-Brasília Highway (1959), the financing of a few major industries, and the administration of financial support for scientific research (Mahar 1979:10; Moran 1983:72).

Life in Gurupá changed little with the SPVEA. Extraction continued to dominate the economy, transportation and communication improved only slightly, and no reform occurred in the agricultural sector. Agricultural production, in particular, continued as an adjunct to extraction because of the weak internal market and a lack of incentive to plant. People living in the town and people living on the tidal várzea were forced to import food. Survival during this period "hung in a delicate balance between starvation and bare subsistence" (Wagley 1968 ed.:300).

By the 1960s Gurupá had changed considerably, although not necessarily for the better. An increase in rural-urban migration boosted the town's population to over 1,000 people by 1960. To accommodate the population increase Gurupá expanded to four streets running parallel to the river, with a fifth taking shape in 1962 (Wagley 1968 ed.:299). Among the motives for rural-urban migration were "push" factors, such as the depressed extractive economy, low returns for agricultural production, and failure of many trading posts that provided the camponeses with imported goods and credit. There were also "pull" factors, such as better access to imported commodities and the improved educational, health, and recreational facilities in town. Other attractions were electricity (six hours a day) and the general *movimento* (movement) or bustle of town life, which included gossip, political campaigns, noise of radios, and daily commercial activities (Wagley 1968 ed.:299).

Once the rural migrants reached the town of Gurupá, however, they found few jobs. Gurupá had no industry, and the municipal government employed no more than forty people. There was a 5-kilometer road opened into the interior (which later became a 12-kilometer road in the 1970s) on which rural migrants planted gardens and sent their produce to town with the municipality's truck and jeep. However, productive land was limited and became increasingly scarce as Gurupá's more prosperous families appropriated larger areas and placed sharecroppers on it (Wagley 1968 ed.:300). Because of limited employment and/or subsistence opportunities, many rural families continued migrating to other towns and cities.

A second major change in Gurupá during the 1960s resulted from triple-digit inflation. Combined with devalued prices for extracted commodities, inflation undermined most merchants' ability to extend credit. Increasingly, trading post owners and regatões found that the value of the debts repaid by fregueses within one to three months did not equal the inflated costs of getting new merchandise. As a consequence merchants depleted their stocks with little or no reserve capital to buy more goods.

Faced with this situation the trading posts and regatões either refused to sell goods on credit (which meant a loss of their fregueses), or sold on credit but raised prices sharply, or went out of business. The stronger commercial establishments managed to survive through various combinations of price increases and credit limitations (Wagley 1968 ed.:301). For approximately 40–50 percent of the trading posts, however, going out of business was the only option. Trading post failure was particularly prevalent in the interior. For example, my consultants told me that on the Mojú River (on the Great Island of Gurupá) there were five active trading posts in the 1940s, but only three by the 1960s. During the same period on the Mararú River (also on the Great Island of Gurupá) five trading posts fell to three, and on the neighboring Murupucú River, two declined to one.

The highly visible class system once prominent during the rubber boom also changed appreciably. This system had been in a long decay since the rubber bust. By 1948 the dominant class consisted of only a few impoverished descendants of the old aristocratic rubber merchant families (Wagley 1976:103). Following the long economic depression of the 1950s and 1960s, these families fell further in their national and local class rankings.

The impoverishment of the dominant class led many Gurupaenses to conclude that by the 1960s Gurupá no longer possessed a class system. Everyone was considered a member of the second class (gente de segunda). In local terms people defined social class by a number of categories, such as occupation, family, ethnicity, education, and wealth. Ideally, the members of the upper class held jobs not requiring any manual labor, came from a good family background, were well educated (high school or college), were wealthy in terms of local standards, and were of European descent. In reality, however, even during the rubber boom, these criteria were rarely met. Following the prolonged depression these criteria were harder to fulfill as most sources of wealth eroded away, opportunities for education disappeared, and family and ethnic lines blurred through intermarriage and migration.

Despite the impoverishment of the dominant class and the local idea that social class had disappeared, the class system in Gurupá continued to function. By the late 1950s and early 1960s there were two classes in the municipality. The first class was the dominant class (merchants, large landowners, professionals, civil servants). Throughout the period it continued to control the economy and politics, although under reduced circumstances. The second class was the working class. There were four divisions within the working class. The first division included landless fregueses. They were principally várzea extractors, although some were terra firme farmers. The second division included autonomous terra firme farmers living on unclaimed land. A trading post patrão controlled these farmers through debt-credit ties. The third division consisted of small landowners on the várzea and terra firme. The small landowners were both extractors and farmers. The fourth division consisted of the urban poor. These people provided various domestic services to the urban dominant class, as well as engaging in seasonal extraction. Some also farmed. These divisions within the working class were not mutually exclusive, and movement between and among them was common.

Besides the four divisions in the working class there was a subdivision that overlapped the other divisions. It consisted of modest, small-scale merchants and moneylenders or "brokers." In terms of material possessions, only slight differences separated the brokers from the rest of the working class. They were always under the control of a member of the dominant class. Yet the brokers did serve as leaders among their working-class division and often dealt with the dominant class in the interests of their class division. These brokers never developed into an upper peasantry since their fellow camponês workers were highly mobile and could escape prolonged exchange manipulation duplicity (dominant class and broker) by switching to another patrão's control, moving to unowned terra firme, or simply leaving the area.

By the 1960s changes occurred in certain cultural traditions. On the one hand, the depression diminished the grandeur of the festivals for Saint Anthony and Saint Benedict. Fewer people attended the festivals, and as a consequence, they generated less revenue for the church. In addition, people no longer performed the *boi bumba* ceremony described by Wagley in 1948 (1976:204–208). The ceremony witnessed by Wagley and Galvão was the last one held in Gurupá, and the people had performed it only at Wagley's request.

At the same time that these traditions were in temporary or permanent decline there were other innovations diffusing into the community. Radios became commonplace possessions of townspeople. Entrepreneurs showed an occasional movie in a large building that also served as a dance hall during festival time. Both of these media increased local awareness of national events. Additionally, several bars opened, boasting kerosene refrigerators. They sold the traditional cachaça alcohol along with cold beer and soft drinks. And finally, people began playing soccer and volleyball by 1962. Soccer quickly became the local passion with two rival teams sporting uniforms and battling each other on Sunday afternoons (Wagley 1964:302–303).

Conclusion

The Cabanagem Revolt marked the birth of the camponês class in Amazonia. The revolt was a protest against the polarization of wealth, the troubling origin of the aviamento system, and an exploitative class system. It claimed the lives of approximately 23 percent of the regional population. After the government subdued the revolt, the camponeses returned to extraction and agriculture activities. They submitted themselves to the labor relations organized through the trading post and, to a lesser extent, the short-lived forced labor program called the Workers' Corps.

The rubber boom that followed brought unprecedented fortune to the Amazon region. Yet the wealth was ephemeral, and sixty years later the region relapsed into economic depression. The boom did establish several salient political-economic patterns that are still shaping Amazonia today. Among them were the domination of an extractive economy with a history of resource depletion, an agricultural sector that served as an adjunct to extraction and led to frequent food shortages, a lack of an adequate internal market to distribute food, persistent labor shortages for all sectors, a class system divided between merchants/landowners and camponeses that was principally maintained through control of exchange rather than land, and the aviamento system that held workers and merchants alike in debt.

The rubber bust and depression period ended in 1964. In the contemporary period that followed (1964–1991), radical changes emerged from state intervention in politics and economics and the penetration of new capitalist firms in an all-out attempt to develop Amazonia. The efforts to develop the region brought many changes to Gurupá. However, as I will show in the following chapters, the ecological and political-economic structures established during nearly four centuries of Luso-Brazilian history significantly affected these processes.

Timber harvesting, Bacá. A heavy log
(center) is tied to two buoyant logs for transportation.

5

REPEATING HISTORY?
ECONOMIC TRENDS, POST-1964

In the hot afternoons people typically abandon the streets of Gurupá. The tropical sun heats the concrete, wood, and metal surfaces to a scorching 110°. Most people stay inside their homes, often napping in a hammock, or find the shade of one of the town's large jambô (rose apple) trees to escape the heat. I often did the latter, passing the time gazing at the river rolling by, enjoying any breeze that might happen to blow, and talking to whomever happened to share the shade with me. While under the jambô tree I remember conversations about development projects occurring in Amazonia. People told of wondrous enterprises they had seen or heard about. There were mines, ranches, dams, highways, and farms generating wealth and prosperity from nature. More than once, however, I asked whether development projects were really helping the people of the region and whether they were destructive and could seriously restrict future use of the environment.

Many were puzzled by my questions. They responded, "How could the enrichment of oneself by using nature's gifts be bad?" Occasionally, though, some would nod their heads in agreement and start naming problems with development projects—deforestation, loss of game, pollution of water, widespread disease among workers, and even hunger for the under-employed and unemployed. When they started naming these types of problems in Gurupá I would scurry for my notebook, for this information is important in order to begin to understand the social and environmental effects of current development trends. I knew the history of resource depletion, labor scarcity, and exploitation in Amazonia. I also knew the level of poverty experienced in Gurupá. The question I sought to answer was whether current development initiatives broke with past limitations, or whether history was simply repeating itself.

The period under discussion begins in 1964. In this year the military overthrew the civilian government of Brazil and took control of the state. For the next twenty-one years the generals maintained a repressive, authori-

tarian regime that aggressively pursued a policy of economic modernization. The regime designed this policy to foster economic growth by attracting foreign investment and expanding the nation's industrial sector through
tax incentives and wage control measures (Schmink and Wood 1992:58).
As part of the overall plan the generals stressed the importance of integrat-
ing the Amazon with the rest of Brazil and developing the region's potential for agriculture, ranching, mineral and vegetable extraction, and industry. The planners assumed that integration and development would greatly
improve standards of living in the region.

The military's policy decisions set in motion a series of processes that
challenged the social and environmental fabric of the Amazon region.
Massive development projects, migration, penetration of the regional economy by multinational corporations, and new demands from the world economic system for products all forced changes and precipitated reactions.
Yet, as I will show, social and environmental features that had been evolving during the previous centuries mitigated these processes. Labor shortages, resource depletion, environmental destruction, and aviamento labor
relations all compromised the lofty designs of modernization. Even following the military's retreat from power in 1985 the economic dynamics of the
region stayed basically the same, although protests against social inequality
and environmental destruction have increasingly punctuated the political
landscape.

In Gurupá the national and regional processes set in motion during this
period at first created an economic "boom" with the introduction of large-
scale timber and palmito extraction, an expansion in government services,
terra firme cattle ranching, a resurgence in the market for rubber, oil exploration, and the promise of earning higher wages through migration to several development projects in surrounding areas. Simultaneously, conflict
arose as various groups contested the control of land, resources, and the
uneasy articulation between the local pattern of labor relations and capitalist firms. Most devastating has been the depletion of resources that threatens to return the community to economic depression. To better understand
these processes and their impact upon Gurupá this chapter will describe the
regional and local economy between 1964 and 1991.

The Military's Development Plans for Amazonia

Geopolitics was an immediate concern of the military regime following the
coup. A history of unsecured borders and underpopulated areas in
Amazonia had led to fears of foreign penetration. In the twentieth century
alone various South American countries have redrawn the boundaries of
Brazil's Amazon five times (Hecht and Cockburn 1990:112). Anxieties
over communist revolution and rumors of plans originating in the United

States on various ways to internationalize the Amazon were examples of more recent concerns. Whether these fears were realistic or not, once in power the military forcefully moved to secure the region. They invoked nationalist imagery of the "conquest of Amazonia" as a venerated mission (Schmink and Wood 1992:12).

Through a succession of regional plans the generals pushed for the building of roads and establishment of military bases. The linchpin of this process was the construction of the Transamazon Highway in 1972, which runs east to west to the south of the Amazon River. This highway is linked to the Belém-Brasília Highway (completed in 1960) and several additional highways built later to connect much of Amazonia to southern Brazil. Collectively, they opened immense areas of land for occupation.

The planners assumed that this land was a demographic void to be filled. They ignored the fact that the roads encroached upon the land of tens of thousands of Native Americans and indigenous camponeses. Road construction and immigration displaced many of these people. Many died once exposed to disease. The government's geopolitical concerns have continued into the 1990s with the drive to build the Calha Norte (Northern Trench), a road running east to west to the north of the Amazon River. Along the road the government wishes to establish several military colonies (Schmink and Wood 1992:110). This road also threatens indigenous populations.

Development was a second concern of the military. Here again a succession of plans was devised for how the government could use the Amazon to solve several pressing problems for the rest of Brazil. Among these were the easing of land shortage problems in other regions by encouraging migration to Amazonia, the opening of a new frontier for beef production to relieve meat shortages in the cities, extraction of resources to finance industrialization in the south, and by the 1980s, extraction of resources to pay international debts. The planners believed these activities would initiate development and lift the regional inhabitants from their long-term poverty.

The generals implemented their goals for regional development in 1966 through a plan called "Operation Amazon." Development was to proceed through a partnership among the government, national businesses, and multinational corporations. The government created state enterprises to provide a variety of incentives (tax breaks, tax holidays, land concessions) and build infrastructure (roads, communication systems, hydroelectric dams, ports) to attract private investment in agriculture, livestock, lumber, mining, industry, and basic services sectors. The principal agency for coordinating development activities was SUDAM, the Superintendência do Desenvolvimento da Amazônia (Superintendency for the Development of the Amazon). Despite plans calling for private investment to bear the brunt of Amazon development, most of the capital came from public sources.

By 1970 a second set of plans named PIN, Programa de Integração

Nacional (National Integration Plan), called for the building of the Transamazon Highway and other routes and the settling of 100,000 small-farming families in various colonization projects along the highways. Migration would solve several problems: It would help populate the region; and it would relieve social and political problems in other areas of Brazil, particularly the northeast, caused by drought, land concentration, population growth, and rural-urban migration.

Within a few years of implementation, however, the government abandoned the colonization programs. Although there were some problems of logistics and bureaucratic red tape, the principal reason for discontinuance was lobbying pressure from elite groups who wished to reserve the Amazon for their own use (Schmink and Wood 1992:77–78). Groups such as the Associação do Empresários da Amazônia (Amazon Entrepreneur Association) successfully, but incorrectly, argued that small-farmer colonization was unproductive and even a destructive use of resources, while the creation of large-scale enterprise, private colonization projects, and cattle ranching were more viable alternatives for development. By 1974 the state changed its course and labeled the colonization project a failure. The government blamed the failure on the colonists (Wood and Schmink 1979).

By 1975 the government began viewing the Amazon exclusively as a "resource frontier" and not a safety valve for population resettlement (Mahar 1979:26). The state created a new plan called Plano de Desenvolvimento da Amazônia (Amazon Development Plan), or PDA. Its centerpiece was a program named POLAMAZONIA (Programa de Polos Agropecuários e Agrominerais da Amazônia [Program of Agricultural and Mineral Poles in the Amazon]), which subsidized big projects in fifteen growth poles scattered about the region. The plan led to a boom in lumbering, cattle ranching, and mining. SUDAM allocated most of its funds to the first two activities. By 1983 livestock accounted for 30.9 percent and timber 50.5 percent of all SUDAM subsidies (Browder 1986:105). Today cattle ranching is the principal economic activity on 85 percent of land cleared in the region. Some 50,000 enterprises raise cattle on ranches that average just under 25,000 hectares (60,000 acres), with a few encompassing over 104,000 hectares (250,000 acres) (Hecht and Cockburn 1990:169–170).

Timber extraction similarly spread quickly throughout the Amazon. Between 1975 and 1980 the Amazon's total wood production increased by 156 percent (from 4.5 million cubic meters to 11.5 million cubic meters). This growth represented an increase in total national output of roundwood from 14.3 percent in 1975 to nearly 31.8 percent by 1980 (Browder 1986:68). The number of legally licensed sawmills jumped from 194 in 1965 to 1,639 by 1981. This number, however, does not include the scores of unlicensed mills (Browder 1986:56–57).

Also under the POLAMAZONIA plan were several large-scale projects initiated in manufacturing, mining, and energy production (hydroelectric dams). One example that was to have an impact on Gurupá was the Jarí tree plantation financed by U.S. shipping tycoon Daniel Ludwig. Ludwig's goal was to build the world's largest tree plantation to produce pulp in the midst of the Amazon forest. In 1967 he purchased a 1,250,000-hectare (3,000,000-acre) tract of land along the Jarí River. He cleared part of this land and planted fast-growing gmelina, pine, and eucalyptus trees. By late 1979 a $270 million pulp mill and wood-fired power plant (built in Japan and towed overseas to Jarí) began operating. Besides the plantation and pulp production there were several secondary operations undertaken including a 14,600-hectare (35,000-acre) rice farm, a cattle ranch, a kaolin mine (a clay used in the production of china and glossy paper), and various food-producing projects.

The infrastructure needed for the project was massive. It required over 4,000 kilometers (2,500 miles) of road and 80 kilometers (50 miles) of railroad. Ludwig imported approximately 2,000 vehicles and various types of heavy equipment (Fisk 1985:18). He built housing for the approximately 6,000 workers directly engaged in the project. By 1980 Ludwig had invested approximately $500 million in the project (Pinto 1986:202). The Brazilian government provided incentives for the investment including an exemption on income tax for ten years and suspension of duties on imported equipment (Pinto 1986:39–40). Despite the massive investment in the scheme the Jarí tree plantation did not produce a profit. By 1982 Ludwig sold the project to a Brazilian consortium for only $280 million, a huge loss (Hecht and Cockburn 1990:131). In the 1990s the only portion of the project earning a profit is the kaolin mine.

The government has also aided such various mining projects as the extraction of manganese in Amapá, cassiterite in Rondônia, bauxite on the Trombetas River, and the largest of all, iron ore at Serra dos Carajás (Bunker 1985:86). Researchers have estimated that investment in Carajás has been somewhere between $1 billion and $4.3 billion (Mahar 1979:111; Dayton 1975, cited in Bunker 1985:86). Infrastructure development has been extensive and includes the construction of the Tucuruí Dam for electric power, an 876-kilometer railway, and port facilities in São Luís do Maranhão. Project planners expect the payoff to be 17,885 million tons of 66 percent pure iron ore (enough to supply world demand for sixty years), 60 million tons of manganese, 2,000 million tons of copper, 48 million tons of aluminum, 88 million tons of nickel, and 100 tons of gold (Cota 1984:74–75; Schmink and Wood 1992:67).

Another mining activity was a massive gold rush in southern Pará during the 1980s. Migration swelled the region and created towns overnight. The gold rush quickly transformed the regional economy, particularly around the Tapajós region. Eighty-five percent of the gold came from placer mines worked by *garimpeiros* (small scale-miners). According to government statistics, a half million people extracted about $1 billion worth of gold a year during this time (Hecht and Cockburn 1990:151). These figures, however, greatly underestimate the activity occurring in the region.

In 1985 the military ceded rule to a civilian government. It was essentially forced out by economic failure, corruption, a long history of repression, and widespread discontent among the populous. Its policies to develop and control the Amazon region were in disarray. Much of the problem lay in the contradictory goals set out by the government. In particular, the military initially supported small-farmer colonization but soon reversed itself and supported large-scale development projects in ranching, timber extraction, and mining. As a result small farmers and large project managers competed violently for land. Organized protests by farmers constrained the expansion of cattle ranches, private colonization projects, mines, and dams.

Additional problems stemmed from the chaos among government agencies in Amazonia. Several had overlapping jurisdiction and contradictory goals. They all overwhelmed economic policy with bureaucratic restrictions. Also, national and international groups criticized the government's environmental policies. They protested the rampant deforestation and potential effects on global climate change.

The civilian governments that succeeded the military have had to contend with environmental issues. In the New Republic's First Amazon Development Plan (I PDA-NA), which came out in 1986, the government planners emphasized economic growth while maintaining ecological balance and reducing social inequalities (see Schmink and Wood 1992:105). In 1988 the Our Nature Plan paid more attention to rectifying environmental disasters and set land aside for national parks and reserves. In the same year the government created the Instituto Brasileiro de Recursos Naturais Renováveis e do Meio Ambiente (Brazilian Institute for Renewable Natural Resources and the Environment), or IBAMA, to enforce environmental regulations. While these policy shifts sounded impressive, implementation proved more complex. In some cases contradictory government polices led to disaster. One example was the government's decision to demarcate and protect the forests occupied by the Yanomami Native Americans. This move was followed by the opening of this land for gold mining and an invasion of some 35,000 miners. After epidemics of malaria and at least one massacre of Yanomami occurred, the government removed the miners. Since then clandestine miners have returned and the miner/native conflict remains. Also troublesome about this phase of development was that the Our Nature Plan was under the control of the military, despite the civilian government being in power (Schmink and Wood 1992:123–124).

By the 1990s the environmental and human rights consequences of Amazonian development had taken the forefront in national and international debates. Camponeses, miners, and Native Americans increasingly organize themselves to protest government policy. Through newly formed alliances with national and international groups concerned with ecological and social issues, they press for alternative forms of development. The proponents of alternative development argue for sustainable use of resources that will leave the forest standing—primarily, extractive reserves. An extractive reserve is a large area wherein local residents conduct extractive activities, subsistence farming, some small-scale livestock raising, hunting, and fishing. People living in the area engage in petty extraction that "involves removal of some part of an ecosystem's material for commercial or domestic consumption in a manner that does not threaten the long-term productivity of the resource" (Hecht and Cockburn 1990:175). "Folk" knowledge permits careful management of forest resources. Local residents plant trees in ecologically appropriate places, use fire cautiously to kill pests and release nutriments into soils, weed competing plants to allow plant and tree growth, fish, and selectively hunt animals (Hecht and Cockburn 1990:176).

Proponents of extractive reserves maintain that the value generated by extraction and associated subsistence activities is always greater than returns from development strategies that destroy forests, such as cattle ranching and colonist agriculture (Hecht and Cockburn 1990:177–178). Whether such alternatives will be successful and will replace the development methods of the past is uncertain. But many who are concerned with environmental and human rights issues now feel there is some hope for the future, although deforestation and violent conflict over land continue.

Development Plans and Gurupá

Regional development plans have never focused exclusively on Gurupá. In large part planners have ignored the municipality, while surrounding areas have received roads, dams, colonization projects, mining complexes, and so forth. Nevertheless, Gurupá has experienced the forces of economic change, primarily in the area of extraction. Because of government incentives and subsidies the municipality experienced several booms—of varying length and intensity—in timber, palmito, rubber, and oil prospecting. More modest changes have occurred in agriculture and the government job sectors. Emigration to large-scale projects surrounding Gurupá has also had an impact on the local economy.

First and foremost among the booms is large-scale timber extraction. This activity began in an intensified form shortly after Operation Amazon provided financial incentives and credit through regional banks. In the late 1960s four multinational timber firms and many national firms set up extraction operations in the municipality of Gurupá. The timber located on the várzeas of the mainland and the Great Island of Gurupá attracted the firms. This timber was easily accessible and inexpensive to harvest because of fluvial transportation. In addition, the timber reserves were located close to the major regional sawmill complexes of Breves and Macapá, saving both time and money in the transportation of logs.

Among the timber firms to conduct business in Gurupá, the most active and influential have been Brumasa (formerly a Dutch company named Bruynzeel, later bought by a Brazilian consortium), Eidai (Japanese), Brasil Norte (Brazilian), and Madeira Tropical (United States). The Jarí tree plantation also bought lightwoods for pulp production. Of the large corporations represented in Gurupá, Brumasa has had the most direct impact (in the 1990s corporate ownership changed, and the new owners renamed the company Trevo, but during the span of my research it was known only as Brumasa). In the early 1970s Brumasa began buying up local land with the benefit of SUDAM's fiscal incentives (Bunker 1985:100n3). By the early 1990s the company owned 95,708 hectares of Gurupá's várzea, or 10.3 percent of the entire municipality.

From the 1970s until the present the timber firms have financed an often frenzied rate of timber extraction. Wood exports increased drastically from a low in 1950 of only 10,548 cubic meters to 450,300 in 1980 and 452,440 in 1989 (IBGE 1956, 1981; Oliveira 1991:107). The timber species most frequently extracted include virola (*Virola surinamensis*), andiroba (*Carapa guianensis*), sucupira (*Dipolotropis martiusii*), and sumaúma (*Ceiba pentandra*). Local extractors also harvest muiritinga, macauuba, louro, and esponja (I was unable to identify these species). Wood has been mostly exported in the form of logs since Gurupá possesses neither adequate sawmills to process the volume extracted nor the technology to produce the much-valued veneers and plywoods. The sawmills that sprang up with the boom have been small-scale, primitive operations that produce only rough sawn wood. Approximately forty have been operating at one time or another in the municipality since 1966.

A second boom that began in the 1970s involves palmito extraction, a foodstuff used primarily as an hors d'oeuvre or salad ingredient. It comes from the top inner portion of various palm trees, including the açaí palm tree (*Eutrepe oleracea*). To prepare it, processors remove the palmito from the palm, slice it into small disks, and can it. It is then exported to the south of Brazil, France, and the United States. There is almost no local consumption. In Gurupá there were several small, mobile canning enterprises operating at different times and one large, stationary factory located in town in 1977. At its peak this factory employed thirty workers. However, the factory ran into financial troubles and the owner left town, bills unpaid, and the business collapsed.

Rubber extraction is another sector that improved during this period. After years of minimal production the federal government imposed import barriers against foreign rubber, which increased demand for domestic supplies. Coupled with a worldwide rise in rubber prices, rubber extraction has become a profitable activity again. Rubber tappers have reopened trails that they had neglected for decades, and the flow of rubber from the municipality has increased.

The final extraction boom to affect Gurupá was oil exploration, which began in 1982 and lasted until 1984. During this period Petrobrás, Brazil's national oil company, contracted a U.S. oil exploration firm, Geosource, to create seismic maps of the subsoil strata surrounding Gurupá. Geosource workers told me that the company hired approximately 400 local men for manual labor. Petrobrás used the maps produced by Geosource to determine if drilling for oil was a worthwhile venture. After two years Geosource moved on and left their findings to Petrobrás. Petrobrás planned no immediate drilling for oil or gas in Gurupá, as the findings were not too promising.

During this period the agricultural sector underwent a few minor changes. Government-sponsored programs for small-farmer loans, a very small colonization project, and technical advice led to modest increases in production during the late 1960s and early 1970s. Yet no food-producing program has had sustainable results, and food production fell off by the 1980s, primarily due to the labor drain to extraction.

Cattle ranching increased slightly during this time. Government loans have allowed ranchers to expand pastures on the várzea. Several landowners have attempted to plant terra firme pastures with grasses developed by government researchers. In addition, some individuals brought in new breeds of cattle and water buffalo (for várzea pastures). Some also made occasional use of vaccines and medicine for the animals. At the time of my research there were thirty-four *fazendas* (ranches) with 1,642 head of cattle and 5,600 head of water buffalo for the entire municipality (IBGE 1981). In addition, some fazendas produce milk, butter, cheese, and cottage cheese in small quantities.

A final area affected by regional development policies is the government job sector. The government created new agencies to administer development programs, which required the addition of many new civil servants. The agencies to appear in Gurupá include: FUNRURAL (Fundo de Assistência ao Trabalhador Rural or Assistance Fund for Rural Workers, which also pays retirement pensions); SESPA (Secretaria de Estado de Saúde Pública or State Secretary of Public Health, which replaced SESP sometime in the 1960s); SUCAM (Superintêndencia de Campanhas or Superintendency of Campaigns, which is charged with control of malaria, yellow fever, etc.); SEDUC (Superintêndencia de Estado de Educação or State Secretary of Education); MOBRAL (Movimento Brasileiro de Alfabetizão or Brazilian Movement for Adult Literacy); INCRA (Instituto Nacional de Colonização e Reforma Agrária or National Institute for Colonization and Agrarian Reform); CELPA (Centrais Elêctricas do Pará or Electrical Centers of Pará); and TELEPARÁ (Telefones do Pará or

Telephones of Pará). Beyond government administrative positions, new jobs have been added in the health sector with the construction of the hospital, in the education sector with the opening of approximately ninety rural-based schools, and with the Bank of Itaú, which operated between 1985 and 1990. In all, economic development activities created approximately 150 new part- or full-time jobs in Gurupá. Local residents received most of these jobs.

Repeating History

While the economic changes sparked by government development initiatives might look impressive, there have been persistent, sometimes debilitating, problems with most programs. Poor planning, limited knowledge, lack of local participation in decisionmaking, and preference given to elite special interests have compromised most projects. More troublesome, labor shortages, environmental destruction, and exploitative labor relations have continued the historic pattern of local impoverishment. By the 1980s it became clear to social science researchers that regional development consisted of gaining massive short-term profits for a few by using socially and environmentally destructive practices. Despite the rhetoric of development and progress offered by government planners and politicians, history repeated itself as nonsustainable economics dominated and the local population suffered the long-term consequences.

The Labor Shortage

The 1950 census estimated that the Amazon region had a population of only 1,844,655 people. As the generals formulated their geopolitical and economic strategies it was painfully obvious that the sparse population would constrain integration and development. One remedy was massive immigration. Just as it had during the rubber boom at the end of the previous century, the government encouraged hordes of migrants to settle in Amazonia and provide it with the necessary labor force. The government colonization program began the process. Soon spontaneous migration followed. It was unplanned and eventually unwanted. As a result the regional population boomed by 202 percent between 1950 and 1980.

Migration did not solve the region's labor problems. Instead, it has created surplus population in some parts of Amazonia and deficits in other parts. The establishment of large-scale projects in mining, timber, and manufacturing, and the promise of relatively high-paying wage labor jobs in these sectors, drew many people from the Amazon's rural interior as well as other regions of Brazil. Even the short-lived government colonization program drew heavily from local inhabitants. For example, Moran (1981:81) found that 36 percent of colonists settling in official colonization projects along the Transamazon Highway were from rural Pará.

At the same time the labor drain from small Amazonian communities has created problems for the local economies, particularly for food production since many emigrants are subsistence farmers. This labor drain has occurred despite large-scale immigration from other regions of Brazil into the Amazon. It has also occurred despite massive problems of land concentration and small-farmer displacement as cattle ranching expanded along the frontiers opened by new roads. Displacement has led to rapid urban growth, problems with unemployment in the new cities, and competition for all wage labor jobs available at the large project sites.

In Gurupá there are two types of labor drain: emigration and reallocation of labor to extraction. In both cases the result has been a reduction in food production leading to food shortages. For example, between 1940 and 1980 manioc production decreased by 51 percent, rice by 88 percent, beans by 68 percent, and corn by 59 percent (IBGE 1940, 1981). The declining food production has led to the steady increase in importation of food and frequent food shortages in town and in the tidal várzea.

Labor shortages created by emigration began in the 1970s. Many rural inhabitants gave up the low returns of camponês life and sought higher wages in such areas as the Jarí tree plantation, the sawmill-mining complexes at Macapá, and the sawmills at Breves. In addition, some people left to work in Belém, along the Transamazon Highway, in gold mines of southern Pará, and at the Carajás mining complex. Exact data on the mobility of the population do not exist. However, data from the 9 percent random sample survey of families in town suggest its widespread practice. The survey revealed that 70 percent of sample families had siblings living in other municipalities. Although labor migration has been a common historical pattern in the Amazon, dating at least to the rubber boom, the recent trend involves a higher volume of people than ever before.

One example of emigration comes from the farming community of Jocojó. When Wagley visited Jocojó in 1948 he reported that the hamlet had a total of nineteen houses. In the following years the hamlet grew to contain approximately forty houses. The number peaked in the early 1970s. According to Gabriel Lopes, a Jocojó native, at this time the hamlet's residents learned of the Jarí plantation that was actively recruiting labor in Gurupá. In the 1970s several boats made weekly stops at Gurupá on their way to Jarí (this direct Jarí-Gurupá connection has now stopped). Gabriel said that a few individuals from Jocojó traveled to the plantation and found steady wage labor jobs. In addition, they found the excitement and movimento of Jarí's growing towns. When this news reached Jocojó more families decided to try their luck at the tree plantation. Some went on a temporary basis and returned home, while others made Jarí their permanent residence.

Why did so many leave the hamlet? Gabriel told me that Jocojó had grown to its limits by the 1960s. The community had used the land surrounding the hamlet to its capacity. Access to more distant land was blocked by a swamp. At the same time the prices for manioc and other food crops were miserably low. As the opportunity to work for wages at Jarí became known, nearly half the households left Jocojó permanently by 1986. Another five or six individuals have continued to migrate seasonally to extract timber at Jarí.

Many interior neighborhoods or hamlets of Gurupá have experienced similar migration pressures. When there is hope of a better future many people do not hesitate to leave their homes. As these people leave no one replaces them in the subsistence food production sector, so food production drops. This pattern persists, although the total population of Gurupá has grown throughout this period, from 12,248 in 1960 to 17,011 in 1989—a modest increase of about 28 percent (IDESP 1989). The key here is that many of the people coming into the municipality are not producing food.

In the 1970s there was one attempt by the municipal government to boost food production by arranging to settle several camponês families from Maranhão along the community's only road. Interestingly, the government could persuade few Gurupaenses to participate in the project (had they learned their lesson from the previously mentioned attempt in the 1960s?). The project placed the Maranhenses (people from Maranhão) on land 5 kilometers from town. There the farmers produced crops for a couple of years and then left the project. They claimed the colonization project was not viable since it made little provision for transportation, credit, and market outlets for produce.

The second problem of labor drain involves the reallocation of labor, a pattern that has manifested itself most visibly in the context of the timber boom. As extraction activities expand a serious drain of labor from other sectors simultaneously occurs. Most critically, people have given up or reduced subsistence agriculture. There are three reasons for the drain. First are the higher wages earned from extraction. An industrious worker can earn a net profit ranging from several hundred dollars to $2,000 for five months of work. A comparable amount of time spent in rubber extraction earns roughly half this amount, while manioc farming earns even less. Because of these wage differentials most able-bodied men and even some women in the interior have extracted timber over recent decades. The interview schedule administered in the four sample hamlets/neighborhoods revealed that 72 percent of men fourteen years and older have worked in timber extraction or lumber production during their lives. In the town survey, 46 percent of men reported working in the wood sector.

The second reason for labor reallocation is pressure from landowners and trading post merchants. The 1980 census data show that extraction earned 218,412,000 cruzeiros, while agricultural activities earned

17,966,000 cruzeiros—a twelvefold difference. To capitalize on this deferential many trading post merchants strongly encourage, sometimes demand, that more time be spent in extraction than any other activity. Simply finding a patrão to finance agricultural production has been nearly impossible for most workers. Trading post merchants opt not to invest in agriculture when they can earn short-term higher returns in extraction. As discussed in earlier chapters, this pattern is several centuries old. Inflation also discourages investment in agriculture. For a crop such as manioc, which takes from one to two years to mature, by the time a farmer is ready to repay loans, inflation has increased the principal of the loan anywhere from 200 to 400 percent.

The third reason for labor reallocation is the lack of an internal market for food. The market in Gurupá is so underdeveloped that it is very difficult to find outlets for any surplus production. Most trading posts refuse to buy produce in excess of the immediate needs of their fregueses. Because of the exchange networks established through aviamento, merchants find it more convenient and sometimes more profitable to import food from other areas to fulfill these needs. The only alternative for farmers has been to trade with regatões or *marreteiros* (riverboat merchants). These merchants, however, have been more interested in extracted commodities than food. They pay very low prices for agricultural goods.

Environmental Destruction

As in the past, current use of regional resources in Amazonia is a predatory venture. Individuals do not seek fortunes through long-term sustainable plans but, rather, through quick assaults on nature and then abandonment of the exploited area. Timber extraction and cattle ranching are prime examples of this activity, although there are other examples from the extraction and fishing sectors. In each case people make few attempts to manage resources.

Timber. Timber extraction has been the classic example of nonsustainable and environmentally destructive activities. Production methods have created ecological problems in three ways. First, timber-extracting firms have tended to be highly selective of species cut. Of a possible 700 known tree species in the Amazon, fewer than 25 species account for 90 percent of present-day wood production (Hecht and Cockburn 1990:158). In 1983 just one species, mahogany, accounted for approximately 54 percent of the volume of all semimanufactured sawn-wood exports (Browder 1986:57).

By concentrating on these species the extraction firms have overexploited and depleted reserves. Once depleted, the firms move on to new areas leaving behind an environmentally impoverished area. Attempts to replant areas have been minimal. There are laws requiring reforestation, but the laws do not specify the reforestation sites. Most large firms that comply with the law subcontract with reforestation firms to plant trees in other areas far from their current extraction sites. Other timber firms avoid reforestation laws by not owning land. They contract for timber with private landowners who do not comply with the law. They also extract illegally from public lands.

Second, extraction methods have been very destructive to surrounding vegetation, particularly on the terra firme. Because of the dispersion of trees in the forest (a natural adaptation to protect against pests and disease), extractors usually harvest only one tree per hectare (2.4 acres). To obtain this tree they must cut or damage many trees that are in the way. It is estimated that to harvest selected species—about 3 percent of an area—extractors kill or harm 52 percent of the adjacent trees (see Hecht and Cockburn 1990:158).

Third, the sawing technology used has been very wasteful, which has led to the need for more harvesting. For example, for export-quality mahogany sawn wood, the sawing process renders only about 35 percent of a log marketable (Browder 1986:80). Through the 1990s many sawmills have lacked the technology to produce veneers and plywoods that are more cost-efficient uses of wood. In 1980 one-half of all lumber exports to foreign markets were rough or semi-industrialized products.

Extractors have employed each of these destructive patterns in Gurupá since the 1960s. Extractive firms have harvested and exported large quantities of only the few species listed earlier. By the 1980s it was clear that the extraction boom for these species was on the wane. Although I have no concrete data on depletion rates, observations made by timber buyers, extractors, and the general public all emphasize that the diameter of trees harvested during the research period is much smaller than it was only a few years earlier. People also comment that extractors are going much farther into the forest to find wood.

The first areas to suffer from depletion were on the várzea. As extractors depleted these reserves, attention turned to the timber on the mainland terra firme. This timber was bypassed earlier since extraction involved higher capital inputs for trucks and for labor to clear roads. By the late 1980s, however, there were approximately ten operations in Gurupá employing trucks and extracting timber from the terra firme. With the combination of the new terra firme reserves and the remaining várzea stands, several sawmill operators estimate that Gurupá can extract timber only into the late 1990s. After that point in time the sawmill operators plan to move their operations to new extraction areas or to change occupations. Most of the timber extractors who are aware of the impending depletion also said that they will either migrate or switch occupations.

Since the timber industry in Gurupá is purely extractive in nature, no systematic attempt has been made to manage or replant trees. Most landowners have cut their trees until depletion occurs. Even the one firm owning land in Gurupá, Brumasa, which claims to have replanted trees as required by law, has not done so in the municipality.

Local extractors and landowners hold varied, often contradictory, attitudes toward timber depletion. Some downplay the consequences, maintaining that the forest will always provide a living. If they deplete one tree species, another will replace it. With time, they assume the original species will naturally return without any attempt at management.

Other people recognize the hazards of depletion. Many of these individuals are small landowners who have exhausted timber reserves on their land. With the loss of timber income they have suffered a substantial drop in standard of living. Still others have seen the destruction of the oleaginous seed collection activities. This occurs as timber extractors remove virola trees, which produce acuuba seeds, and andiroba trees, which produce andiroba seeds. Since the 1800s these oleaginous seeds have been one of Gurupá's principal exports. Seed extractors exported the seeds or processed them into oils for local use. However, by the 1980s it was rare to find these once-abundant seeds. The disappearance of the seeds and oils made from them destroys both a valued medicinal remedy and a source of badly needed income.

Palmito extraction.   Brazil is the largest producer of palmito in the world. Most of it has been exported to the international market since the 1950s. Large-scale Amazon production of palmito began in the 1970s after predatory extraction depleted reserves in the south and southeast (Oliveira 1991:127–131). The same pattern of depletion in Amazonia has spread westward from the city of Belém ever since.

Palmito extraction in Gurupá has created considerable problems. The principal source of palmito in Gurupá is the açaí palm, which also produces the much-valued drink made from palm nuts. Extraction of palmito requires destruction of the tree. But the tree stump, if cut properly, will produce regrowth and fruit within five to six years. Therefore, if landowners and workers carefully manage palmito extraction, açaí will not be eradicated.

But such resource management is not practiced in Gurupá. For regrowth to occur, extractors must cut the tree at the base. Palmito-extracting firms in Gurupá cut trees at the top, destroying the chance of regeneration. Cutting trees at the top makes harvesting easier for the extractor, who can move from tree to tree without descending and without worrying about untangling the entire tree from the forest canopy. However, when harvesting occurs in this fashion extractors permanently destroy whole areas of açaí production. The process is systematic and results in depletion of palmito from worked areas. Several nearby municipalities, such as Breves, have nearly eliminated palmito in this way. The government is concerned enough about predatory extraction to send out biologists to collect açaí for a seed bank. It hopes to guard against the future extinction of many varieties of the tree.

Although conservation efforts by extraction firms are nonexistent, camponeses do plant the trees for their açaí. Planting techniques are usually limited to scattering seeds around one's house. More rare in Gurupá is a systematic planting of trees. One exception was a young entrepreneur who experimented with açaí production. This entrepreneur, Edson Povo, was one of my key consultants and grandson of Jorge Povo. Edson had accompanied a government biologist on a trek through Gurupá to find the most productive açaí trees and collect their seeds for a seed bank. With the technical advice gained from this experience, Edson bought several hectares of land just outside town and planted 1,000 açaí seedlings from the seeds he had helped collect. Edson raised the seedlings with care, planting them in small cups containing manure. When the seedlings were 25 centimeters high he transplanted them into the ground. He planted the trees several meters apart to protect against the easy spread of disease and pestilence. In the future Edson told me that he planned to expand his endeavor and to plant cacao in between açaí to further reduce the chances of the spread of disease and pestilence.

For his efforts Edson was the source of jokes. Few people could see the logic of planting açaí when it grows naturally in the forest. However, in conversations with me Edson responded that already there was a shortage of açaí in town. Individuals who own açaí presses (electrically powered machines that remove the pulp that is then mixed with water to make the drink) have to rely on an uncertain supply from the interior. Days often pass without enough açaí to meet demand. The press owners claimed the shortage was only temporary due to an unusually high number of toucans migrating through the area that year. The toucans feed on açaí. However, Edson maintained that with increases in palmito extraction and competition from açaí buyers from neighboring municipalities who are willing to pay high prices, the shortage was sure to intensify. With his açaí farm he hoped to cash in on the demand.

When I returned to Gurupá in 1991, I asked Edson about his açaí. He lamented that a grass fire had destroyed most of the plants. He had abandoned his plans for açaí production and had turned to raising water buffalo. Toward this end he had planted grass and raised a couple of animals. The future of his small pasture, however, was uncertain because of ecological limitations. I could not help feeling that with this turn of events Gurupá had lost a promising entrepreneurial undertaking.

Cattle ranching.   Cattle ranching on the terra firme has produced a major ecological disaster in the Amazon. It stands out as one of the most promoted, but most destructive, of the development possibilities. The military government allocated approximately $1 billion and numerous tax breaks over a twenty-year period to business firms and wealthy individuals (mostly from the south) to deforest massive areas of the region, plant pasture, and raise cattle. The transformation of forest directly or indirectly to pasture is responsible for approximately 90 percent of all deforestation in Amazonia. All totaled, deforestation has destroyed an estimated 16,700,000 hectares (some 40,000,000 acres) of rain forest—about 10 percent of the Amazon (Hecht and Cockburn 1990:54).

The clearing of large areas of forest for pasture exposes the thin topsoil to erosion from torrential rainfall. The remaining nutrients for the grasses are quickly used or lost by leaching from heavy rainfall. Shrubby weeds and plants toxic to livestock invade the pasture. Soils are compacted (Hecht 1983:173–176). The cost to recuperate degraded pastures after only ten years of use is prohibitive, so most ranchers simply clear more land (Hecht 1984:388; Hecht and Cockburn 1990:174). By the 1990s ranchers had abandoned more than 50 percent of land cleared for pasture. The land is now practically useless for human activities (Hecht and Cockburn 1990:174). Ranchers contend with these limitations by simply expanding pasture into uncleared forest. In reality, cattle ranching is slash-and-burn ranching—a destructive and nonsustainable practice.

Cattle ranching as a whole in Amazonia is an irrational endeavor. Few if any ranches generate a profit. Production rates are only one head per hectare (0.6 per acre), which means production costs usually exceed the selling price (Hecht and Cockburn 1990:169). Thirty percent of the cattle ranches established after the 1960s have been abandoned, and 40 percent have sold no products (Hecht and Cockburn 1990:171). Cattle ranching is exceedingly illogical in economic terms until one considers the value of the government subsidies and rising land values. Both elements compensate for inadequate production. Land values, for example, may increase by as much as 2,000 percent in a few short years (Hecht and Cockburn 1990:170). Simple clearing of forest cover, which is often done to lay claim to land, increases land value by 30 percent. Deforestation and the pretense of cattle ranching have therefore been profitable for southern business firms. The result, however, is a degraded environment of little future use, all for short-term profit.

What is lost in this process of wealth accumulation? There is incredible loss of biodiversity that might have potential uses for agriculture, industry, and medicine. For example, complex chemical compounds present in tropical flora have a long history of use in Western medicine. Drugs originally extracted from tropical forest materials are now worth $12 billion a year. The National Cancer Institute in the United States suggests that the Amazon may have five plant species with the capacity to generate superstar drugs against cancer; in fact, 70 percent of all plants known to have anti-cancer properties are found in lowland tropics (Hecht and Cockburn 1990:61). Beyond these utilitarian losses, there are problems with disruption of water cycles caused by deforestation, losses of countless species of animals and plants that biologists have never classified, and destruction of complex ecosystems that ecologists do not fully understand.

Cattle ranching on the várzea of Gurupá has been ongoing for at least 100 years. The small number of cattle and their grazing on natural grasses has not appeared to create too much ecological damage during this time. Even when landowners introduced new grasses and water buffalo into the ecosystem in the 1970s, no outward sign of environmental destruction was apparent. Terra firme ranching, on the other hand, has indeed created problems. In the 1970s several individuals cut down forest and planted grass on Gurupá's mainland terra firme. One of the first experiments occurred along the dirt road to Pucuruí. It quickly ended in failure as the animals fared poorly. The owner blamed the failure on the lack of water for the animals. By the 1980s the pasture was unused and heavily overrun by a variety of weeds. It was very questionable if the pasture would ever have any ranching or agricultural use.

Landowners have planted additional pastures in the municipality. Over time each experienced some sort of problem—nutrient depletion, soil compaction, toxic weed invasion—leading to poor results and abandonment. Overall, the pastures have had little impact on beef supply in the municipality. In terms of ecological impact, the small number of terra firme ranches attempted in the municipality has limited problems created by pasture failure. The small number of ranches is likely related to the lack of a road that would allow land speculators easy access to the area.

As an interesting side note, the chronic beef shortage motivated one small group of individuals to rustle cattle from the Jarí plantation and sell the beef in Gurupá. The cattle-rustling ring successfully supplied Gurupá with beef for nearly half a year in 1984. When the authorities finally uncovered the ring and arrested its members, Gurupá's principal supply of beef ended, and the town again suffered chronic shortages.

Fishing.   Fishing is another area that has suffered recent assault. There have been two threats to Amazon fisheries: destruction of habitat and commercial overfishing. Habitat destruction has occurred as extraction of certain várzea tree species takes place, as deforestation to establish várzea cattle ranches occurs, and as pollution increases. Deforestation is critical, as many fish species feed upon fruit and seeds dropped by a variety of tree species. Removal of these trees disrupts the feeding cycle of these fish. Loss of fish also disrupts patterns of seed dispersal, as fish no longer eat and then redeposit seeds in their waste in new areas. Urban and mining pollution have also taken their toll on the habitat. For example, gold miners typically dump mercury (used to separate gold from other materials) into local streams and rivers where it remains in the ecosystem for centuries. This creates health problems and death all along the food chain, which includes fish and humans. Although little data on the impact of deforestation and pollution upon fish habitats are currently available, these processes undoubtedly are creating long-term problems.

Commercial fishing is a second problem. Between the 1950s and 1970s the introduction of monofilament fiber gill nets and seines, diesel-powered boats, ice production, and Styrofoam insulation greatly transformed commercial fishing (McGrath et al. 1993:176). These innovations enabled fishers to travel farther and preserve fish longer. Regional, national, and international markets for Amazon fish also expanded during this time. SUDAM responded by financing commercial fishing in the hopes of feeding the growing urban population. It also hoped to earn foreign revenue, for national balance-of-payment problems, through export to the international market (Loureiro 1985:148). In the late 1980s the estimated harvest was 198,000 tons per year (Bayley and Petrere 1989).

Researchers believe that the intensification of commercial fishing is depleting the fish populations, although there are no precise data on this trend (Goulding 1983; Bayley and Petrere 1989). The pattern of harvesting only a few species is particularly damaging. This practice not only depletes the targeted species, but also damages other species caught in the nets. These waste fish are discarded and often die. Discarded fish average nearly 70 percent of all fish caught (Oliveira 1991:153). One result of declining fish catches is increased conflict between commercial and subsistence fishers, particularly over control of fish in várzea lakes (McGrath et al. 1993).

Fishing fleets began entering Gurupá's waters in the early 1980s. The regional authorities allowed the commercial fishers to fish indiscriminately with no restrictions on quantity of catches or on the type of nets used. Although no scientific studies exist, nearly all residents acknowledge an observable drop in fish caught for local consumption (see Wesche and Bruneau 1990:62 for similar observations). More damaging is the fact that few residents of Gurupá have been involved in commercial fishing (with the exception of shrimp harvesting); nearly all of the fishers come from coastal cities (Oliveira 1991:155). Therefore, fish stocks for local consumption are reduced, aggravating food shortages, while local residents cannot even benefit from the wages paid for fishing.

The Future

The economic changes experienced by Gurupá in the 1964–1991 period promise to be both limited in scale and ecologically destructive. As in the past, extraction often continues until it depletes resources. This is the probable future of timber and palmito extraction. Management of resources is virtually nonexistent. New booms occur only as extractors discover new resources or the world market creates a new demand. Yet each boom and depletion cycle impoverishes the environment, which creates increasing limitations on future human use (Bunker 1985:55). A recent and highly visible sign of this process is the depletion of andiroba and viola trees, which resulted in the elimination of the andiroba and acuuba seed trade from Gurupá. This pattern of predatory extraction will likely continue, despite the new language of the civilian government and the Our Nature Plan, because of national concerns with fostering industrial development in the south and paying international debts. Unless there is a radical change in policymaking, an alteration of the demands for the world system, or successful grassroots organization to resist this trend, the Amazon people will have limited hope of escaping the centuries-old pattern of poverty.

6

LABOR AND LAND
IN A CHANGING ECONOMY

In June 1985 I met Ricardo Silva, a fifty-five-year-old administrator of the SESPA health agency. Ricardo came to Gurupá to help inoculate people against yellow fever, a sometime fatal disease spread by mosquitoes that was penetrating the region. Armed with his inoculation gun, Ricardo and a local team of health workers were traveling the municipality to treat as many people as possible.

I traveled with Ricardo on several of his outings into the interior. The trips were by boat and tended to be long, drawn-out voyages. Along the way Ricardo and I passed the time conversing. I remember in particular one exchange about the poverty of communities like Gurupá. Ricardo, a native of Belém, kept insisting that people in the interior communities in Amazonia are poor and backward because they are lazy and unintelligent. He stopped short of suggesting they are racially inferior. The people, he said, impede development and progress.

I pressed him to better explain his opinion. He responded that people in the interior communities do not work hard to industrialize, maybe they do not know how. Without industrialization they cannot modernize and progress. He said, look at all the development activity around here—highways, colonization projects, mines, dams, and some industry. People are investing in this region. But do the local people prosper? No, he said, it is all wasted on them.

At this point I asked whether he thought there are any structural limitations to improving standards of living. I asked if stratification, exploitation, land conflict, or nonsustainable use of resources by outside interests for quick profit affected standards of living. His response was a sharp no, "caboclos" (the pejorative term for rural inhabitants) are the only ones responsible for their own misery. With that he promptly changed the subject.

Ricardo's opinion is unfortunately a very common one in the Amazon region. It is a view that blames poverty on illusory cultural, social, or

113

genetic flaws of poor people, while simultaneously denying any role for privileged social groups. The view mystifies all kinds of structural limitations placed upon populations. In contrast I have tried to show in the previous three chapters how the structure of the regional and local political economy has created or maintained poverty over the last four centuries. In this chapter I wish to address the issues of labor relationships, land conflict, and how changes in these areas have affected Amazonia and Gurupá, focusing on whether these processes create, maintain, or alleviate poverty.

Capitalist Labor Relations

In the 1960s' development designs, the government planners assumed that capitalist labor relations would structure Amazonian development. Through this system employers would pay laborers competitive salaries that would increase demand for consumer items. Increased demand would stimulate industrial production and lead to regionalwide development. Economists and other social scientists often describe capitalism as an economic system organized through markets that operate by supply-demand price mechanisms. But more than this, capitalism is a worldview that interprets political economy on the basis of the belief that everything has a market value. Land, wealth, and even labor have price tags and can be bought and sold as commodities, which are goods produced not for use, but for sale (Wolf 1969:277).

From this perspective workers in capitalism are viewed and treated as objects to be used to generate profit. Personal or social considerations in treatment of the labor force are downplayed, unless labor organization can force "benefits" or "job security" to be part of the market price of their work. Ideally, this system organizes a workforce lacking direct access to the means of production (land, resources, and tools), which obligates the labor force to work for owners of these means in exchange for paid wages. Owners then accumulate wealth through market exchange (as proponents of capitalism maintain) or through exploitation of labor by means of underpaid wages (as critics of capitalism maintain).

Social relations under capitalism are markedly different from social relations in other political-economic systems. The commodification of everything allows the replacement of social relations among people with impersonal economic relations that are mediated by things (often wages). This is an entirely unique process in terms of human history. For better or worse, capitalist labor relations are clearly the most radical form of organizing human productive labor ever devised.

In Amazonia it is clear that certain economic sectors use capitalist labor relations, particularly in the big projects and on some large cattle ranches. But as a whole labor organization in the Amazon is still decidedly not capitalist. Yet there are major changes taking place in the structure of labor relations. One of the most important is the articulation, or rearticulation, of the noncapitalist systems with capitalism.

Today most Amazonian peoples extract resources, grow crops, and engage in exportation/importation of goods through the traditional aviamento system or recently developed variants of it. Many capitalist firms operating in the region have found it advantageous to use this system to generate profits instead of restructuring it along more pure capitalist lines (e.g., wage labor). By articulating with the preexisting system the firms successfully siphon off wealth from the local populations at low costs. The consequence, however, is the same as it has been for four centuries: Amazon wealth enriches groups outside the region, while local populations benefit little. In this section I will describe labor relations and the role they play in maintaining local poverty in the extraction, sawmill, food production, and oil exploration sectors.

The Extraction Sector

In Gurupá the extraction network operates similarly to the old aviamento system with only a few modifications. Today many large extraction firms deal directly with trading post merchants and landowners and eliminate the middle positions (import/export houses, aviadores). In doing this the firms deal in cash payments, not in merchandise as the old rubber traders did. Merchandise passes through the traditional channels among import/export firms, aviadores, and trading posts. There are also new commercial channels supplying a growing number of retail stores in Gurupá.

Another modification involves credit. Most firms do not extend credit as the old rubber traders did. The firms are not interested in establishing long-lasting ties to their clientele. This is especially so with timber and palmito since the firms will eventually deplete these resources and then move on to other areas. Considerations about inflation also affect the extension of credit. The firms do, however, extend prepayments to help finance extraction. In these ways the labor relations for extraction have diverged from the traditional economic relations.

The actual organization of the indigenous camponeses to extract, though, has not changed greatly. Patron-client ties through the trading post continue to organize most timber, rubber, and palmito extraction. The merchants advance cash, food, and tools to the fregueses for extraction. When the fregueses deliver the timber, palmito, or rubber in a month or so, the merchants balance the accounts. The trading post pays workers in goods with a 79–100 percent markup for inflation, transportation costs, and profits. With the boom economy and relatively high prices paid for wood, palmito, and rubber, along with the increased availability of cash, there is usually an outstanding balance in favor of the extractor. The merchants pay the balance in cash. There are still cases of unscrupulous patrões manipulating exchange rates and workers mismanaging money so that a long-term debt relationship ensues. In the 1990s, however, the instances of indebted fregueses who participate in extraction are growing rarer.

The patron-client system appears to suit the needs of the extraction firms. They rely on the merchant/landowner to organize and control labor through their *freguesias* (the total number of fregueses working for a trading post merchant). By dealing with the trading post merchant, the firms save themselves the complicated task of finding scarce labor, assigning workers to the scattered resources, and financing workers in the manner to which they are accustomed (credit toward food, tools, and clothing).

One example of a trading post patrão's success in timber extraction is that of Oscar Fernandes, who maintains the Casa Gato trading post in town (see Wagley 1976:95, 104). Dona Dora Andrade was the former owner of the post. As she aged, she turned the family business over to her brother-in-law, Oscar, in the 1960s. Oscar and his sons kept the business going through the economic depression of the early 1960s, although the post often suffered from a shortage of goods (Wagley 1968:301). The Fernandeses shielded themselves from the worst effects of the depression by diversifying their economic activities. They owned approximately 12,570 hectares of land with many fregueses producing rubber, cacao, and food crops. They also possessed a cattle ranch on a várzea island.

When the first timber companies came to Gurupá, the Fernandeses' landholdings and access to workers quickly attracted their attention. The family became one of the first to extract large quantities of timber from their land. With the profits earned the Fernandeses' business prospered as much as it had during the rubber boom. Oscar Fernandes reported to me that the trading post's freguesia grew to nearly 300 by 1986, by far the largest in the municipality.

With the new capital and secure contacts made, one of Oscar's sons, Antônio, took a full-time interest in timber extraction. He organized several labor parties and financed them through the family's trading post to extract from the Fernandeses' lands. He sold the logs to Brumasa, which then helped him finance a truck for terra firme extractions on the public lands behind the town. Once on the terra firme, Antônio extracted all year. The Fernandeses also used their political influence (Oscar was a former mayor and vice mayor) with other local elites to have a road extended into the interior. Funds for construction came from a federal grant, while funds for maintenance came from the *prefeitura* (county government). The local elites said they built the road to service the agricultural colony, mentioned previously, and to eventually connect Gurupá to the Transamazon Highway. However, road construction accomplished neither of these goals. In the end local elite families used the road primarily to extract timber and to plant pasture for cattle.

Antônio continued extracting timber until 1986, after which time he abandoned extraction having depleted marketable timber from his land and much of the accessible unowned terra firme land. Antônio now spends his time overseeing his family's cattle ranches and running a newly opened bottled gas depository.

Gurupá's trading posts, such as that owned by the Fernandeses, are an important element in carrying through the timber boom. Yet there are now only twenty-six major trading posts left in Gurupá, down from an estimated fifty in the early part of the twentieth century. The twenty-six major patrões are not able to monopolize timber extraction as their predecessors had done with rubber extraction. This inability to monopolize the boom market has also been aggravated by an influx of cash into the economy combined with relatively high wages for extraction. When workers have cash in their hands they can avoid permanent debt and bypass the trading post to make purchases. At the same time there is an increasing number of regatões and retail stores servicing Gurupá that are willing to do business with the cash-carrying workforce. Increased worker mobility, through access to diesel motorboats, also allows workers to "shop around" instead of having to rely on the nearest trading post. All these processes have led to a decline of trading post control over workers.

Because of the weaker control over workers there is room for alternative forms of labor recruitment. In the timber extraction sector, semi-independent contractors, or *compradores* (buyers), have entered the business and now play an important role. These compradores are local entrepreneurs or entrepreneurs from the south of Brazil. They work as intermediaries or agents for the timber, palmito, and rubber firms. They maintain a variety of relationships with the firms. In a few cases they are direct employees of firms, especially the timber firms of Brumasa and Eidai. These compradores receive a commission on the amount of timber delivered. More often they deal with a variety of large and small firms, selling to the firm offering the best price.

There are two types of compradores in Gurupá, although the two are not mutually exclusive categories. The first type of comprador arranges the sale of resources from small- and medium-sized landowners. Frequently, the landowners extract timber, palmito, or rubber themselves, and the compradores arrange shipping and payment. On occasion the compradores finance the extractors with small cash loans or tools. Through this system compradores only partially maintain the credit and debt system. The extractors more frequently receive cash with which they buy goods from trading posts, stores in town, or regatões.

The second type of comprador hires workers to extract. These compradores, known as *gatos* (cats) in other regions of the Amazon, organize labor to extract from public land or from the land of private landowners who either lack extractors or lack a trading post. The compradores either hire workers in town or *moradores* (occupants) on the land, or they bring workers in from surrounding municipalities. The extractors receive their wages in cash with some minor financing and advancing of money. In a few cases well-known and trusted compradores who have relatives in town arrange for their workers to establish credit in a town store. This system also serves to partially duplicate the traditional patron-client, credit-debt relationship.

The compradores who hire extractors work under precarious conditions. Unlike the trading posts, they are unable to develop strong patron-client, credit-debt relationships to retain labor. They usually deal in cash with "free" workers who are prone to desert the comprador at most inopportune times. In addition, landowners are likely to default on contracts with a comprador if a better buying price can be found. At the same time extractors and landowners have sufficient cause to be concerned about compradores. In many instances compradores take resources and never return to pay extractors or landowners for them.

An example of a comprador and the various dealings of his trade is the case of Wennuildo Flavio, whom I met while conducting research in the rural hamlet of Camutá. Wennuildo, or "Mineiro" as people call him, was in his twenties in the mid-1980s. He had traveled to Gurupá from the state of Minas Gerais in the south of Brazil. Initially, he represented a small firm in Belo Horizonte, specializing in road asphalting, that wished to enter the timber business. Mineiro volunteered for the job since he was involved in a money scandal that had tarnished his reputation in Belo Horizonte. Mineiro first traveled to Belém, where he established ties to a large sawmill. Next he went into the interior to scout for timber. After several years of doing business he came to Gurupá in 1985 and decided the municipality was a good spot to extract timber. He stayed in town trying to secure his first contract. Mineiro complained that early on he got little help from local extractors and fellow compradores. There was considerable competition to control timber contracts and some resentment toward an outsider coming to extract Gurupá's wealth.

Mineiro's first break came during a Worker's Week seminar sponsored by the Catholic Church. He met several groups of autonomous farmers/extractors and small landowners who agreed to sell timber to him. These individuals were happy to deal with a comprador since they could escape some of the price gouging common in dealings with trading posts. Mineiro contracted to buy sucupira wood. Once he finalized the contract he began advancing the extractors some cash, equipment, and spare parts. One group he did business with was from the hamlet of Camutá on the Pucuruí River. This community had managed to buy a truck and two chain saws and was busy extracting timber at the time (see Chapter 9 for a further discussion of Camutá).

With Mineiro overseeing extraction and Camutá's diligent workers, the order was near completion within a month. Meanwhile Mineiro had contracted for a barge from Belém to come and pick up the logs in Gurupá. Once the barge arrived in Gurupá problems arose. First, the barge arrived with a large leak. The crew had to wait for materials from Belém to repair the barge. As long as the barge was damaged the extractors were unable to load logs. Second, the extractors of Camutá were in need of money and had grown tired of waiting for their final payment from Mineiro. They had accepted a second contract and a small loan from a rival comprador and began extracting timber simultaneously for both compradores. The additional extracting further retarded fulfillment of Mineiro's contract.

The damaged barge and extraction slowdown left Mineiro in a difficult position. He had rented the barge for only one month. If it stayed out any longer he had to pay a significant fine. Mineiro had to place constant pressure on the extractors until the order was finally completed and the timber delivered to Belém. For all his troubles Mineiro made a small profit on the shipment. He explained that the firm expected to earn a 120 percent profit on investments. He took a cut of this profit. In addition, Mineiro maintained that it was common practice for a comprador to withhold some wood to sell himself. This withholding was to pay for various expenses incurred, such as buying alcohol.

By the end of 1985 Mineiro sought to be more independent in his contract dealings. He abandoned his old firm and took a loan from a stronger local comprador and financing from the Brumasa timber company. With this capital he hired his own crew to extract timber from unowned land located on the Pucuruí River. By directly hiring extractors he hoped to earn more profit and avoid any conflicts of interest or work slowdowns. Unfortunately, Mineiro found that hiring workers increased his problems. First, he had no direct access to a trading post so he had to pay the extractors in cash. His workers expected Mineiro to finance them or at least give them small cash advances—something strong compradores always did. Mineiro's cash reserves were limited, and often he could not comply with these expectations. As a result his extractors would quit without warning. He commented that the strong compradores, who always had money on hand, would spoil the workers. Weaker compradores like himself just could not keep up with financing extractors.

Since Mineiro lacked control of workers through debts, control of land, or patron-client relationships, he had no way of retaining labor for long periods of time. His turnover was high, especially around festival times (June–July and December). He complained that in December 1985 he had a barge ordered and a contract nearly ready when the Saint Benedict festival began. All of his extractors abandoned him to attend the festival, which lasted two weeks. Without workers he could not load and deliver the timber. The barge sat at the extraction site for the two weeks, and Mineiro was forced to pay a large fine for delaying it.

While in a sense Mineiro was at the mercy of his extractors, there have been other cases where workers have suffered mistreatment by compradores. During the period of my research there was one such case among palmito extractors. The case is unusual due to its severity, but it falls within the general range of possible labor relations in Gurupá. The case involved a German comprador, nicknamed Gigante (giant), who extracted for a French palmito exporting firm. Gigante used extractors from Breves. These workers were out of jobs and had been desperately seeking employment since the collapse of the sawmill industry and the depletion of palmito in Breves. Gigante brought the workers to Gurupá and put them in the forest on the Great Island of Gurupá. They were isolated in the forest and totally dependent on Gigante for delivery of food and other supplies. At this point Gigante began abusing the extractors. When workers did not meet production quotas because of difficult terrain or land conflicts with occupants (see Chapter 9), or because of a capital shortfall, Gigante delayed sending food and supplies to the extractors. The workers were in a difficult situation. They ran short on food but were without money and too isolated to make leaving the extraction site an easy venture. Most of them stayed and hoped for Gigante to fulfill his obligations.

This situation continued for several months. People in Gurupá started to comment on the desperate situation of Gigante's workers, but no one could or would intervene. Finally, Gigante's business conduct got him into trouble, and eventually the French palmito firm fired him. However, it was not his mistreatment of workers that got him fired. The firm fired Gigante because he sold the firm's palmito to another palmito firm for his own personal profit. Once the firm dismissed Gigante, the extractors were left stranded and had to make their way back to Breves as best they could.

Beyond the compradores and trading posts, there is a third method of organizing labor for extraction. An example of this method occurred on the land bought by the Brumasa timber firm. In the 1970s Brumasa bought 95,708 hectares, or approximately 10 percent of the municipality of Gurupá. On this land there were many occupants who were former fregueses of patrões who controlled the area. The corporation decided to allow some of these occupants to stay on the land since the company needed workers to extract timber. The occupants were encouraged to extract timber from part of the reserve with the strict understanding that they deliver the timber to Brumasa. The company also prohibited the occupants from opening new gardens, since this might destroy valuable trees. Brumasa agreed to pay cash for the timber cut. However, the corporation made no provisions to supply workers with goods or to finance extraction. In essence, the timber firm replaced the traditional labor relations with strict capitalist wage labor relationships.

The company's attempt to impose wage labor relationships met with failure. The occupants of Brumasa's land resisted in ways reminiscent of rubber boom and depression days. For example, the occupants discovered that at times they could receive higher prices for wood by selling secretly to trading posts or compradores. Even if the prices for wood were the same or slightly lower, the trading posts and compradores offered to finance the extractors in cash or goods. An ongoing credit relationship, and even a partial advancing of cash, gave the extractors an added sense of security. They considered this far superior to the impersonal dealings with the timber firm. As a result occupants began extracting timber and selling it secretly to trading posts and compradores.

To curtail this activity Brumasa hired several overseers to patrol the land. Since the company also hired these overseers as compradores earning commissions on timber delivered, they had a special interest in stopping the illegal sale of timber. A few of the more zealous overseers used intimidation and violence to curtail illegal selling. One notorious overseer became well known after he threatened a pregnant woman, who fled by jumping into the water. My consultants told me that this same overseer also tied a cable around an extractor's house and then used his boat to pull it into the water.

Although overseers caught many people selling timber illegally (these cases filled the court records in the decade of the 1970s) and the police expelled a significant number of people from the company's land, Brumasa was unsuccessful in halting the practice. It was not until extraction began to deplete timber reserves that the problem subsided. Possibly because of this experience the company stopped buying land and concentrated on acquiring timber from private landowners and through compradores. This system proved to be less conflict prone and more cost effective.

The Sawmill Sector

There are three ways in which sawmills structure labor relations. The first two ways involve the small interior sawmills. In these mills either a patrão organizes the workers and provides them with provisions and some cash through a trading post, or the workers own the mill. In the former case, the patrão advances merchandise and loans to the workers. The workers receive a small percentage of the market value of the wood sawn from which they pay their debts. In some, but not all, cases workers can earn a surplus paid in cash. In other cases patrões manipulate the prices of food and imported goods to keep workers in debt, or at least manage not to pay them in cash. Despite these drawbacks, workers can establish patron-client ties that offer them some financial and job security. Job security is especially important since the interior mills tend to close down after several years of operation. Good patrões will provide their workers employment in another economic sector.

Workers possessing their own sawmills organize themselves differently. These individuals are frequently small landowners who accumulate enough capital from timber extraction to purchase a diesel engine and small circular saw. Some of these individuals have received small government loans for their mills. Labor for the mill, as well as for extracting timber, is generally drawn from their own extended families (kindreds) or friends. Fictive kinship often strengthens the ties between nonrelated co-workers. The family collects the profit from these mills or partitions it out to co-workers, depending on the time spent in production. Extractors receive a fixed rate for each log delivered. Most of these extractors maintain alternative sources of income to fall back upon, such as gardening, extraction, and livestock raising. Alternative livelihood activities are important because of the fragile nature of the lumber industry and the gradual depletion of marketable timber species.

The third form of labor organization is a hybrid wage payment, the form employed by the town sawmill. Gurupá's mill paid workers an hourly wage ranging from one-half the regional minimum wage for underaged boys (from twelve to fifteen years old) to several times the minimum wage for adult women and men workers. At the same time, however, the sawmill ran a small trading post that offered workers the option of buying goods on credit. In addition, when the company trading post could not handle demand, the local stores and trading posts extended credit to the sawmill workers, something to which they agreed because several of the sawmill's management staff were native sons of Gurupá who had close personal ties to the local elite. In a sense the sawmill articulated with the traditional trading post/patron-client system. In a few cases management and workers established direct patron-client relationships. Management had an interest in these relationships since they were local residents who could benefit from the economic and political advantages of having clients.

The traditional economic features incorporated into the structure of the sawmill were adaptations to local needs. For the workers there was an increased sense of security in dealing with a patrão, or pseudopatrão, represented by management or management's ties to town elites. Credit offered by the company store or through arrangements with town stores also added to worker security. For management, the traditional features enhanced labor control as debt relations motivated people to work. One consequence was a low turnover rate for workers. Also, management could lower the actual wages paid by price manipulation in the company trading post. Patrões and credit also smoothed over many delays in the payment of wages by the sawmill. When business complications delayed payment by weeks, the credit offered in town served as a safety net to support workers.

Despite the sawmill's adaptations to the local economy, weak national and international markets and some mismanagement slowed the sawmill's production. This eventually caused prolonged delays in workers' pay that ultimately turned the workers against management. The worker/management conflict came to a climax in 1984. At the time an American named Peter Hoffman, who had married into a southern Brazilian family, owned the sawmill. He had hired several relatives of Gurupá's mayor to manage the mill for him. Things were running smoothly between 1983 and 1984. Peter told me that he had $70,000 invested in the mill. At its best the mill grossed close to $20,000 a month, and workers received their wages on time. Then a series of mishaps occurred. First, a mill contractor bought junk wood that the mill could not sell. Next, a shipment of lumber waiting for export became stained and thus unsellable. Peter reported losing $15,000 on the stained shipment alone. Another setback occurred when a contracted barge failed to show up in Gurupá for a large shipment. Peter lost his contract on that job altogether.

As these successive failures occurred the sawmill began delaying payment to workers, as well as to landowners who supplied the mill with timber. Workers were first paid weekly, next biweekly, then monthly, and finally, in 1984, wages were three months behind. Because of the large debts incurred by the sawmill's workers at the town's trading posts and stores (which were compounded daily by high inflation) and the nonpayment for timber extracted from many landowners, the whole community was in an uproar. Many store owners who were themselves threatened with going out of business from unpaid debts were forced to refuse further credit to workers. Loss of credit severely affected workers dependent on sawmill wages. For some workers a period of hunger followed as they had no money and no access to gardens for crops. All the while Peter was heavily indebted to banks and attempted to pay off these debts before paying his workers.

Meanwhile, rumors arose in town that Peter had taken the workers' wages and invested in a gold mine. Others arose that he sent all his profits to the United States. People were sure he had lots of money and was cheating his workers. Peter's practice of renting private airplanes to taxi him to and from Gurupá was all the proof that many workers required of his hidden wealth. The perceived extravagance by Peter and the growing hardships from nonpayment of wages led to a series of retaliations against the American. He received many death threats and was nearly run down by Gurupá's only taxi. Peter began visiting Gurupá less and traveling with companions for protection.

Finally, tensions peaked when a large shipment of lumber ready for delivery was set on fire. The fire started on a Saturday night and was put out by townspeople only to start up again. The second blaze burned for two days. A fireboat sent to Gurupá from Breves finally extinguished it. Following the fire some looting of the mill occurred. Most people in Gurupá assumed that the fire was arson. The only disagreement among them was over who set the fire—disgruntled workers or Peter's own men to end workers' claims to the large debts owed.

After the fire at the sawmill, workers, store owners, and landowners gathered the support of local politicians to seek a legal remedy for the unpaid debts. They hired a lawyer from Breves, and the courts forced Peter to begin paying his debts. In part he did so by selling the sawmill's machinery. He also had his management run a skeleton crew to saw logs to pay for debts. The managers hoped to buy the mill for themselves, paying $15,000 for it through profits from sawing wood. However, shortly after the mill restarted it ran into marketing problems and began delaying wages again. By 1986 the sawmill completely shut down. Local authorities impounded the remaining machinery to pay debts. With the closing of the sawmill, Gurupá's brief experience with hybrid wage labor in the lumber/timber sector ended. Labor organization returned to the realm of the trading post/landowner and the semi-independent comprador.

The Food-Production Sector

Traditional labor relations dominate the food-production sector of Gurupá's economy. There are two types of arrangements merchants/landowners have with farmers. The first involves farmers living on a patrão's land. These individuals pay rent for use of the land. The rent is most frequently paid in extracted commodities since most farming families have members participating in extraction during half the year. The patrões and workers view extraction as the primary activity to be taxed. Agriculture, by contrast, holds a secondary status and is usually undertaken only for the farming family's maintenance.

The second arrangement is between a trading post and an autonomous farmer (small landowner or occupant of unowned terra firme). The trading post owners usually agree to trade for only the amount of food needed to supply their fregueses. This practice leaves the farmer in a precarious situation when demand for food is low. Barter is the principal form of payment. Because of the traditional markup in prices in the trading post, there are few consumer goods for which the farmer can afford to trade with food production.

Pedro Chuva, a full-time subsistence farmer in the rural hamlet of Bacá, commented one day to me on the low returns for farming. He has never worked in extraction and has suffered the consequences. In conversations with Pedro he lamented the poor returns from manioc, his principal crop. He compared his situation with that of a neighbor named Manoel who extracted timber. By never working in timber, he said,

> Look at what I have. I can never afford to build a nice house like Manoel has [Pedro's house was made of palm thatch, Manoel's of wood]. Nor can I buy clothes, a bicycle, or even a stove. When my family is sick I have no cash for medicine and must ask for loans. I even have a hard time buying shells for my gun. If I don't have shells, we don't eat meat.

The trading post also structures the labor relations for the larger cattle ranches. Patrões deduct food, tools, and other materials from workers' pay. If there is any surplus salary, the workers receive cash. The custom of paying ranch workers with a few of the newborn animals each year, which is the standard form of payment in other areas of Brazil, is not a common practice in Gurupá. On the smaller ranches workers are often members of the owner's family. They distribute profits within the family according to varying personal arrangements.

The Oil-Exploration Sector

The final type of labor relation applies to oil exploration. The firm Geosource differed radically from the trading posts and most firms by seeking pure capitalist relations—that is, a flat wage for labor. The wages were high by local standards, being slightly above the minimum wage. Additionally, when productivity was high the workers earned bonuses that could double their salaries. Also, the firm paid the workers' federal insurance fees and offered a health post. The health post treated many injuries, including seven poisonous snakebites in its first year of operation. Geosource personnel told me that it spent $2,000 a month in medical supplies alone. The work schedule devised by Geosource was two months in the forest followed by ten days off. This schedule allowed men to return home to visit and help care for their gardens if their family was maintaining them.

Because of the high pay, benefits, and work schedule, Geosource had little trouble attracting large numbers of workers. Yet it could not retain workers for extended periods of time, averaging a 30 percent turnover rate per month. Men tended to work for a few months then take a few months off until their savings ran out, at which point many asked for their jobs back. The highest turnover rates coincided with festival times.

Geosource's inability to retain workers is related to the difficulties experienced by the independent timber compradores. For example, Geosource's control over workers was based solely on payment of wages. The company had no credit-debt ties to obligate people to work. Workers were also alienated from the firm because of the lack of patron-client ties. As an alternative many workers sought to establish these relationships with store owners or trading posts in town. The workers saw these ties as crucial for survival. The ties offered future security for workers and their families when there was a need for health care, education, food, clothes, or small loans. The workers could not count on Geosource to provide these services, beyond immediate health care for the worker (not the family). When Geosource left Gurupá in 1984, it left behind nothing for the workers' future beyond wages paid.

The labor force hired by Geosource was not separated from the means of production (land, resources). Most workers had families maintaining subsistence gardens, and there were always opportunities to hunt and fish. This allowed workers the freedom of refusing to work for wages in companies such as Geosource if they so desired. Many workers worked only long enough to save money for consumer items, for emergencies, or for festival time. Beyond these needs, compulsion to work for wages was minimal.

Land Conflict

Another way capitalism is affecting Amazonia is through the commodification of land. Historically in many parts of Amazonia, resources on the land, not land itself, had value (Bunker 1985:27–28; Schmink 1982:346–347; Foweraker 1981:47). This was an integral part of the extractive economy. With the latest penetration of capitalism this pattern has changed. Land now has an exchange value above its use value. A booming land market has developed, and land is becoming highly valued as an investment. This commodification of land and the emergence of a larger land market have created tension and conflict as different actors contest control, access, and ownership of the tropical forest.

The present-day pattern of land conflict began with the opening of vast areas of the Amazon frontier to development in the 1960s. This created a tremendous land rush. Newcomers entered the area and claimed nearly 42 million hectares (approximately 100 million acres) of land as private property (Hecht and Cockburn 1990:107). Some sought land for development purposes, while others sought it for speculation purposes or as a hedge against the nation's rampant inflation. Competition for land has been fierce. National and international firms, individual landowners, and land grabbers (*grileiros*) have aggressively pursued landownership. Many firms and individuals have resorted to expropriating land from the immigrant camponeses, indigenous camponeses, and Native Americans. The level of expropriation has been high. For example, during the late 1970s social scientists estimate that nearly 4 percent of the total small-farmer population of the Amazon was evicted yearly from contested land (CONTAG cited in Branford and Glock 1985:26–27). In 1987 over 13 million hectares and 109,000 people were involved in land disputes in the region (Hecht and Cockburn 1990:195).

The new landowners have concentrated their expropriated and otherwise acquired land into huge estates. At least eight of these estates consist of 1 million hectares each (Hall 1989:97). This process of landownership concentration in Amazonia essentially reproduces the grossly uneven land tenure patterns of *latifúndio* and *minifúndio* found throughout the rest of Brazil (Hall 1989:96–97; Hecht and Cockburn 1990:169).

The Amazon land rush has occurred with much violence, particularly as owners of large cattle ranches have forcibly expropriated land from the camponeses and Native Americans. One example of land conflict, among many, occurred near Conceição do Araguaia in the south of Pará. Cattle ranchers expelled immigrant camponeses from land they occupied to make way for new ranches. Measures used to expel occupants included beatings, shootings, poisoning of streams, and burning of fields and houses. There were some 200 murders, most unrecorded by the state, between 1969 and 1981 (Foweraker 1981:20). Another example involves the mining complex at Carajás in Pará. Here large landowners used violence to prevent small farmers from occupying land, as well as to encroach upon land already farmed. According to Hall (1989:82ff.), between January 1985 and October 1987 there were eighty-four "recorded" fatalities involving rural violence with many additional unrecorded murders as small farmers simply disappeared. Among the dead were a Catholic nun, a priest, a lawyer, several hired gunmen, and several military police.

Land Conflict in Gurupá

Land conflict in Gurupá takes on a different form than the frontier conflict described above. The lack of a road, heavy immigration, large cattle ranches, and an extensive land market has mediated the level of land expropriation and violence. Nevertheless, there is great disparity in landownership. Gurupá's 1980 census data for landownership distribution exceeds land concentration found in the frontier regions of eastern Pará. In Gurupá only 0.1 percent of landowners possess 69 percent of the land. In eastern Pará 2 percent of landowners have 56 percent of the land (Hecht 1983:178; IBGE 1981).

This, however, does not mean there is a land shortage in Gurupá. A large portion of terra firme in the municipality consists of unowned state land and is open for legal occupation. The Instituto Brasileiro de Geografia e Estatística (IBGE) estimates that 63 percent of the municipality is unowned state land, while INCRA estimates that only 39 percent is unowned state land (IBGE 1981; INCRA 1985). Furthermore, many of the small landowners in Gurupá have access to and use more land than they legally claim. There are also many occupants who have never legalized their land claims. Until recently, the incentives to obtain legal title to land have been few. Obstacles, however, have been many. For example, occupants must deal with the government bureaucracy, the lack of legal advice, the cost and time involved in the process, and the need to pay land taxes once land is formally owned.

Although land is available there are problems discouraging its occupation. For instance, unowned land is often less desirable because of its isolation. Bureaucratic and legal difficulties, and intimidation by the former owner, complicate acquiring private land. However, in comparison to the land problems experienced on the frontier areas of Amazonia (the south of Pará, Acre, Rondônia), these are not severe obstacles.

Gurupá also has some problems with expropriation and eviction, although these problems are less severe than in the frontier regions. For example, there are multiple cases of eviction of fregueses and occupants from land claimed by large landowners. This is part of a centuries-old tactic used by landowners to discipline unproductive or nonconforming workers. This type of expulsion is not the same as land expropriation along the frontier, since the Gurupá landowners have prior claims to land, usually dating back three to five generations. Eviction of clients and occupants is not a principal tool used by local large landowners in Gurupá to amass new land-holdings.

There are other types of land conflict in Gurupá that revolve around timber extraction. The principal way that timber extraction generates conflict is to call into question vague property boundaries or communal holdings established during the rubber boom. Unlike rubber extraction where a permanent rubber road demarcates a large area, extractable timber can cover the entire expanse of land and requires precise demarcation as a proof of ownership. Vague boundaries between holdings, and especially the nonexistence of back boundaries from the rivers and streams, lead to ambiguous and overlapping claims to trees. Adding to the problem is the growing instance of intentional poaching of timber from other people's property.

In addition to these problems is the introduction of a limited land market that gives exchange value to land itself, not only to resources upon the land. Brumasa is the principal initiator of the land market, as the company has purchased nearly 10 percent of Gurupá's land. Brumasa bought the land for timber extraction and as an investment and hedge against inflation (ample government incentives and subsidies helped finance the purchases). The later two features are alien to the traditional economy wherein people typically increase their economic power by expanding exchange opportunities (hiring more extractors) rather than purchasing land. To legalize its purchases, Brumasa needed precise land demarcations and proper land titles. Since both of these were lacking, the company resorted to the court system to clear up problems. When this proved inadequate, the company allegedly bribed local officials to alter or create the proper documentation needed.

The land market system introduced by Brumasa has not transformed the entire land tenure system in Gurupá. Beyond the company's purchases, only a few individuals have bought modest amounts of land to serve as a store of value or hedge against inflation. A larger land market system has not developed in Gurupá because of the continued economic domination of vegetable extraction and the lack of large-scale productive economies such as agriculture and cattle raising. Agriculture and ranching give value to land, while extraction gives value to resources on the land. As stated before, agriculture and ranching have not developed extensively in Gurupá because of the lack of an internal market and the lack of an overland connection to the Transamazon Highway.

The growth of timber extraction has created many conflicts over timber ownership since the late 1960s. Many of these conflicts end up in the court system. Gurupá's judge told me that in the 1970s and 1980s she constantly held hearings on overlapping claims to timber. Sorting out the claims is next to impossible because of the legally deficient land titling system in Gurupá and often the lack of titles altogether. In most cases the judge's ruling is unacceptable to one or both parties. When a conflict reaches this level, extralegal intimidation or violence usually settles the matter.

This is the case of Flor Gonçalves, who lives on the Mojú River of the Great Island of Gurupá. I talked to Flor during one of my excursions into the interior. He spent several hours explaining his story. Flor said he had lived on his land for nearly thirty years. He has a title to his land, although it is vague on boundary demarcations. Throughout the timber boom Flor resisted depleting all of his timber, unlike many of his neighbors. Instead, he planned to save as many trees as possible for his children to harvest. Flor also planted cacao, orange, and rubber trees and always maintained a subsistence garden.

Flor had problems with one of his neighbors, João Mendes, who extracted timber from land claimed by Flor. João had sold all of his timber shortly after the timber boom began. He then became a timber comprador. When the market became difficult in the 1980s, João and his family began extracting timber from the contested land. Flor contended that they crossed over a stream that was the boundary of his property and cut a good number of trees. At first Flor complained directly to João's sons. An argument occurred, and one son threatened Flor's life. The poaching of trees continued. Flor next went to the judge in Gurupá. Since the judge was not regularly visiting Gurupá, there was a series of delays. When the judge finally arrived and heard the case, she made no decision since the land titles were not sufficiently clear. The judge offered a compromise that Flor rejected since it gave João rights to extract timber on what Flor was sure was his land. Flor left the court bitter. He was determined to get his own justice. He warned that any more poaching of timber would result in death. He armed himself and watched closely over the disputed land. Up to the time I concluded my research, Flor's strategy seemed to be working, as João had taken no more timber.

Other cases of conflict occur when people extract timber from unowned land far removed from the riverfront, especially on the terra firme. In these cases land is frequently owned along the waterways. This ownership blocks access to the interior. Timber extractors may trespass on the privately owned land to reach distant timber. When this occurs the landowner or even an occupant may complain about the trespass. In other cases the landowner may claim ownership of the distant land since there are often no back boundaries to property. This land often serves as a common area. Several families may use it for hunting and extraction. To alleviate this problem timber compradores have begun "renting" a road (or paying a fee for access to land) from the owner of property along the waterway. If a landowner continues to object to extraction from the distant land that is ambiguously claimed, compradores often seek access to the timber through another landowner and ignore the protests. Policing distant timber is difficult, and the victor is usually whichever party has more determination, political ties, success in court, or in rare cases even guns.

Another type of conflict has occurred between Brumasa and the former owners and occupants of the land acquired by the company. When Brumasa began amassing land, it bought it very cheaply. People in Gurupá had no idea of the value of the timber on their land and were pleased to get some cash for what they considered nearly useless land. Gurupá was still in a depression, so any quick source of cash was very welcome.

João Cruz, a successful businessman whom I got to know over the course of my visits to Gurupá, told me of his dealings with Brumasa. In the early 1970s he sold his land on the Baquiá River to Brumasa for a low price. He then moved to another piece of property along the Mojú River and opened a small store. When the timber boom began, João sold timber from his Mojú property and was able to greatly expand his operation. Looking back to his transactions with Brumasa, João lamented that if he had only known the value of timber on his Baquiá property, he would not have sold it and would have been a richer man today.

Other people were not as lucky as João. Some sold all their land and moved to Gurupá or a larger city. Of these, most did not find employment and soon ran out of money. Since they had no land to return to, they were forced to join the growing mass of urban poor.

Brumasa used various methods to secure the forest reserve it wanted. For the most part company representatives bought land without difficulties. In other cases there were problems with land titles of questionable authenticity. Nearly all land titles were vague on precise boundaries and many overlapped with neighboring properties. As a result land squabbles arose. In these cases Brumasa did not hesitate to use the court system, to use its political influence on local officials, and according to various consultants, to use the local police force to intimidate or expel troublesome occupants.

One case of disputed landownership occurred on the Baquiá River of the Great Island of Gurupá. One of the participants in the dispute related the story to me. It seems that two landowners lived adjacent to each other in a place where the river took a sharp bend. The titles of both landowners failed to specify a back boundary to their properties, which clearly overlapped because of the river's course. But until the point at which Brumasa asked to buy the land there was never any conflict between the neighbors since neither family used the land for economic pursuit beyond hunting. One of the landowners accepted Brumasa's offer to buy the approximately 100 hectares of overlapping property. When the second landowner discovered the firm's intentions to cut timber from this land, he protested vigorously. The conflict ended up in Gurupá's court where Brumasa's access to lawyers and its political influence resulted in an easy victory. The second landowner lost the timber on all of the disputed property.

More difficult problems for Brumasa arose on land occupied by families with no titles at all. These occupants had either been living on the land of others for decades or had informally inherited the land when the owner left, especially after the rubber bust. When Brumasa attempted to buy this land, it often found overlapping claims. In one case a family claimed ownership of a large area. They sold the land to Brumasa without ever producing a title. When Brumasa came to extract timber, it found a second family occupying the area. This family explained to me that they had occupied the land for fifty years. They knew nothing of the land sale nor of the selling family's claims to the land. Upon learning of the deal they refused to allow Brumasa access to the timber. Brumasa immediately commenced legal proceedings to have the second family expelled from the land. The case remained in the court for six years. The judge finally decided in favor of Brumasa. The second family was forced to vacate the property.

Throughout the early 1970s Brumasa continued to buy land. People in Gurupá repeatedly reported to me that when so required, Brumasa used its influence and money to shortcut the legal system. Others allege that the county record keeper (*cartorário*) received various gifts for speeding along the processing of land titles. On the meager civil servant's salary that supported him poorly for years, he was suddenly able to build one of the best houses in town and to spend a sizable amount of money on health needs. All this occurred after Brumasa came to town. People also tell of how Brumasa and the previous town mayor had a close, mutually advantageous relationship. Several of my consultants alleged that, for a portion of Brumasa's business, the ex-mayor used his influence to ensure that land acquisition and extraction proceeded smoothly. This included Brumasa's easy access to the few military police stationed in Gurupá to expel troublesome land occupants.

A third development to affect the level of land conflict in Gurupá, although not directly tied to timber extraction, was a series of laws giving land rights to occupants (*posseiros* or squatters) of the land. Laws to protect rights to land that is occupied and utilized have been in place since the nineteenth century (Santos 1984), but in the second half of the twentieth century the federal government enacted several laws that strengthened occupants' rights. For example, in 1970 the federal government claimed jurisdiction over all unoccupied lands in the Amazon (Santos 1984:454).

The government made provisions for any family occupying and farming or extracting on state land for a year and a day to qualify for ownership of up to 100 hectares (reduced to 50 hectares after 1981) of that land, the modular size for land claims in Pará. In Gurupá this provision covered much of the terra firme. People had ignored this land until the 1980s when terra firme timber extraction began. Since there were few people living on this land, little conflict arose with this new law.

The recent awareness and use of two other laws, however, have created tension in Gurupá. The first law requires landowners who expel occupants to give cash redemptions or indemnifications for improvements made to the land. The second gives occupants possession of 100 hectares (reduced to 50 hectares after 1981) of privately owned land if they reside on and work it for ten years (now five years).

Use of the redemption laws cut into landowners' power over fregueses. No longer can landowners legally expel individuals without paying a price. Of course, many landowners simply ignore the law. Few occupants challenged landowners until a rural union movement in the 1980s began informing occupants of their rights. Still, today landowners can count on a sluggish legal system in Gurupá to delay judgments on the value of land improvements and delay deadlines to pay. Usually, inflation reduces the true value of redemptions so that the landowner pays very little. Despite all these drawbacks, the laws do afford some degree of security for landless fregueses that improvements to houses and time spent in planting crops will not be lost outright to a disapproving landowner.

Like the law on redemption, the law on occupants' rights to privately owned land has led to change in land tenure. In Gurupá's 1985 land registration (INCRA 1985), fifteen individuals and two timber businesses claimed 66.7 percent of all land privately owned—40 percent of all land in the municipality. Most of these individuals, however, do not have proper documentation. Many lack land titles altogether. If the land is untitled then theoretically it reverts to state control. Anyone who has worked the land for one year and one day can become the legal owner. As such, these landholders are at high risk to lose their land.

This new threat to landownership has led to a concerted effort on the part of landowners to move fregueses around so they cannot qualify for landownership. In addition, there is renewed incentive not to let fregueses plant permanent crops (cacao, rubber, palmito) that they can use as proof of land occupation. Despite this, nearly all large landowners have many fregueses on their land who easily meet the ten-year residency requirement and can legally claim land. For these fregueses the threat of claiming land is a newfound check on patrão power.

Still there are serious limitations to this check. First, there is the overwhelming bureaucracy involved in applying for land title and challenging rights of the previous owner. Second, if individuals get land, then they need to pay taxes on it. In Gurupá it is common to be delinquent in paying land taxes. In fact, 90 percent of the landowners registered in the 1985 land census owed back taxes (INCRA 1985). Nevertheless, nonpayment of taxes can lead to confiscation of land, especially when individuals have angered local officials. Third, the legal claim to land was a maximum of 100 hectares, down to 50 hectares today. To support a family pursuing a livelihood of extraction and some subsistence agriculture, this amount is often not sufficient. This is especially true as the family expands with the maturation of succeeding generations. As a result many fregueses engaged in conflict with their patrões over land rights complain that the act of claiming the 100 or 50 hectares is actually a victory for the landowner. A large landowner can easily afford to give up 100- or 50-hectare slices of land and still have vast tracts left. On the other hand, the fregueses will overexploit their land as their families grow over the generations.

The persistent land conflict of the past two decades has contributed to a growing threat to the camponês livelihood. Although land concentration in Gurupá has not changed much since the rubber bust, except for Brumasa's holdings, some landowners have impeded workers' access to land by expelling them from land, moving them around on land, and prohibiting them from planting certain crops or planting in new areas. Poaching of timber has pressured other workers. These threats combine to create a growing apprehension over access to land. The actual or perceived threat to land and resources thus joins the problems of resource depletion and food shortages in threatening camponês subsistence.

The Future

Despite the penetration of capitalist firms and a cash economy, the institution of the trading post still dominates Gurupá's labor relations. Attempts to sidestep the trading post, as in the cases of Petrobrás and Brumasa, have met with serious problems of labor turnover and poaching of resources. Capitalist hybrids, such as the town sawmill, that have incorporated debt-credit and patron-client ties along with wage labor have proved more successful. In the near future the trading post and hybrid capitalist form of labor organization will likely dominate. Although they are exploitative from the camponeses' point of view, they nevertheless form the most efficient and cost-effective system given current circumstances.

Two developments may challenge these traditional and semitraditional forms of production relationships. The first is the large-scale penetration of the area by capitalist firms that will occur if Gurupá receives an overland connection to the Transamazon Highway. If this indeed occurs, then Gurupá may undergo the kind of radical change witnessed in other sites along the Transamazon Highway (see, e.g., Velho 1972; Ianni 1978;

Schmink and Wood 1984). The second is the development of workers' cooperatives, which can bypass the trading post. By the 1980s there had already been several attempts to develop workers' cooperatives, a novelty examined in Chapter 7.

Economic changes have also created ambiguity and conflict over resource and landownership. The timber boom and Brumasa's introduction of a market value for land have called into question vague and undocumented land possession. This trend will continue if economic growth continues. With the introduction of an overland connection, the problem would likely explode with violence. Additionally, with recent land tenure laws granting occupant rights to land, there is great potential for further land conflict, a potential also examined in Chapter 7.

7

ADAPTATIONS TO POVERTY

I remember one sunny, humid afternoon on which my friend and key consultant Nicanor Alves sat his thin body down on the shady roadside curve in front of his deteriorating house. The 6-kilometer walk to and from his small manioc garden in the scorching tropical sun, plus several hours of digging, peeling, grating, and toasting of manioc to produce a week's worth of food for his family, had left the sixty-six-year-old man exhausted. Yet he was in good spirits as always. He gazed down the hill, past the row of tattered wooden shacks of his neighborhood, to the expansive, muddy brown water of the Amazon River. For a few minutes he was deep in thought, then, unexpectedly, he smiled and turned to me to tell a joke: "When people ask me why this town of Gurupá is so poor, why people have to work so hard just to feed themselves, I tell them just think of the name, *guru—pá*!"

He cackled loudly at his joke. After his laughter subsided, I told him I did not understand. He repeated the punch line, "*guru—pá*!," using hand motions to add emphasis. But he saw in my face that I still did not understand, so with great patience he explained. "*Guru* is when you plant a seed and it dies in the ground before sprouting" (a regional phonetic variation of the verb *gorar,* which means to miscarry, go wrong, or make ineffectual). "*Pá* is pá" (a diminutive form of *rapaz*—boy—used as an exclamation). "So," he concluded, "Gurupá never had a chance. It was doomed to be backward from the start."

Nicanor did not make his fatalistic assessment of Gurupá with malice. Rather, he had formed his opinion through a lifetime of frustration. He has struggled hard to find good land to farm and from which to extract forest products, as well as adequate wage labor to support his family. As I was to learn during my research, many Gurupaenses share his experience and viewpoint. Collectively, they feel that progress, development, and prosperity, however conceived, have all passed them by.

Given the current threats to livelihood, I often wondered how the population copes. How do the people endure poverty, resource depletion, land

135

Impromptu Carnaval ensemble, Gurupá

conflict, and exploitative labor relations? What types of cultural, social, and psychological adaptations have they devised to survive?

While examining this quandary I discovered a multitude of adaptations devised by Gurupaenses, some rooted in centuries of struggle, all shaped by contemporary crisis. These adaptations enable people to deal with problems through social remedies, symbolic acceptance of their situation, supernatural explanations, protest, or a variety of diversions. Principal among these adaptations are finding a patrão, labor flexibility, kinship flexibility, folk views of poverty, manipulation of the supernatural, and an array of distractions from soccer to television. In this chapter I will examine each of these coping mechanisms.

Finding a Patrão

Although patrão-freguês ties are unequal and exploitative many in Gurupá still consider them a necessity for economic and social survival. The ties serve as a type of insurance policy for the freguês during bad times. Loans, credit, food, medicine, and work can be secured through a good patrão-freguês relation.

Nicanor Alves, the manioc farmer quoted above, commented to me that once a family has found a good patrão they have far fewer worries in this world. He continued:

> When someone is sick and in need of help, you go to the patrão. When you need a little more food to eat, you go to the patrão. If you need land to extract or grow crops, you go to the patrão. Even if you own your own land, it is good to have a patrão that will buy what you produce and give you credit in his store. A bad patrão can hurt you, but still you can get supplies from him that no other store will give you.

Since Gurupá lost well over half its trading posts following the rubber bust, there has been a severe shortage of patrões in the municipality. I heard many people lament the loss. One farmer said that he had even traveled to several nearby municipalities in search of a patrão to work for, but without success.

The desire for a patrão-freguês relationship pervades most types of labor relations. As shown in the previous chapter, the most successful types of labor organization for Gurupá have been those that include some variation of a patrão-freguês tie. Pure wage labor relationships (such as with Geosource or at Jarí) have resulted in high worker turnover. Nicanor also commented on wage labor:

> The pay is good at these companies, but it is not always enough. What happens when someone is sick or cannot work, who pays for food or

medicine? At least with a patrão you get credit. In the companies you get laid off.

Nicanor was referring to salary levels that do not cover total family expenses or provide sick leave. Although wage labor jobs pay relatively high salaries by regional standards, they are usually below the level of reproduction. The result is that a worker's family must subsidize the worker receiving wages, which is done by pooling labor in such activities as farming, extraction, or petty domestic production. In a sense family labor subsidizes the wage earner whose low wages then subsidize the company. Many find this system unacceptable and avoid it if possible. When circumstances force individuals into low-wage jobs, they prefer to work for short periods and then return home until funds are exhausted.

Labor Flexibility

By "labor flexibility" I refer to two important features of indigenous camponês life: occupational flexibility and geographic mobility. Occupational flexibility involves the diversity of jobs that members of a household or a single individual will hold simultaneously or consecutively over a span of years. This flexibility may be seasonally based or opportunity based. In the former many individuals hold a series of jobs through which they rotate during a calendar year. The most common combination of activities is extraction and gardening. According to the extensive survey conducted in Gurupá by Oliveira (1991:209), 61.5 percent of rural families reported conducting some combination of agriculture and extraction as part of their means of subsistence. Within the extraction sector, individuals may engage in timber, rubber, palmito, and occasionally Brazil nut extraction. Additional forms of economic activity include small animal husbandry, subsistence fishing, and working in rural industry such as in a sawmill or palmito processing. Table 7.1 lists the range of economic activity in Gurupá.

Occupation flexibility also enables the population to shift among many activities as necessity demands. During a boom they may engage only in extraction, while during economic depression they may rely on subsistence agriculture, fishing, hunting, and animal husbandry to survive. The key here to coping during depression years is access to land and, hopefully, to a patrão. Even during the worst of times people in Gurupá can always eke out a living on unoccupied land.

Closely associated with occupation flexibility is geographic mobility. As mentioned previously, people in Gurupá, as in much of Amazonia, are very mobile. Males in particular migrate throughout the region to find wage labor jobs. Migration may be seasonal, temporary, or permanent. This

Table 7.1   Combination of Economic Activities Among Camponeses of
             Gurupá

Productive Activities	% of Families
E	14.9
A	0.4
AP	1.1
F	2.2
RI	1.1
E-A	5.5
E-AP	4.4
E-F	3.3
E-RI	1.1
E-A-AP	25.1
E-A-F	1.1
E-A-RI	5.2
E-AP-RI	2.0
E-AP-F	1.8
E-F-RI	0.4
E-A-AP-F	10.7
E-A-AP-RI	10.6
E-A-F-RI	0.4
E-AP-F-RI	0.4
E-A-AP-F-RI	2.9
A-AP	0.4
A-F	0.4
A-RI	1.3
A-AP-F	0.4
A-AP-RI	1.1
A-F-RI	0.4
AP-F	0.3
AP-RI	0.4
OA	0.7

Source: Adapted from Oliveira (1991:209).
Notes: E = extraction (timber, rubber, palmito, cacao, nuts); A = agriculture (manioc, corn, rice, beans, bananas, etc.); AP = animal production (chickens, pigs, cattle); F = fishing; RI = rural industry (sawmills, palmito processing); OA = other activities

pattern has allowed the relocation of scarce labor to areas of greater economic activity. Gurupaenses have left to seek work in Jarí, Macapá, Breves, Belém, Carajás, along the Transamazon Highway, and in the gold mines of southern Pará. They have also left when debt relations with a patrão become intolerable.

People who migrate try to maintain ties to their families and friends back home. Even in the case of permanent migration, family members maintain contact through letters, telephone calls, gifts, and visitation. These contacts are crucial in establishing important exchange networks. For example, migrants to urban areas will frequently obtain a variety of medicines or consumer items available only in the city and send them to the countryside. The rural family sends agricultural produce such as manioc or fruit to the city family.

The urban-rural networks also serve to support members when traveling and in need of a place to stay. This proves most important when rural members are sick and need medical treatment available only in the city. Friends and relatives provide room and board free, a cost that would otherwise keep individuals from attempting the trip and their treatment. These networks also allow a rural family to send their young to school in the larger towns. In return, the urban family members retain a "home" to return to if jobs are lost or other troubles arise. They also have a place to stay during vacation time when it is customary for city people to travel to the interior.

Kinship Flexibility

In Amazonia, as in much of the world, kinship networks not only function as primary sources of socioemotional gratification and personal identity, but also operate as essential sources of economic and political aid. Amazonians make the most of this aid by continuously defining and redefining kin networks in ways that best respond to need and opportunity. In doing this, kinship group formation goes far beyond simple genealogical relations to include criteria such as geographic proximity, wealth calculations, social prestige, and ethnic backgrounds (Nugent 1993:145).

Among the indigenous camponeses and townspeople of Amazonia the kinship unit is the kindred, an ego-centered kinship network based on bilateral descent (people trace kinship through both the male and female lines). Principal members of a kindred include grandparents, parents, parents' siblings, spouses, siblings, children, and grandchildren. People may or may not include other relatives in their kindreds such as cousins, nephews, nieces, siblings' spouses, spouses' parents, and children's spouses.

At its broadest level people may call their kindred *gente* (people), although this may include nonkin symbolically linked to the kinship group. The term *parentes* (relatives) is more restrictive in its application to biological kin, although some nonkin may still be incorporated, and includes kin whether they live in close geographic proximity or are distant. The term *família* (family) is the narrowest category and generally refers to the unit of the household (Nugent 1993:144).

Flexibility occurs in the kinship system when people include or exclude relatives at the família and parente levels. It also occurs through the use of "honorary" kin terms that diverge from genealogical reality. For example, a person may call a cousin an *irmã* or *irmão* (sister or brother) and say she or he is família. This occurs when a person is particularly fond of the cousin and interacts on a daily basis with him or her. The person calls the cousin família even though the cousin does not reside in the household.

In the same fashion a person may use the term *primo/prima* (cousin) for a well-liked, but genealogically distant, relative, or even for a nonrelative. The person may also consider the primo as família.

On the other hand, an individual may refer to a disliked cousin as simply parente or gente. This shows a lack of intimacy and a symbolic distancing. In other cases of kindred formation flexibility, individuals may ignore their primary kin or call them parentes (implying less intimacy) if they live far away and interact infrequently, are poor, or have less desirable physical features (skin color, hair color). By contrast, people may use the term "família" for less closely related kin and nonkin if they live nearby and interact frequently, have wealth, or desirable physical features.

People use kinship flexibility as a tool to cope with the rigors of Amazon life. Kinship flexibility enables individuals to manipulate the kinship idiom to justify a request for, or a rejection of, financial assistance, access to land, housing, labor, food, or job acquisition. For example, while collecting genealogical information I asked one of my key consultants to list his primary kin, or his família. Among the people listed was his brother-in-law, whom he called brother. Although the two men lived separately, one in town and one in the interior, the continuous mutual aid they gave each other—agricultural labor, loans, and places to stay while visiting—created a greater sense of kinship closeness. On the other hand, this consultant labeled one of his sisters-in-law as only parente. The woman was a single mother of three who appeared to suffer from a mental disorder and could not support herself or her children. She would periodically visit and ask for assistance. The family would grudgingly give the aid and then have to ask the woman to leave after a week or so.

Flexible kinship also aids in meeting the seasonal demands of the agricultural/extraction cycle and the life cycle of households. During a year a particular household may divide as certain members leave to extract timber or rubber in another part of the municipality and then rejoin later to continue farming. At each transition the family adds or subtracts relatives from the household's composition. The flexibility of the kindred smooths over this change.

People also manipulate the language of kinship to encourage the presence of individuals at certain times of the year. For example, when members of a family need the labor of a distant relative, they can address her or him as primo or irmão. This action increases the social pressure upon the individual to help the family. In the same way additional members may be added or lost to a family during its growth cycle. For example, a family that has only infants can ask a teenaged female cousin to live with them with the expectation that she will help care for the children.

A person may also extend kinship networks to nonkin to expand one's potential source of aid. In these cases the term "primo" is employed for nonkin. Extension of kinship networks is also done through the establishment of ceremonial or fictive kinship ties, particularly compadresco relations (godparentage/co-parentage), or through adoption.

Compadresco relations are based on the tradition of Roman Catholic baptismal sponsorship in which a godparent assumes spiritual and often economic responsibility for a child. It sets up a pseudokinship relationship that may include strong personal ties, not only between child (*afilhado* or godchild) and sponsor (*padrinho* or godparent), but also parents and sponsor (*compadres,* or co-parents). Members of compadresco networks provide mutual aid to one another that may overlap the types of aid offered by kindreds—financial assistance, access to land, housing, labor, food, and job acquisition.

Compadresco relationships may be between social and economic equals or between unequals. Where social class is different, the fictive kin tie serves as a social safety net for the lower-class member. This person can use the ties to petition the padrinho/compadre for emergency loans, jobs, protection, or help with a child's education. For the higher-class members, they can use afilhados/compadres to ensure themselves of a dedicated clientele for business, a reliable workforce for economic production, political support, and a group of people to do odd jobs. The relationship is asymmetrical, with the higher-class member benefiting more from the tie. The lower-class member, however, does accrue important measures of social, political, and economic security. This type of relationship is common between trading post merchants and their fregueses, although anyone with greater amounts of wealth may offer such ties (Wagley 1976:157).

Fictive kin networks may be extensive. For example, Zecá Marajó, a retired lawyer and businessman with whom I shared a house for part of my stay in Gurupá, once boasted to me that he had 330 afilhados with many more compadres. I used to sit and observe his interactions with people passing in front of his house. Repeatedly I would see young and old people stop, address him as padrinho, and ask for his blessing (*benza*). Asking for a blessing is a common gesture of respect to one's godparent. Whenever Zecá had an errand to run, such as buying food or other necessities, he would stand by his window and wait until one of his many afilhados passed by and then ask them to do the errand. Compliance was unwavering.

In Gurupá there are several ways to establish compadresco relations—through baptism, weddings, confirmation, and even during festivals in honor of saints. In the latter case adults establish fictive kinship without any children involved. I participated in such a ritual. During the festival for São João (Saint John) during June, I requested to "pass over the bonfire" with Zecá Marajó to become *compadres de foguerio* (co-parents of the bonfire). Zecá consented, and we underwent the prescribed ritual of passing our joined hands three times over the fire while repeating, "Saint John said, Saint Peter confirmed, that Our Lord Jesus Christ ordered us to be co-parents in this life and in the other also."

With this relationship we strengthened our friendship. It also helped me build rapport. In the case of Zecá, he found a new source of loans. The morning following Saint John's day Zecá came to my window, greeted me with a big smile and a handshake, called me his compadre, and then proceeded to ask to borrow $10. As I was to learn later, compadres have the right to request loans of one another. I gave him $15.

People do not take all fictive kin relationships seriously. Just as with kindred ties, individuals may choose to ignore fictive kin ties (see Wagley 1976:153). Others are formed simply for entertainment purposes. This happened to me once while visiting the rural hamlet of Camutá during a Saint John festival. A teenaged girl approached me and requested that I pass over the bonfire to become *amigos de fogueiro* (friends of the bonfire). The ritual was the same as described before. Afterward, the girl held the right to call me "friend" whenever we happened to meet. In this form the ceremony served as little more than an innocent type of flirtation.

The practice of adopting a child (*filho de criação*) is another common way of expanding kinship ties. People in the Amazon use the term "adoption" in a broad sense since nearly any child raised by someone besides her/his biological parents—an aunt or uncle, grandparent, godparent, or friend—may be considered to fall under this category. Adoptions may be done through the legal system, but most frequently they are done through informal arrangements. People adopt for a number of reasons: to care for children whose parents have died; to send children to live with others who can offer more in terms of education or wealth; to send children to live with couples who are childless; to have the adopted children care for younger children, single adults, or the elderly; or to gain access to adopted children's labor. In the latter case, adoption may develop into a master/servant relationship.

During my fieldwork a married couple, who were two of my key consultants, asked me and my wife if we would adopt their fifth child, a two-year-old girl. They made the offer for several reasons. It was a sign of friendship in that the family trusted us with the child. It was likewise an act of goodwill in that we had no children of our own at the time, and the family suspected that we were infertile. They also hoped that we would raise the child in the United States and give her all the material and educational advantages found there. And finally, the adoption would tie our two families together and effectively expand their kinship network, that is, if contact could be maintained long distance.

The offer flattered us, and we were indeed tempted to adopt the beautiful little child. However, we had to decline, explaining to the family the legal problems of adoption, getting a passport and immigration papers, not to mention my lack of a job. These technicalities seemed to be lost upon them. When I next explained that they would rarely see the girl because of prohibitive travel costs, and that when they did she would speak Portuguese like I did—something they found very humorous—they agreed that the adoption might be too troublesome to attempt. I have always felt that the realization that their child would be linguistically and culturally transformed by the adoption made the rejected request easier to accept.

Folk Views of Poverty

People throughout the world have been known to endure great hardship when they can give symbolic meaning to their suffering, for symbolic meaning can explain and/or justify hardships and aid acceptance of one's condition. In Gurupá I wished to learn how people understand their poverty and how they give meaning to it, so I asked a series of questions to elicit folk views on quality of life and reasons for it. I made use of the recent introduction of television with its constant images of upper- and middle-class life in southern Brazil to spark conversation on affluence and poverty. For those who had little exposure to the medium I asked about their impressions of life in Belém. I also asked whether people considered Gurupá developed and whether life seemed better to them in Gurupá or in Belém.

The Gurupaenses answered these questions in a variety of ways. A minority of people felt Gurupá was not particularly underdeveloped or poor. Individuals responding in this manner tended to be from the interior with little or no exposure to other communities, lifestyles, or the mass media. Most people, however, considered Gurupá poor and backward on the basis of the lack of good jobs (nonextractive jobs), of good wages, of the ability to consume industrial goods, and of access to adequate health care and education. When I asked why Gurupá suffered from poverty, people gave me a variety of reasons that generally fell into five nonmutually exclusive categories, several of which I mentioned in Chapter 3.

One view explains the community's poverty as a curse: It is said that a disgruntled former resident had buried a donkey's head in Gurupá, and the burying of the head has thus caused businesses to falter, development projects to fail, and personal misfortune to plague innovators. It amused me to hear the U.S. sawmill owner, Peter Hoffman, also repeat this tale after his business had failed. He swore to me that Gurupá must be cursed. Along the same lines is the joke told earlier about "guru—pá" (a seed that rots before sprouting). The notion underlying the joke is that the very name of the community has cursed it.

A second explanation blames the community's poverty on the character inadequacies of the population. I found this viewpoint most frequently among Gurupá's dominant-class members, as well as among many middle-class individuals in cities such as Belém. As exemplified by Paulo Silva's comments in the last chapter, people holding this view see rural inhabitants of Amazonia as culturally or racially inferior. Their faults have led them to underachieve and remain in poverty, while superior peoples (usually people of European descent) overachieve and prosper greatly.

This type of prejudice is expressed in the pejorative cover term for Amazon people, "caboclo," a sort of subset of mestizo. People variously characterize them as lazy, less than human, tricky, corrupt, ugly (meaning having Native American features), cunning, traitorous, despicable, unreliable, coppery mongrels, half-breeds, poor and unhappy individuals, perfidious characters, and imbeciles (Wagley 1976:141; Nugent 1993:25). The term not only succinctly symbolizes all kinds of negative attitudes toward the population, it also serves to justify poverty in naturalistic terms. People seem to imagine an evolutionary sequence where civilized/urban (superior) is distanced from semisavage/rural/caboclo (inferior). Native American Amazonians, from this perspective, are the true savages. Caboclos, therefore, cannot help their condition because it is the natural order of things for them to be inferior. Ideologically, this attitude aids in the unquestioned, continued political-economic domination of the region by outside groups.

I recorded many examples of prejudice held against caboclos while doing fieldwork, particularly among urban, middle-class Brazilians. Consistently, I found that these people felt the government squandered public resources on the rural caboclos (public health, economic development, and education). They felt that it was much better for the government to direct scarce funds to the city or to large capital-intensive projects in the countryside. National and regional planners likewise take this view. They often see rural populations as "technologically backward and destined to disappear," or as a social pathology and the main reason for the contemporary underdevelopment and poverty of the region (Anderson and Ioris 1992:366; Nugent 1993:47; see also Schmink and Wood 1992:6).

A third explanation blames the community's backward state on a lack of good natural resources and its poor location. Gurupá has no gold, no iron, no oil, and the land has poor agricultural potential. The lack of natural resources has hobbled the community in its attempts to develop industry, which the Gurupaenses see as the principal way to raise standards of living. The community's location further damages local standards of living, for Gurupá is far from urban and industrial centers and lacks an overland connection. This forces people to import goods by river transportation, a very slow and costly mode of transport. People are very sensitive to the price markups they pay for imported goods. Many told me their poverty is a direct result of high prices in Gurupá.

A fourth explanation explains poverty as a result of local dominant-class exploitation of the poor. Individuals espousing this viewpoint maintain that Gurupá has had many opportunities to develop industry, create jobs, and prosper. The main barrier has been a corrupt dominant class that has allegedly embezzled municipal funds and blocked economic development to preserve its privileged position and power.

Politicians usually receive much of the blame in this view—part of a historic, pan-Brazilian distrust of politicians. One indication of this distrust in Gurupá is the response elicited when I asked people to rank the desirability of certain professions on a scale from 1 to 3, where 3 meant "good," 2 meant "all right," and 1 meant "bad." Calculating the averages of the responses, politicians ranked relatively low (2.49), below the occupations of engineer (2.94), truck driver (2.84), businessperson (2.75), and bricklayer (2.75). The only occupation ranked lower than politician among the choices the respondents were given was that of bookie for the popular lottery, known as *jogo dos bichos* or animal lottery, which scored 2.05.

The final explanation for Gurupá's condition is based on a radical critique of capitalism in which poverty is seen as a result of the capitalist economic system. Proponents of this view interpret capitalism as a socially antagonistic form of wealth accumulation. The elite gain wealth through exploitation of workers (underpaying wages), accompanied by political repression of dissenters. Great concentration of wealth in the hands of a few comes at the cost of creating poverty for the masses. The system is the cause of poverty. People, therefore, must transform the system before conditions will improve.

This view is surprisingly well articulated in Gurupá. In part this derives from local experience with the world economic system and its uneasy articulation with the camponês political economy. As stated previously, tensions arise over competition for land, resource depletion, low earnings, and price gouging by trading posts. The view also stems from the introduction of social Catholicism and its views on Christian justice. Authors of liberation theology have developed an effective critique of exploitation and stratification within capitalism and call for its alteration.

Each of the above folk views gives different meanings to poverty. Each view also leads to different types of coping. In the first three views (supernatural cause, an inevitable cultural or biological quality of the people, a problem of natural resources or location) people resign themselves to accept fate as it has been dealt to them. After all, how can one change magic, human biology, or the environment? They often see Gurupá's poverty as the will of God. The other two views (a consequence of corrupt local officials, a systemic problem caused by a powerful economic system) cry out for change to take place. As I discuss in Chapter 8, these views lie at the base of recent political activism.

The Supernatural

For a long time social scientists have recognized that beliefs in religion and magic are important adaptive mechanisms used by all cultures to deal with social and psychological stress. Belief in the supernatural provides meaning and structure to the world and enables people to reduce anxiety and increase control over the unforeseen, unpredictable, and unintelligible dimensions of life. Through prayers, offerings, music, dance, manipulation of objects, alerted states of consciousness, drama, telling of myths, divination, sorcery, or witchcraft, the world becomes discernible and even controllable. In Gurupá there are four principal realms of the supernatural that function to either explain the unexplained or to manipulate fortune or misfortune: the forest and river *visagens* (malignant spirits), the Catholic saints, *Umbanda* and spiritism, and magic.

Visagens

Eduardo Galvão (1955:88–117) and Charles Wagley (1976:224–241) described in detail a realm of supernatural that originated with Native American cosmology. People believe that this class of supernatural lives in the fauna of the forest, streams, and rivers and have labeled this class *bichos visagentos* (magically malignant animals). These spirits adversely affect the lives of those who venture into their domains, particularly those who are exploiting the natural environment.

Bichos visagentos may take many forms. For example, there is one forest spirit known as Anhangá, a demon that takes the shape of an animal (usually a bird known as *inhambu* or tinamou) and hunts humans. It may kill a person or steal one's soul, causing illness and eventual death. Howler monkeys (*Alouatta caraya*) may also be visagentos and steal one's soul. The *mãe de bichos* (mother of the animals) is another supernatural entity that takes different animal forms. It protects the animals from overhunting and overfishing by taking the soul of a person who hunts or fishes to excess.

Many people told me of close encounters with spirits. In one case the mother of a local restaurant owner told me about a near miss with a *visagem* (the singular form of "visagens") the day after it occurred. It seems the woman was working in her roça in the interior. At dusk she decided to return home. As she walked she heard the kind of peeping sound a chick makes. It sounded as if it were directly below her feet. She stopped and looked but could see nothing. She kept going. Again she heard the peeping sound right next to her, but could see no animal. By the third time she was sure that a visagem was following her. She tried to scream but could not. She ran home as fast as possible and upon seeing her husband managed to scream and warn him. Her husband yelled back, and the visagem, never seen by either of them, went away. The woman later said to me that on occasion the devil opens the doors of hell and sends a visagem to bother or scare people. She was very happy that her husband was home and able to scare the demon away.

Visagens may take human form as well. People told me of various sightings during my fieldwork. One example occurred as a group of children waited for one of Olga's nighttime English lessons, which she held in the old SESP health post. She had canceled class that night, but the children were unaware of this. While waiting in the dark in a downpour one girl leaned up against a door that then sprang open. This startled the group, so they ran across the street. Looking back they saw a light in the building, then a woman leaving the building with an umbrella. This scared them more, and they ran to our house to tell of the visagem they had seen. In their excitement they told story after story of visagens around town. The children said some guarded buried gold, while others simply tried to steal one's soul (*assombrar*). I later inquired about these visagem stories and found the belief to be widespread in adults as well.

Another supernatural forest creature is the *curupira*, a small black-bodied animal, humanlike in form, except that its feet point backward. It emits a shrill cry but can also imitate human voices and lead people into the forest where it kills them. Its backward footprints function to deceive people into thinking they are running away from it when they are actually running into its ambush. The *cobra grande* (big snake) is yet another supernatural creature found in the forest. It is a boa constrictor that grows too large to live on land, forcing it to dwell in the river. People say they see it at night as it travels along the river, its two luminous eyes glowing brightly. The cobra grande will capsize boats and eat its inhabitants. Fishers are particularly wary of this supernatural beast.

People in the Amazon say the *boto* (freshwater dolphin) has the power to transform itself into human form. Once in this form, either a handsome man or a beautiful woman, it will seduce men or women with disastrous outcomes. If a man succumbs to a female boto's seduction, he will copulate until he dies. If a woman has intercourse with a male boto, she will bear a child of the boto—recognizable by a blowhole on the top of its head. This belief is widespread in Amazonia. During my research period there was a case reported in the newspapers of a woman in another part of the Amazon returning a child to the boto; that is, she threw the child into the water where it drowned. The notion of boto seduction sometimes serves as an explanation of unwanted, out-of-wedlock pregnancies.

The wife of a local boat owner once told me a story about the boto and her mother. As the story went, the mother was alone in her house in the interior while her husband was away on business. In front of the house was a narrow raised walkway that extended out onto a stream. Whenever someone walked on the walkway the logs moved and made a squeaking noise. One afternoon the woman heard the walkway squeak. She wondered who was there but did not look. She quickly forgot this incident until the next day when it happened again. This time she looked out the window and saw a man nicely dressed in a long-sleeved yellow shirt, long pants, and a large straw hat. He looked and walked like her husband but was not her husband.

Fearing that the man might be a boto, she hid and began praying. Luckily, she said, God sent a neighbor's dog, which scared the man away.

Later that same day the woman's brother-in-law came by for a visit. She told him the story, and he decided to stay the night and see if it would happen the next day. When nothing happened on the following day they figured that the boto knew that the man was there. So the brother-in-law decided to trick it by pretending to leave, then sneaking back into the house. This he did and then waited with his gun ready. Sure enough they heard the walkway squeak. The stranger/boto walked right into the house. The brother-in-law leveled his gun and shot at it. He missed and the boto fled outside. The brother-in-law pursued and fired three more times, all missing. The boto jumped into the water and never again returned.

Among the random sample I interviewed in town and in the interior, 22 percent of the respondents acknowledged they had seen a visagem; 61 percent said that visagens existed; 67 percent said curupiras existed; 94 percent said the cobra grande existed; and 74 percent said the boto could transform itself into human form. These widespread beliefs collectively help explain misfortunes that occur in the forest, river, or even town. For those who believe, they also serve to curb excessive exploitation of forest/river fauna for fear of reprisal. For those who disbelieve or doubt, the telling of harrowing encounters with visagens, told late at night in the dark, at a minimum serve as a source of endless entertainment.

Catholic Saints

Although Catholic cosmology is broad, complex, and varies from culture to culture, I wish to focus on a particular aspect most relevant to this discussion: the veneration of the saints in Latin American folk Catholicism. Throughout Latin America people pray to and petition the saints and the Virgin Mary to aid them in their everyday lives. Believers pray primarily to the saints and the Virgin because they feel God and Jesus are too distant and too elevated in the spiritual hierarchy to deal with the details of the lives of ordinary people (Galvão 1955:39). In Gurupá people see the saints as benevolent powers or protectors who intervene in the lives of the populace. Each saint has an array of powers and specializes in certain human problems. In return for their aid the saints require respect, which involves prayers, celebrating the day of the saint in the appropriate manner, and fulfilling promises or vows made to them (Wagley 1976:220).

People in Gurupá commonly use promesas to deal with misfortune or uncertainty. As explained previously, a promesa is a petition, or contract, made with a saint in which a reciprocal exchange occurs. For example, a person may ask a saint to perform a miracle, like healing a sickness, finding a job, finding a lost object, or protecting one's life, and in return for the miracle, the person will repay the saint with something of value. Repayment can take the form of offering money to the saint's church, decorating the statue of the saint, making sweets to give to children, making a pilgrimage to the saint's church, participating in a novena (nine nights of prayer dedicated to the saint), or walking in a religious procession for the saint. Social scientists interpret the saints' festivals as a form of collective payment for the well-being of a community (Galvão 1955:42).

In Gurupá promesas are most commonly made to the community's two most important saints, Saint Benedict and Saint Anthony, both housed in the church. Saint Anthony, the patron saint of Gurupá, is located behind the altar, and Saint Benedict is off in the right wing. Despite Saint Anthony's official status as patron saint, Saint Benedict is the most cherished saint. Saint Benedict is a dark-skinned saint who is the protector of river travelers, rubber tappers, and the poor. People make promesas to him to protect them, particularly in river travel. A very common method of repayment for safe passage is to set off fireworks each time one is traveling in a boat that passes in front of the church. The sound of popping skyrockets emanating from boats on the river in front of the church is a daily occurrence in Gurupá.

People in Gurupá tell of many cases of saintly miracles. Particularly during Saint Benedict's festival time (in December) people will sit and tell of all kinds of astonishing events attributed to the saint. I collected many stories of saints' powers, including many of the same ones recorded by Wagley and Galvão thirty years earlier. A common story told and retold was the sighting of Saint Benedict and Saint Anthony walking the streets of Gurupá at night. When confronted the saints would disappear. Careful inspection of the saintly icons in church the next day would reveal sand on their feet from their outing. A second version of this story describes how a police officer shot at the two saints in the dark. The next day people found a bullet hole and blood on the arm of Saint Anthony. Since this occurred, the story goes, the saints have not ventured out of the church.

Many people told me of the healing power of Saint Benedict. Broken limbs, deep gashes, infections, and terminal illnesses have all been miraculously cured after the afflicted appealed to the saint. Interestingly, the therapeutic function of these beliefs was not lost upon the town's doctor. In many cases she was unable to treat illness because of a lack of medicine, the general poor health of a patient, or the advanced state of the illness when the individual first came in for treatment. When Western medicine had nothing to offer, she would suggest to her patients that they seek the aid of the saints.

Another much talked about example of Saint Benedict's powers concerned the theft, sinking, and recovery of the boat owned by Gurupá's priest. I describe the context of the theft in detail in Chapter 9, but in brief, it appears that someone cut the boat's mooring ropes and perforated the hull, which caused the boat to sink. The strong current of the Amazon River then carried it downstream. For weeks devotees of the church dragged the river bottom with very little hope of finding the boat. When they surprisingly discovered the boat, many Gurupaenses proclaimed it a miracle granted by Saint Benedict. The priest's status grew among the populace.

There are many ways to repay a saint for miracles. Some people will dedicate their lives to the saint. This entails participating in all of the saint's celebrations and carrying out a number of functions to maintain the icon and the church. Men join the irmandade, or brotherhood, of Saint Benedict. In the past this was a strong association that planned and carried out the celebrations, dances, music, auctions, and processions for the saint. The brotherhood even had its own separate cemetery.

Today, with a priest in residence, the brotherhood has lost much of its control over the proceedings to the church administration. Its membership has dwindled, and most members are in their fifties or older. The brotherhood still holds an occasional dance that features drums and takes place in a shelter dedicated to the saint. The dance I witnessed, however, was cut short because of rowdy youth. One brotherhood member who plays the drums confessed to me that he no longer likes to participate in the dances because young people do not know how to behave. They tarnish the honor of the saint. Despite these problems, membership in the brotherhood still bestows honor and prestige upon its members. Membership also qualifies individuals to carry the saint or saintly paraphernalia during the all-important religious procession.

Another form of repayment for saintly miracles is the making or purchasing of an ex-voto and sending it to the saint. Ex-votos are images of afflicted body parts healed by a saint. They include limbs, heads, hearts, and so on. The images may be miniature or life size. People purchase metal and wax ex-votos, or they use wood to carve their own. Believers then take the icons to the church and present them to the saint as a payment for the promesa. I heard many tales of how individuals delivered ex-votos by placing them in the river far downstream from Gurupá. Miraculously, overnight, the images found their way upstream to the shore in front of the church.

The main focus for repayment of promesas is the religious procession for St. Benedict held in December. During this time the population of the town of Gurupá triples in size as people from all over the lower Amazon region converge to pay homage. The climax of the religious celebration is a procession. Devotees parade the image of the saint through the streets of Gurupá, then take it on a fluvial procession by boat in front of the town— called a meia lua, or half moon. These activities are followed by a Mass.

During the town procession, thousands of devotees repaying promesas and wishing for the saint's blessings envelop the saint. They walk with the saint, sometimes barefoot, sometimes crawling the last portion of the route that leads into the church. People of all ages participate. Children dress as angels (homemade wings, halos, and white frocks) and carry candles. Along the way people sing, recite prayers, and shoot off fireworks. On occasion a stand of a hundred or more fireworks will be set off, which may last five minutes and choke the air with gray smoke. The procession will stop and wait while the skyrockets fire into the sky.

The meia lua that I witnessed in 1984 had a total of forty-seven large and small boats participating. Devotees placed a second, smaller image of the saint on the lead boat. The boats then followed the lead boat as it passed three times in a half-moon pattern in front of the town. A continuous stream of skyrockets streaked from the boats. Boat owners participated in the meia lua to bring some assurance that misfortune would not occur in the upcoming year—particularly, the sinking of a vessel.

People told me Saint Benedict took this commitment seriously, as evidenced by a recent example of a boat owner who made a promise to Saint Benedict that he would participate in the meia lua every year in exchange for the safety of his boat. The boat, *Fé en Deus* (Faith in God), functioned well for five years and earned the owner good profit from the transport of cargo and passengers. The owner then decided to stop participating in the meia lua and skipped two years. By the third year mechanical problems plagued the boat and it seldom ran on time. Community consensus held that the saint was punishing the owner for failure to live up to his promise. During the next Saint Benedict procession the boat was prominently in the lead in the procession with numerous skyrockets flaring from its decks.

As this case shows the saints do not always act benevolently. If a person offends them or breaks a promise they are likely to punish the guilty. Thus many people told me it was dangerous to work on a saint's day, for the day is holy and people should respect it. Yet an exception can be made when a patrão forces one to work on a holy day. Under these circumstances the saint feels pity for the worker and does not punish.

Sebastiana Alves, Nicanor's wife, told me of two cases in which the saints castigated individuals not honoring their days. In the first, one of Sebá's *comadres* (co-mothers) decided to go fishing on Saint Peter's day. A number of people advised her against it, but she did not listen. While fishing she had an accident and drowned. The second case involved a man who extracted timber on Saint John's day. People warned him not to do it, but he too refused to listen. While in the forest the tree he was cutting fell on him and killed him. These two examples were enough proof for Sebá to deem saints' days as holy, and she thus makes sure that no one in her family acts callously by working on them.

Umbanda and Spiritism

Although Roman Catholicism is the official religion of Brazil, there are several alternative religions that coexist or are syncretized with it. Among these are the spirit mediumship religions, which are religions based on the idea of spirit possession. There is a continuum of such groups that vary in belief, ritual, social class, ethnicity, and geographic origin. In Gurupá there are two of these religions, Umbanda and spiritism.

Umbanda is a uniquely Brazilian religion that formed through the syncretized rituals and beliefs of Africa (particularly Yoruba and Dahomey cultures), Native America, and Europe (Catholicism and spiritism). Although the religion had its origins among the African slaves, it has long since expanded to all ethnic and social groups in Brazil. Today there are many regional variations and regional names for the belief system, although "Umbanda" is becoming the most ubiquitous form. In its cosmology there is a pantheon of African gods, called *orixás*. Believers have syncretized these gods with the Catholic saints, the Virgin, and Jesus. Below the orixás are a variety of spirits, such as *pretos velhos* (elderly African slaves), índios (Native Americans) or caboclos (in this context, also Native Americans), and children. The orixás and spirits have special powers that they use to aid or harm humans. Believers make contact with the supernatural through spiritual possession. They summon spirits by drumming, singing, hand clapping, and/or dancing. Umbanda specialists/mediums, called *pais, mães,* and *filhos de santo* (fathers, mothers, and children of the saint, respectively), receive the spirits during religious and curing ceremonies. With the spirits' aid, they divine, tell futures, heal, find objects, create or end romance, and thwart or send evil magic for their clients.

Umbanda came to Gurupá in the 1960s via Belém where a version known as *batuque* exists (see Leacock and Leacock 1972). Since its introduction believers have practiced the religion only sporadically. None of its adherents has been able to maintain a *terreiro* (loosely translated as church) for very long. My consultants could name only three people currently living in Gurupá who practiced Umbanda. All were women. One, known as Dona Socorro Pena, operated a terreiro for a while then stopped. A second, Dona Anaí Castanha, was rumored to have had her special powers (*corrente,* or current) taken away by a pai de santo in Belém. The pai de santo accused her of abusing her power by using money she earned from clients to support a drinking habit. The third, Dona Marta Costa, set up a private practice to heal, divine, tell the future, and do magic for a small group of clients.

The second variant of spirit mediumship religion in Gurupá is spiritism. It is based on the works of Allen Kardec, the pen name of French schoolteacher Hippolyte Léon Dénizard Rivail. The movement began in the 1860s and diffused to Brazil in the 1900s. Today the religion is most frequently practiced in the south of Brazil, principally among middle- and upper-class people of European descent. Spiritist belief is highly variable and may overlap with Umbanda in some cases. However, there are four fundamental principles common to most groups that identify themselves as spiritists: communication with the dead via mediums, the existence of a spiritual body, healing through spiritual energies, and gradual purification of the soul across various incarnations in a process governed by the law of karma (Hess 1994: 11-12).

Gurupá has one self-declared spiritist named Mercedes Monteiro. He also belongs to the Flores Brasileira Umbanda Spirit Foundation of Belém, which shows the overlap with Umbanda. Mercedes told me that he holds ceremonies twice a week from 8:00 P.M. to 9:00 P.M. in which he receives several spirits of famous lawyers and physicians. Both advise clients. The physicians may even perform supernatural surgery, mimicking an operation above a patient's body. Mercedes also heals illness with *passe* (pass), a therapy similar to "laying-on" of hands that strengthens one spiritually, and with magic water (*água flórida,* or perfumed water). Additionally, he performs dispossessions in which he summons a troublesome spirit and then educates or enlightens it to stop causing trouble for the living.

Magic

Magic is the manipulation of supernatural forces for a desired result. It differs from religion, at least heuristically, in that it is a mechanistic process, while the former is an uncertain petition to the supernatural. With magic, if the right thoughts occur, the correct words are spoken, the proper ritual performed, or the appropriate ingredients mixed, applied, or ingested, the result is assured. In reality magic is often intertwined with religious belief, making a hard-and-fast distinction between the two difficult. In Gurupá magic is done for good, particularly for healing sickness, or it is done for evil, witchcraft and sorcery.

Healing is an important use of magic, especially considering that the community's hospital and one doctor are unable to deliver health care to all who need it. In short, Western medicine is unavailable to many. So people must rely on alternative healing practices that include religious healing (spiritual intervention through Catholicism, Umbanda, or spiritism), medicinal remedies (several stores in town and even the pharmacies sell roots, leaves, and extracts with purported healing properties), magical healing, or a combination of all three. There are several specialists in Gurupá who cure through magic and religion. In the past these specialists included *pajés* (individuals with shamanistic powers—a tradition of Native American origin), *benzedeiros* (blessers), and *parteiras* (midwives). Today only benzedeiros are commonly found in Gurupá, although the hospital trains midwives in Western medical practices to assist in births at home in order to reduce the workload of the hospital personnel.

People in Gurupá estimate that there are somewhere between twenty to thirty benzedeiros operating in the municipality. They are both male and female, although the ones I talked with were all female. They cure one's afflictions by using a combination of massage, blowing smoke, prayers, offerings, and medicinal plants, the first two being common healing methods among Native Americans. The prayers and offerings originate in Catholicism, Umbanda, or spiritism. Prayers used during curing, however, serve as incantations rather than petitions to the supernatural. I interpreted them as more magical in nature than religious. Benzedeiros also treat people to prevent harm or to strengthen them against a range of maladies such as arthritis, ulcers, the "evil eye," *inveja* (envy or jealousy), *assustamento* (fright), *panema,* or sorcery/witchcraft (see Wagley 1976: 248–252; Galvão 1955:122–128). The only major addition to the folk healing practices found in Gurupá since the 1950s is the assimilation of Umbanda and spiritist rituals and beliefs.

The activities of Marina Santos serve as an example of the contemporary eclectic nature of healing practices used by benzedeiros in Gurupá. Marina is in her forties and has lived in Gurupá about ten years along with her husband and two children. She lived directly behind us when we resided in the adjoining house to Zecá Marajó. We quickly got to know her and her family, and she became one of my key consultants.

Marina is known along her street as an accomplished blesser. She has treated people for a long list of ailments, including malaria, undernutrition, and the evil eye. She cures using a combination of techniques: massage, prayers, and offerings to syncretized Catholic saints/Umbanda gods. I experienced her skills firsthand when I fell ill with blood poisoning during the later stages of my field research and sought her help. I also went to the hospital where I got a steady dosage of antibiotics. My affliction was in both legs. An abrasion on each little toe—obtained by wearing shoes while playing basketball after six months of wearing only sandals—became infected during a canoe trip where my feet were constantly in water. Both legs swelled to a point just below my knees, making walking painful.

Marina diagnosed my ailment and prescribed a treatment, *cortar izepla* (meaning to cut izepla). The idea of izepla is related to the Native American view that illness results from the penetration of a malignant object into the body. A curer must remove this object or cut it by supernatural ritual. In Gurupá people combine this concept with Western medical etiology to create a dualistic treatment regime. The physician treats an ailment's physical cause, while a benzedeiro treats the supernatural cause. The prevailing view is that the physician either does not know about the supernatural cause or ignores it, putting one at great risk.

For my cure Marina had me sit in her only chair in front of her makeshift altar. On the altar were a variety of statues and pictures of saints and Umbanda orixás. She lit a candle as an offering, made the sign of the cross, and then said a prayer to a picture she had of Saint Anthony—on horseback slaying a dragon. Next Marina knelt down and used her thumb to trace the sign of the cross on my feet. She recited a prayer too quietly and garbled for me to understand. Her eyes were closed as she concentrated on her task. She massaged each leg, which I vividly remember because of the intense pain it caused. Then, while grasping a feather, she again made the sign of the cross on each foot and recited another set of prayers. In fifteen minutes the treatment was complete, and she assured me I would get better, which I did in about two weeks. For her healing services I gave her some eggs and manioc flour.

Magic is also used in Gurupá to send or protect oneself from evil. Evil appears in several forms. As mentioned above there is evil from bichos vis-agentos that can make a person ill or die. The afflicted may call upon ben-zedeiros or *Umbandistas* (practitioners of Umbanda) to save a person from these maladies. There is also an animatisic force known as *panelança* or *panema*. Panema is an impersonal, soulless, supernatural force that brings bad luck and it forms in objects or people. If a fishing pole has panema, for example, it will not catch fish. If a gun has panema, it will not kill game. If people have panema, they will become sick and may die.

I observed a case of panema during the course of my fieldwork. It involved a young bank functionary and his wife, both from Belém, whom I got to know in 1985. During pregnancy the wife contracted German measles. She refused to abort the fetus. The fetus was stillborn, and the mother lapsed into a coma. People commented on the tragedy, saying such occurrences are frequent when a man with a pregnant wife gives meat, fish, or fruit to someone else who carelessly lets a dog or a pig eat the bones or seeds/peels. This gives the woman panema and causes birth defects in or death of the baby.

To eliminate panema, objects, animals, or people can undergo ritual cleansing by benzedeiros, Umbandistas, or spiritists. My consultants cautioned me that the best treatment is simply prevention. One should avoid unlucky things and take care with discarded food.

Witchcraft and sorcery are additional sources of evil. Anthropologists heuristically separate the two, defining "witchcraft" as evil done with mental powers alone (it is thought) and "sorcery" as evil done with materials and incantations. One must be born with the power to do witchcraft, while anyone can learn to do sorcery. In Gurupá people join the two concepts. Both fall under the title *feitiço* (evil magic), and according to the town and rural samples, 55 percent of Gurupaenses said that feitiço existed as an authentic supernatural force.

People who believe in feitiço claim that it is at the root of most misfortune and even luck. Most believe that envy and jealousy are the most frequent reasons for one to use it. There are three main practitioners of it—witches proper, benzedeiros, and Umbandistas/spiritists—although there are many people who dabble in the occult as novices.

My consultants could identify only a few witches in Gurupá. They are all elderly women living by themselves who lack supportive kindreds, are eccentric, and are considered social outsiders and therefore dangerous in a supernatural sense. They can injure people out of spite or can be hired to harm people for a small price. Yet no physical violence is directed toward them, and people generally tolerate them even as they fear them.

I met one self-proclaimed witch, Dona Elena Azar, who lives in a collapsing house on Saint Anthony Avenue. She boasts of her abilities to anyone who will listen, telling of good and bad deeds she has performed. One of her favorite stories is her alleged battle with a former priest in Gurupá. The priest disliked Dona Elena and condemned her practice of witchcraft as Satan's work. Publicly insulted, she fought back. As the story goes, she drove the priest mad and made him defecate all over the church. When I asked about the outcome of the struggle, she smiled and said, "I'm still here and that priest is not." When I asked about her relations with the current priest she responded that he knows of her power and is careful not to offend her.

Sebá Alves told me of several conflicts she had with feitiço. One case occurred when she lived along the Mararú River on the Great Island of Gurupá. She was young then and a good worker and midwife. Her skill caused jealousy (inveja) in one of her neighbors, who was afraid she would lose her husband to Sebá. The neighbor, who dabbled in sorcery, sent feitiço to Sebá. This caused Sebá to have tremendous pain in her teeth. At the same time the envious neighbor sent feitiço to one of Sebá's comadres. However, this feitiço errantly attacked the woman's three-year-old daughter, who happened to be standing outside the house at the time of the transmission. They found her all coiled up like a snake and suffering greatly.

Sebá and her comadre decided to fight back. They went to a benzedeiro, who identified the source of the feitiço. The benzedeiro cured Sebá and the child through prayer and rubbing cotton soaked in alcohol on their heads. As the benzedeiro did this to Sebá, a buzzing cicada flew out of her body (this is part of the Native American cosmology where the intrusion of a foreign object or animal causes illness). The benzedeiro caught it and asked Sebá and the woman if they wished to send the feitiço back to the individual who sent it. Returning feitiço, Sebá commented, is always fatal. They agreed. Soon after the envious woman got sick, and six months later she died. Sebá and the child eventually got better, although Sebá admitted going to the town's dentist and having all her teeth removed and replaced with dentures.

The second source of evil magic or sorcery comes from Umbandistas and spiritists. Although these individuals did not publicly admit practicing sorcery to me, many people told of potions, amulets, offerings, and animal sacrifices obtained from them. *Macumba* and *quimbanda* (evil magic) were the terms applied to these practices. Occasionally, my consultants pointed out small collections of candles, feathers, and blood left at crossroads as a sign of macumba activity. Whether the people making these offerings intended to do harm, to help, or to simply make an offering to an orixá or spirit was rarely clear to my consultants. Nonetheless, my consultants were clearly nervous of the practice.

Mercedes the spiritist told me about several close calls he had with people accusing him of evil magic. He adamantly stated that he only does good magic (*corrente branco*). Nonetheless, people do not always trust him. In one case a town drunkard died. The mother of the deceased could not accept that her son had died of alcohol abuse. She blamed Mercedes for using his magic against the son and threatened revenge. In another case a young child disappeared in the interior. People blamed Mercedes and threatened his life. Mercedes's friends concluded that the woman was simply careless with the infant, who fell into the river and drowned.

Diversions

As in all cultures the people of Gurupá have devised a number of ways to entertain themselves. These diversions serve myriad functions such as recreation, relaxation, release of anxiety and tension, creation of shared values to increase social solidarity, and so forth. All these functions enable people to better cope with the hardships of life. In Gurupá there are many such activities that I interpreted in this light, among them the celebration of festivals, saints' days, dances, circuses, parties, weddings, birthdays, soccer tournaments, and sport contests. Other pleasures include listening to the radio, playing dominoes or cards, gambling, singing, artwork, and even alcohol consumption. Of course, this list is hardly exhaustive.

Television is another important form of diversion. It has only recently been introduced to the community. Despite its short time in Gurupá, television promises to have an important influence upon sociocultural life as it not only entertains but informs people about regional, national, and international events in a way never possible before. To understand the potential of television to shape the discourse on the political economy, a discussion of the medium's impact in Gurupá is warranted.

Television

The research presented here is part of a larger study directed by Conrad Kottak that analyzed television's impact in six communities in Brazil (this section is adapted from Pace 1993). The goal of the research was to understand the role of television in shaping sociocultural change and in forming national cultural identity, particularly in rural areas. Brazil was chosen for study in part since it has the world's fifth largest television audience size with some 75 percent of households possessing sets (Miranda and Pereira 1983:48). At the same time the country's high level of illiteracy, underdevelopment, and the relative isolation of rural areas made it likely that rapid and profound changes would occur from exposure to television. Researchers in each of the six communities conducted ethnographic research and administered interview schedules. The interview schedules covered a wide array of topics and included commonly asked questions used in U.S. television research. (For the complete results of the project, see Kottak [1990] and Pace [1993].)

Among the sites chosen for study Gurupá is the most geographically and culturally isolated, as well as the community with the least exposure to television. From the early 1600s until the 1950s Gurupá's principal source of information on national and world events was conversations with itinerant river merchants and travelers. Their sporadic visits, plus a scarcity of printed matter and high illiteracy rates, meant a great deal of isolation from not only current events, but also pan-Brazilian culture in general. This situation began changing in the 1950s with the introduction of the battery-powered radio. With radio, people in Gurupá could hear news, sports, and even soap operas on a daily basis. However, it was not until the arrival of television, and six hours of electricity daily, that high levels of exposure to world events and pan-Brazilian culture were obtained.

The first televisions to receive satisfactory reception in Gurupá were installed in 1982. Despite the sometimes erratic reception, the televisions attracted much attention as exciting new forms of entertainment in town. The owners of the sets proudly displayed them as status symbols. During soccer games and nightly *novelas* (Brazilian soap operas) people arranged their sets before windows to face outward into the street. There large crowds could gather to catch glimpses of the programs. Social pressure was brought to bear on anyone not allowing public access to the television in this way. The community considered televiewing a form of public entertainment.

Soon after 1982 more families began acquiring televisions. By the summer of 1983 when I first arrived in Gurupá there were eight working sets. This increased to twenty-seven by 1985. In 1986 the government installed a satellite dish in Gurupá, which ended the need for individuals to purchase a costly antenna and reception booster for their sets; this also enabled many less affluent families to afford TVs. In 1986 there were 86 television sets and by 1991 over 200.

With only a few years of viewing in the community, the amount of exposure to television is still quite low. According to the urban and rural surveys of 1985 and 1986, 88 percent of the sample reported less than one year of televiewing, 11 percent less than five years, and only 1 percent more than five years. The mean for the sample was 0.8 years of televiewing. In addition, I classified 45 percent of the sample population as nonviewers of television (no exposure), 46 percent as light viewers (by Gerbner's [1967] definition, less than three hours a day), 9 percent as medium viewers (two to six hours a day), and 0 percent as heavy viewers (six or more hours a day). The mean hours of television watched by the sample population was 0.8 hours a day. It is important to note, however, that all of these figures are biased toward more televiewing than actually occurs in the community because of the proportionately low number of rural residents, who lack access to television, included in the sample population.

Even though low television exposure is the norm for most people in Gurupá, community perceptions of the value of television are overwhelmingly positive. In the survey, 87 percent of the sample positively evaluated television, 4 percent neutrally evaluated it, and 9 percent negatively evaluated it. In the United States the rates are approximately 69 percent positive, 16 percent neutral, and 15 percent negative (Comstock 1978:129). The types of positive effects that Gurupá respondents listed include entertainment, information, education, and increased social interaction. Negative effects include that it teaches bad habits, is addictive, enslaves economically, and brings disturbing news.

Questions asked on the survey about program preferences and programs watched indicate that the novela, the news, and sporting events (soccer being the most watched) are of greatest importance to the sample viewing audience. Brazilian-produced novelas air six times a week, end after six or seven months, and are generally of high quality. People throughout Brazil follow them passionately. The same holds true for Gurupá. However, the program content of novelas does more than simply entertain: It also gives the people of Gurupá their first glimpse of middle- and upper-class lifestyles in Brazil, particularly in Rio de Janeiro and São Paulo where producers film most novelas. Since the community of Gurupá is overwhelmingly lower class, information on middle- and upper-class lifestyles and affluence is very limited. Even when people from Gurupá travel to urban centers such as Belém there usually is little contact with people of higher socioeconomic status. The images of higher classes that are presented on the nightly novela, therefore, are often completely new experiences for the Gurupaenses.

Beyond views of middle- and upper-class lifestyles, television provides novel information about the world. Through the news, variety shows like *Fantastico* (Fantastic), and documentaries, exposure to global cultures and lifestyles has created a greater awareness of the world beyond Gurupá. This change is evident in public and private topics of conversation heard in the community. Before the spread of television, conversation often focused on local events, gossip, soccer, or an occasional diffuse comment on regional or national politics. For example, during my first visit to Gurupá in 1983 people often asked me vague questions such as what kind of jungle grows in the United States, whether all Americans are rich, and what cowboys are like. With the spread of television, however, conversations take on a more cosmopolitan, more diverse nature. In the mid-1980s I remember discussing the details of events occurring in North America, Europe, and the Middle East. People scrutinized national politics (1985 was the year that the military regime that ruled Brazil for twenty-one years gave power back to a civilian government). I found myself discussing the goals of the American space program, the ideology of President Reagan, poverty in the United States, international terrorism, and the geophysical causes of earthquakes.

Exposure to world events via television stimulates a real quest for additional knowledge. Gurupaenses seek out reading material and radio broadcasts to supplement their few hours of daily televiewing. One possible indication of this thirst for additional knowledge is found in the positive statistical correlations between a higher number of televiewing hours and higher levels of exposure to print media, literacy, and the number of hours spent listening to the radio (Kottak 1990:151).

People in Gurupá reacted to this information in varied ways. There appears to be an association between higher television exposure and lower evaluations of the community's standing. I speculate that the glimpse of wealth and affluence brought into people's homes has increased an awareness of Gurupá's lowly status nationally and internationally. This has led many people to seek better answers or to better articulate their explanations of poverty. In this sense television has aided in increasing social class awareness. As a consequence it has possibly augmented class tensions in the community—tensions created by economic and political processes.

Conclusion

In this chapter I have endeavored to show how the people of Gurupá have adapted to the social conditions of poverty and underdevelopment. They have structured their lives to make the best of a low standard of living. Key aspects of this adaptation are finding a patrão, job flexibility, kinship flexibility, folk views of poverty, use of the supernatural to explain uncertainty and manipulate the world, and indulgence of diversions—of which television has created significant short-term changes. Despite the diversity of adaptations, increasing numbers of Gurupaenses are dissatisfied with their life conditions, particularly the worsening economic and ecological circumstances. I think the knowledge gained from television has only strengthened the existing discontent and has led to new forms of questioning. Combined with political problems and social movements arising throughout Amazonia over the last thirty years, Gurupá's struggle for a better life has taken on overt political dimensions. The next two chapters examine the political struggles of the community.

8

THE RISE AND FALL
OF AUTHORITARIAN POLITICS

In early 1978 I was visiting a friend in the Japanese section of São Paulo, called Liberdade, when I happened to glance out of the apartment building window to the side street several stories below. By chance a heavily guarded motorcade was passing by at that moment. As I strained to look inside a large limousine in the middle of the cavalcade an unforgettable face appeared. It was then-president/dictator of Brazil, General Ernesto Geisel. The scene startled me. I found it hard to believe that I was seeing in person a leader who so polarized political opinion in Brazil at the time. Some considered him a heroic guardian of the patrimony, fighting against the subversive threats of communism and anarchy while pushing hard to industrialize and modernize the country. So many others, however, considered him an oppressive dictator directing a systematic campaign of political repression to further the military's view of modernization. Among the techniques used for repression were widespread uses of torture, murder, and economic exploitation.

As the motorcade whisked away I had no idea how profound the human rights abuses were during the military's twenty-one-year reign of power. Only in the following decades did the full story begin to emerge. Nor was I aware of the profound long-term impact that political changes wrought by the military rulers were to have, even in such faraway places as Gurupá. This impact continues, even after the reemergence of civilian rule in 1985, as the military's policies proceed to generate tremendous political and economic reverberations. In this chapter I will discuss the rise and decline of the military state and the corresponding consequences in Gurupá.

Post-1964 Politics

During the 1950s and early 1960s Brazil entered a political crisis period created by rapid economic change, growing industrialism in the south,

163

shifting balances of political power, increasing centralization of power at the federal level, and growing class conflict. Social tensions came to a climax in 1964 during the populist government of President João Goulart. The military was very apprehensive about the growing social disorder, particularly protests for land reform by peasant leagues. It also grew wary of the threats to economic growth gained from its modernization policies, particularly calls for redistribution of wealth. On April 1, 1964, the military reacted to the political disorder by overthrowing the government and establishing a centralized authoritarian regime (O'Donnell 1978:7).

During the following twenty-one years the military regime sought to strengthen the economic development policies initiated in the 1950s. Much of this development revolved around a policy of import-substitution-industrialization, wherein local production of consumer goods replaces imported goods. To achieve this goal the military allied itself closely with international businesses and banks and openly encouraged foreign investment. To create a secure investment atmosphere the military kept a tight control on labor unions and their right to strike, eroded working-class wages to ensure a cheap labor force, and destroyed the capacity of the national bourgeois groups to oppose its economic policies (Ianni 1970:191; O'Donnell 1978). To augment the internal market for luxury commodities that Brazilian industry was producing (automobiles, appliances, and so forth) the military promoted income concentration in the middle and upper classes (O'Donnell 1978).

The military constructed a bureaucratic-authoritarian state (BA state) to enact its economic and social policies. O'Donnell defines the BA state by the following characteristics:

(a) higher governmental positions usually are occupied by persons who come to them after successful careers in complex and highly bureaucratized organizations—the armed forces, the public bureaucracy, and large private firms; (b) political exclusion, in that it aims at closing channels of political access to the popular sector and its allies so as to deactivate them politically, not only by means of repression but also through the imposition of vertical (corporatist) controls by the state on such organizations as labor unions; (c) economic exclusion, in that it reduces or postpones indefinitely the aspiration to economic participation of the popular sector; (d) depoliticization, in the sense that it pretends to reduce social and political issues to "technical" problems to be resolved by means of interactions among the higher echelons of the above mentioned organizations; and (e) it corresponds to a stage of important transformations in the mechanisms of capital accumulation of its society, changes that are, in turn, a part of the "deepening" process of a peripheral and dependent capitalism characterized by extensive industrialization. (1978:6)

The military government extended the BA state apparatus into all regions of the country. As it entered Amazonia in the mid-1960s it drastically altered the region's political status quo. The state imposed highly complex centralized bureaucracies on the region and forced political realignments. This simultaneously satisfied the needs of the developing industrial base in the Brazilian south, particularly generating foreign revenues, and the changing needs of the state, particularly maintaining legitimacy by allocating public resources to private groups (Bunker 1985:79). Through this process Amazonia lost its regional autonomy and became an institutional, administrative, and political periphery of the Brazilian center (Bunker 1985:124). The new dominant groups that arose in the Amazon were completely dependent on the initiative and support of the powerful nation-state and on large corporations investing in the region (Bunker 1985:82).

The transition from traditional political control to BA state–aligned control occurred through several processes. For example, the BA state eroded the Amazonian political elite's power by the transfer of much of the local decisionmaking process to the national center. Particularly in areas with valuable extractive or agricultural resources, local decisionmaking was kept to a minimum. Some of these areas were designated national security areas and were occupied by the military. Gurupá lies on the margins of one of these areas. Although the military never occupied it, the military regime did have a role in appointing Gurupá's mayor in 1966.

Another way the traditional elite lost power was through economic change. With the construction of new highways and the introduction of new or renewed economic activities such as timber extraction, mining, and cattle ranches, often under the control of southern-based business or international business, old monopolies based on extraction and exchange were broken. This undermined the economic foundations of local political power. In Gurupá a number of timber firms penetrated the local economy and, as described in Chapters 5 and 6, swayed local political policy and judicial decisionmaking in their favor.

The old dominant class also suffered from a loss of control over land that affected political hegemony. The federal government appropriated all unclaimed lands within 100 kilometers of existing or planned highways and then set up the INCRA agency to administer the land. Land in this category accounted for approximately 3,112,653 square kilometers, or 63 percent of the legal Amazon region (Santos 1981, cited in Emmi 1985). Within this land was the southern part of the municipality of Gurupá.

In addition, with the penetration of the capitalist mode of production into the area, land title, not simple rights to land use, became important in controlling land. The lack of land titles destroyed some dominant-class members' claim to land and, as shown in Chapter 6, created growing tensions over land claims.

To enact BA state policies the military regime organized and manipulated the ARENA (Aliança Renovadora Nacional, or National Renovation

Alliance) political party. In the Amazon ARENA defended the interests of the BA state and of southern and international businesses. In return, the government allowed the party to establish political hegemony over the region. Internal disputes, however, plagued the party, and by the 1970s it split into two factions. The split was not ideologically based, as both factions had the military regime's confidence. The split merely represented two elite groups fighting for power (cited in Emmi 1985).

ARENA's political control extended into Gurupá where one political faction used its support, and that of the military government, to gain and maintain political control of the municipality. This faction carefully followed the social and development policies of the military regime by facilitating domestic and international businesses' access to natural resources and labor while quelling local social dissent. In the following sections I will discuss the relation of this faction to the traditional political elite and its place within the social class system, as well as its role in the local political process.

Social Class in Gurupá

Until recently, a small local dominant class has controlled the political system of Gurupá. From my consultants' and my own estimates, this class accounts for approximately 5 percent of the municipality's population. I determined that the dominant class consists of two divisions that are rarely mutually exclusive. The first consists of merchants and large landowners. The major source of power for this division, as discussed in Chapter 5, is the control of exchange and, to a lesser extent, control of land. The merchant and large landowning members organize, control, and expropriate wealth from their workers through the institutions of credit-debt lending and patron-client relationships. The second division of the dominant class in Gurupá consists of a few professionals residing in town (judges, lawyers, doctors) and civil servants. The latter are always relatives or friends of the merchant and landowning families. The professionals and civil servants control access to government jobs, government services, and government revenue, as well as having considerable influence within the local legal system. Usually, the two divisions of the dominant class pool their resources to further the interests of the class and to maintain the political status quo.

Subordinate to the political apparatus of the dominant class is a large and diverse working class, which accounts for approximately 95 percent of the municipality's population. The working class consists of people who engage in some type of manual labor as their principal form of livelihood. People in this class operate under a patrão (trading post owner or landowner), a wage employer who controls exchange or access to the means of production, or are autonomous. As discussed previously, the working class consists of four divisions and one subdivision, a delineation based on my observations. People in Gurupá, however, do not necessarily distinguish these groups.

The first division consists of the poor town dwellers who are employed part-time or underemployed in wage labor, and/or seasonally employed in extraction and/or farming. Wage labor jobs held by these urban poor include lumber production in sawmills, semiskilled artisan jobs such as carpentry and masonry, unskilled municipal jobs such as street cleaners, weeders, and garbage collectors, and other service-sector jobs such as maids, cooks, nannies, and laundresses. The second division of the working class consists of landless fregueses. These people farm or extract for a landlord/trading post merchant. The third division includes the autonomous terra firme farmers on unowned land. These independent farmers still maintain close ties to a trading post merchant and often migrate seasonally to extract for that trading post merchant. The fourth division consists of the small landowners. These small landowners engage in extraction and farming.

Finally, the one subdivision that crosscuts the other working-class divisions is that of the brokers. The brokers live in both the rural and urban areas. They engage in extraction, farming, and wage labor under a dominant-class patrão. However, they also function as modest, small-scale merchants, moneylenders, and intermediaries between their fellow workers and patrões over matters of produce exchange and land access.

None of the four divisions of the working class is mutually exclusive. Individuals often change membership in them several times during a lifetime. This occurs most frequently among the urban poor, landless freguês, and terra firme farming divisions. Despite this fluidness the working class is still differentiated and segmented in terms of political behavior. In general the urban poor and landless fregueses tend to submit more readily to the economic and political demands of their patrões if they have one. Their conservative behavior is due to their relatively powerless position vis-à-vis their patrões, who control access to the means of subsistence and the means of exchange. Less submissive, but not totally autonomous in action, are the independent terra firme farmers on unowned land. These people have freedom of access to the means of subsistence but are dependent on patrões for exchange. Politically, these farmers' actions range widely from conservative to radical depending on individual circumstances.

The small landowner division, by contrast, is the most independent in action. These landowners control the means of subsistence, often on the economically valuable várzea. There is some pressure on this group to submit to the wishes of the trading post patrão who controls exchange. However, the small landowners are in a better position to resist these conservative influences, especially since the timber boom and rubber resurgence have increased their wealth. At the same time there is the potential for highly successful small landowners to increase landholdings, recruit fregueses to work for them, and establish trading posts. Through this mobility a few small landowners enter the merchant/landowner division of the dominant class—defined as those people controlling production or exchange of their workers. This limited potential for mobility, superimposed upon the relative freedom of political action, divides the small landowners into a small conservative faction aligned with the dominant class and a larger radical faction pursuing its own interests.

Freedom of economic and political action is an important element in political change within the working class. As I show in the next chapter, the direction and intensity of change depends on both a group's ability to resist the dominant class and its ability to unite individuals with conflicting class interests. A key to this process is the leadership of the broker subdivision. The brokers are instrumental in persuading their followers to participate or to not participate in the political resistance movements.

The dominant social class in Gurupá during the 1980s consisted of no more than thirty to forty families. These families were set apart from other classes by their control over the means of production and exchange. In terms of wealth, education, appearance, or customs, however, the distinction between the dominant class and the working class was hard to discern, especially for outsiders such as myself visiting the community. This is the result of years of economic depression and impoverishment of elites, as discussed previously.

In the 1980s I found no one using the phrase "gente de primeira" (people of the first, or upper, class) in Gurupá, as observed by Wagley (1976:104–105). Many people insist that there is no class system left. In the "folk" view everyone is considered equal, although there are individuals who fare better in material wealth and prestige than others. Other Gurupaenses remain aware of class relationships but demote the dominant class to the classification of gente de segunda (people of the second class) along with the working class. They still recognize the "superiority" of the dominant class by calling it *gente de primeiro seleção* (people of the first selection), *gente formada* (educated or mannered people), or simply *comerciantes* (merchants). They call the working class *gente de segundo seleção* (people of the second selection) or *lavradores* (specifically, manual laborers in agriculture, but in Gurupá people expand the meaning to include extractors as well).

Despite the blurred distinction among classes by both local residents and outside visitors, when I systematically observed social behavior I found careful maintenance of class boundaries among most groups (class boundaries between some small landowners and merchants/large landowners are less well maintained). These observations were not difficult to make, as I was categorized as "upper class" in local terms and received differential treatment. Common examples of class maintenance I found include addressing a superior as Seu or Senhor (mister or sir) and Dona or Senhora (mistress or madam). It is also a common practice for individuals of "low status" to avoid direct eye contact with "superiors," to sit on the floor and offer chairs to superiors, and to experience vergonha (shame) in the presence of superiors.

People also maintained social distance during indoor and outdoor public festivals. Prominent individuals pay relatively high fees (over U.S.$2) to rent tables and chairs while the poor have to stand. In addition, people maintain class distinctions by dance hall patronization. Several dance halls have gained reputations for catering to higher-status individuals or to lower-status individuals. For example, people commented to me about the smugness of the one elite dance hall and the high entrance fee charged to separate the poor from the rich. Other people commented about the rowdiness of the various poor dance halls where every dance is sure to bring on a fight.

Another example of maintenance of class distinctions involves skyrocket displays during religious processions. As discussed in Chapter 7, shooting skyrockets is a traditional method of paying homage to the saints. People typically fire them from riverboats passing the church of Gurupá to pay a promesa to Saint Benedict for a safe journey. In addition, people use them during processions to pay promesas and to honor the saint. Given the importance and visibility of the skyrockets, in 1986 a few prominent families decided to improve the status of the Saint Anthony procession (the saint of many town elites) vis-à-vis the Saint Benedict procession (the saint of the poor) by buying and setting off several hundred skyrockets. The expensive fireworks display, which consisted of nearly fifteen minutes of solid rapid-fire explosions, surpassed the corresponding display for Saint Benedict. I interpreted this event as symbolically demonstrating Saint Anthony's superiority and, by extension, the elite's superiority in Gurupá. When I suggested this interpretation to some of my dominant-class consultants, however, they disagreed.

The Politics of the Dominant Social Class

Of the approximately thirty families that make up the dominant class in Gurupá only eight are active politically in that they campaign for political parties and run for office. These families form an inner circle of power within the municipality. The inner circle, however, does not always function harmoniously. There are frequent squabbles and even open hostilities among factions. The conflicts within the inner circle are usually personal or family disputes, or disputes over access to resources. Rarely are there major ideological differences.

The extent to which the dominant class' squabbles were manifested

varied throughout my research period. Before and after the military dictatorship the squabbles were commonplace. During the dictatorship, however, dissent was strongly curtailed, as one faction in Gurupá seized and
maintained political control. One man, Alberto Viana, headed this faction.
Alberto used his connections to the regional, and by extension, national,
regime to become the virtual *coronel* (town boss) of Gurupá.

Alberto Viana is from one of Gurupá's "fallen" aristocratic families.
His mother, Dona Branquinha, was the prim and proper schoolteacher and
the church *beata* (overseer) described by Wagley (1976:106–109, 121–122,
157, 167–168). Since the 1940s the Viana family has maintained its position in the dominant class through landholdings in the interior and a trading
post in town. Alberto's father also ran the telegraph station in town. Alberto
entered politics while still young. He was active within the newly formed
ARENA Party immediately following the military's seizure of power.
Because of his political connections and his willingness to align himself
with national and international businesses entering the area, ARENA
appointed Alberto *prefeito* (mayor) of Gurupá in 1966. Once in office he
consolidated power by ingeniously using personal persuasion and the
repressive powers given him by the new government. A diverse cohort of
his supporters and detractors told me that by the end of his first term as
mayor, Alberto had co-opted or silenced his opposition.

Alberto used a variety of legal and extralegal methods to maintain
political power. All were typical actions politicians took throughout Brazil
at the time. For example, people in Gurupá told me of several positive
enticements he allegedly offered to gain allies. He procured funding for
projects favored by elite families such as the timber extracting road into the
interior. He kept a supply of cash on hand to buy support or quiet dissent.
He also controlled access to most government jobs, which he strategically
handed out to supporters. Alberto was careful to fill most of the government positions with individuals he could easily manipulate. In this way he
was assured of minimal competition or resistance from within his administration.

At the same time Alberto had many methods for retaliating against
those who opposed him. For example, people openly alleged that he manipulated local tax laws and seized opponents' land or store merchandise for
back taxes. Others alleged that he blocked payment of delinquent taxes by
his rivals by arranging for the local tax collector to refuse to accept payment. The only recourse for his rivals was to travel to Belém to pay back
taxes. Other alleged methods of retaliation against opponents included
using the local police to intimidate them. He also had access to the federal
police, which he used to ensnare the troublesome local priest on several
occasions.

After Alberto's first term as mayor his acquired political power
allowed him to control Gurupá's ruling party and to handpick his successor

in 1971. Alberto remained in the government, strategically positioned as the municipal secretary. From this office people maintain that he controlled the mayor's actions. During the following administration, 1973–1976, internal dissension and the split in the regional ARENA Party turned Alberto against the mayor he had initially supported (see Miller 1976:321–322). However, by 1976 Alberto regained political control and was elected mayor again. One of his first actions was to stop all the projects of the previous administration, a common practice in Brazilian politics. Of particular note was the discontinuation of the street-paving project after only two streets were completed. The cement purchased for the additional two streets and various cross streets was left unused and hardened in the humidity of the rainy season.

By Alberto's second term as mayor his reputation for total command of the local political system and his extensive corruption had become legendary. People told me of state and federal grant appropriations released to Gurupá for construction of a new municipal dock, a sewer system, street paving, a school in the interior, and a small sports center. Little or nothing was done to complete these projects, yet the money disappeared. Another scandal involved the regular delaying of government pay to municipal employees. Many municipal employees reported that Alberto withheld this money for up to three months at a time while investing the money in Belém for a nice profit. When he finally issued the delinquent pay, it was usually less than the amount owed. In one extreme case Alberto managed to avoid paying the vice mayor's salary for six years. Alberto took these alleged wage-skimming rights so seriously that he swore to many people that he would leave Gurupá if ever a bank were established in the municipality to directly distribute wages. Alberto was also rumored to have used municipal funds and workers to clear land and plant pasture on his property. In addition, various people made allegations that he appropriated much of the municipality's machinery and spare parts for his own use.

Alberto took a special interest in interacting with timber, palmito, and Petrobrás firms. He encouraged them to operate in Gurupá and then provided them with numerous favors. For example, in Gurupá it is common knowledge among the people that Alberto persistently pressured the local notary public to speed up land purchases and property titles for Brumasa. In addition, there were several cases of individuals resisting the company's land appropriations and timber-extraction activities who received messages from Alberto demanding them to give in to the company. I saw one of these letters.

In return for such favors, several companies allowed Alberto to become their principal business intermediary. In the case of Petrobrás Alberto became a local labor recruiter. He used this position for political purposes, reminding recruiters that he gave them a job as a favor. This favor needed to be repaid through political support during election times.

I interviewed Alberto in 1983 in Belém before my first trip to Gurupá. When rereading my notes of this interview to prepare this book I was surprised that Alberto had repeatedly complained about outside economic forces, particularly U.S.-based multinational corporations. He said that the multinationals were robbing Gurupá of its wealth. Always the politician, he never mentioned to me that he was a labor recruiter for the multinationals.

Through Alberto's access to government funds and his dealings with various extraction companies he amassed a sizable amount of capital. Outward signs of his prosperity in Gurupá were found in his extensive landholdings and in his ownership of a sawmill, a bakery (the largest in town), a truck, and an expensive house (by local standards). In Belém he maintained a second house, cars for his children, and for a while a small fleet of taxis. He educated his children and, through the help of the state governor, obtained a prestigious government job in the nation's capital of Brasília for one son.

Alberto's critics pointed out to me that he did his best to keep Gurupá subservient to his control. He understood that as long as Gurupá remained isolated and underdeveloped (except for extraction activities) he could prolong his political hegemony. Toward this end people alleged that Alberto used his power to prevent or postpone the establishment of banks, diesel stations, and better port facilities, and he even discouraged the construction of a connecting road to the Transamazon Highway.

Alberto's undisputed control of Gurupá continued into the early 1980s. At this point, however, major shifts in local, regional, and national politics abrogated his power. I discuss these shifts below.

The Political *Abertura* and the New Republic

By the late 1970s and early 1980s the military regime had initiated a gradual lifting of some aspects of its authoritarian rule en route to a transfer of power to a civilian government by 1985. This political *abertura* (opening) was a response to growing dissatisfaction within the dominant class with the exclusionary political and economic policies of the regime, widespread corruption, the worsening economic status of Brazil, and persistent popular resistance—increasingly organized by the Catholic Church. The military regime began reducing censorship of the media and allowed the formation of opposition political parties for local municipal and city elections in 1982. By 1985 the military allowed the Senate to elect the first civilian president in twenty years, Tancredo Neves, who died before taking office. Neves's vice president, José Sarney, replaced him. Several civilian governments have followed since.

In Pará, as in the rest of Brazil, the abertura led to a proliferation of political parties. The Partido Democrático Social (Social Democratic

Party), or PDS, replaced the ARENA Party as the principal supporter of the status quo. However, defections from the party along old factional lines led to its defeat in the next Pará elections. The major opposition party to the military rule, the Partido do Movimento Democrático do Brasil (Democratic Movement Party of Brazil), or PMDB, took control. Between 1982 and 1985 there were a growing number of political conversions from the PDS to the PMDB throughout Amazonia. This was part of a national trend that eventually led to the election of opposition candidate Tancredo Neves.

Several other political parties formed during this time. One of particular note, both nationally and in Gurupá, was the aforementioned Partido dos Trabalhadores (Workers' Party), or PT. The PT formed in the industrial sectors of São Paulo where it had strong ties to labor unions and the progressive sector of the Catholic Church (discussed in the next chapter). Its political agenda emphasized workers' rights, correcting Brazil's income disparity, and later on, land reform.

In Gurupá these political shifts greatly affected Alberto's undisputed control of municipal politics. The demilitarization of the national government led to a decrease in local censorship, political restrictions, and repression. Without these types of extralocal support Alberto's ability to govern declined (this was a major reason people were so willing to tell me of his alleged misdeeds). By the early 1980s Alberto had to resort to creative political shenanigans to preserve power. One instance of this was his manipulation of the formation of the PMDB: He actually encouraged one of his political underlings to found the party in Gurupá, and he was even rumored to have helped complete the complicated forms required for party formation. With his own man leading the opposition party, Alberto was assured of a weak opposition.

Similarly, Alberto persuaded Cecília Porto Albuquerque, daughter of the former mayor Jorge Porto (see Wagley 1976:150) and a popular figure among the local population, to run for mayor in his new party, the PDS. Using her family's good name, her popularity, and Alberto's backing, she overcame strong gender prejudice and a field of eight candidates from three parties to win the 1982 mayoral election. The candidate from the PT actually received the most votes, but a law allowing the leading candidates to pick up votes from defeated candidates in their own parties gave Cecília the needed cumulative total for victory.

Despite Alberto's success in the 1982 elections, part of his power base had been permanently lost because of the abertura, as it greatly restricted his ability to contain opposition through police harassment, tax manipulation, and judicial noninterference. Alberto's loss of repressive powers enabled many silenced enemies to retaliate for the first time in eighteen years. Immediately following the elections the opposition members of the new town council made a motion for a state inquiry to audit past government expenditure abuses. Several of my key consultants told me that Alberto used his political connections in Belém and Gurupá to stop the inquiry. However, the mere fact that his opponents made such a public motion indicated that Alberto's political power was deteriorating. Changes in the state government to the opposition party, the PMDB, also weakened Alberto, as he remained loyal to the PDS. His administration received few state funds and favors from the opposition's governor.

A third major blow to Alberto's political power was a schism that developed between him and his handpicked successor, Cecília. Before being elected mayor Cecília had worked in the FUNRURAL office, administering retired workers' pensions. Since she had no political background and was from a family closely aligned with Alberto, the outgoing mayor hoped to manipulate her and essentially run the prefeitura as he had in earlier years. Toward this end, after Cecília's inauguration, Alberto was still directing government business and asking municipal workers to report to him before seeing Cecília. Alberto even persuaded Cecília to pay off the debts he had accumulated while in office—the same debts that Alberto's opponents wished to investigate for possible charges of embezzlement.

By 1983 Cecília and her husband grew tired of Alberto's interference. Cecília's husband and Alberto got into a heated argument, and they exchanged death threats. From that point on Cecília's administration distanced itself from Alberto. In retaliation Alberto used his political influence to create problems for Cecília. One example involved the 1985 election for president of the municipal council. The council consisted of four members from the PDS and three members from opposition parties. Cecília's party, the PDS, had the majority and would have won if not for Alberto's heavy-handed pressure on one *vereador* (council member) from the PDS to vote for the opposition candidate. The victory for the opposition candidate caused considerable embarrassment for Cecília and for the PDS.

In 1988 Esmarelda Madeira, Cecília's vice mayor, won the mayoral elections. Esmarelda was from a family closely associated with Alberto's. Not surprisingly, she found room for him in her administration as municipal secretary. This created further strains within the dominant class since most felt the position should have gone to the outgoing mayor, Cecília.

The combined effects of the demilitarization of government and the abertura, the end of local repression, the ascension of the opposition party nationally and regionally, and the personal schisms within the PDS were important in breaking Alberto's political hold on Gurupá. If there had been no other mitigating events the political system would likely have returned to one controlled by a number of competing factions within the dominant social class. However, the rise of a camponês political movement, organized through the PT, the rural union, and the Catholic Church, created changes that significantly altered the traditional political and economic power structures of Gurupá.

The Origins of the Workers' Party

Until the late 1980s the PT's national political agenda clearly emphasized problems associated with the urban industrial labor force. There was no clear link to rural concerns of small farmers, such as land reform or food-production problems. The rise of the PT in Gurupá, therefore, might appear to have been a peculiar occurrence. Two factors, however, account for the party's rise: the lack of a true opposition party because of Alberto's alleged manipulation of the PMDB and the influence of the Catholic Church among the indigenous camponeses.

The role of the Catholic Church was the critical factor in bringing the PT to Gurupá. The local church had labored for years to raise the political consciousness of the indigenous camponês class in an attempt to have the people "liberate" themselves from oppression and poverty (see the next chapter for details). As this endeavor started to succeed, members of the fledgling movement sought alternative avenues for political activism. Through involvement in regional and national union meetings, political conferences, and church assemblies, many individuals came into contact with members of the PT. During this period the PT was gaining considerable strength in the south of Brazil. By the late 1980s and early 1990s the party began to win legislative positions in state and federal assemblies and important mayorships—including São Paulo's—and it had made a very strong run for president of Brazil.

When the Gurupaenses learned of the ideological and political agenda of the PT they recognized common, if somewhat vague, goals and became interested. The PT, in turn, encouraged the Gurupaenses to form their own branch of the party. With the aid of PT representatives in Belém, Gurupá established its own PT in time for the 1982 elections.

Gurupá's PT developed a vague platform for political economic reform. The leaders talked generally of promoting small-producer agriculture through loan programs and by obtaining technical advice. They mentioned organizing a market cooperative to distribute manioc and other commodities produced on the mainland to the islands of Gurupá. The cooperative would bypass trading posts and develop an internal market for agricultural goods. The leaders also talked of support for rural workers in securing land rights. However, the bulk of the PT's campaign rhetoric consisted of critiques of the dominant class' privileged position in Gurupá and its abuse of power. In particular, they focused on Alberto Viana and the well-known allegations of corruption against him. The PT promised that under its administration misappropriation of funds, abuse of payrolls, and political favoritism would not occur.

The reason the PT had such a vague platform was due in part to the national composition of the party. Throughout much of the 1980s the PT remained essentially an urban-based party dealing with problems of the industrial labor sector. The party's line on agrarian problems was undeveloped. By the mid-1980s critics maintain that the party's line on agrarian problems eventually became insensitive to peasant issues (Henfrey 1986:15). This void in party ideology forced the PT of Gurupá to borrow heavily from other institutions, such as rural unions and the Catholic Church, to formulate its views on agrarian problems.

Despite this problem of an unclear platform, Gurupá's party has had little trouble attracting its sizable following—about 40 percent of the eligible electorate according to election results. The PT's remarkable success in voter recruitment stems from several factors. One is the increasing threat to the camponês livelihood posed through increases in resource depletion (oleaginous seeds, açaí, timber). The second is fear of dispossession from land. This threat overcomes the traditional segmentation of the camponês class, particularly among the small landowners, the independent terra firme farmers, and to a lesser degree, the landless fregueses. The urban poor suffer from these problems too, but they tend to intensify ties to the dominant class to overcome these pressures. The party also has grown rapidly because it can align itself to preexisting grassroots organizations found within the Catholic Church (see next chapter for details). Finally, the PT is strong because it is the only viable alternative to the dominant-class-oriented PDS and PMBD.

In the 1982 elections the PT presented a full slate of candidates. For mayor they chose Renato Fonseca. Renato is a well-liked manioc farmer and extractor from the interior. In the mid-1970s he came to live in town and worked as a caretaker in the church. When I interviewed him, Renato told me that initially Alberto had asked him to serve in ARENA and run for council member. Renato declined, preferring to remain apolitical at the time. Renato continued working in the church and soon got a position in the archives. By this time Renato's direct exposure to the church and its progressive message had effectively politicized him. He became an active catechist and obtained a good understanding of social Catholicism. In the padre's absence he often held services in the main church. He became very visible to the public.

When the PT formed, Renato decided to work in its directorate. Alberto, upon learning this, rebuffed Renato, saying he felt he had lost a son. Nevertheless, Renato continued his endeavors. When candidates for political office were being chosen, Renato seemed an attractive candidate. The PT drafted him to run for mayor. He left his church job during the campaign but still preached in church. Renato's opponents in the mayoral elections sharply criticized his close association with the church, charging that he used Mass to campaign for votes.

In the mayoral elections Cecília of the PDS won by combining the total sum of PDS votes (which included those for three other candidates).

Renato, however, received the greatest number of votes for a single candidate. The PT also made impressive showings in the council member race, winning two of the seven seats. These political gains profoundly altered the status quo in Gurupá. The dominant class, weakened economically by years of inflation and depression, now found its political hegemony broken and its very future in question. By the next round of elections in 1988 the PT did even better, capturing four of the nine council member seats. It failed to win the mayor's office because three political parties pooled their votes for one candidate, Esmarelda. Gurupá did have the distinction, people told me, of being the only municipality in Pará that voted for the national PT candidate for president—Lula—in both the initial and runoff elections.

The mounting success of the PT has created a number of reactions within the dominant class. At one extreme some members of the dominant class now seek to make amends with the Workers' Party, particularly Alberto Viana. With the rise of the PT Alberto has lost considerable power. On the one hand, this has occurred because the PT has heavily eroded Alberto's following in the interior. On the other hand, the extensive allegations of corruption and political abuse against Alberto have gained him many enemies within the dominant class. After the break with Cecília, Alberto's support dwindled even further. Being a clever politician, Alberto attempted to regroup his support by aligning himself with the PT, at least in appearances. Toward this end he asked the party for forgiveness and began broadcasting sympathetic messages about the PT over loudspeakers. The PT, however, completely rejected Alberto's ploy. In fact, the party directorate passed a resolution protesting Alberto's disguised interference in its affairs.

At the other extreme several members of the dominant class have intensified their criticism of the PT. They persistently label the party "communist" and warn the public that the communists will commit atrocities if elected. Among the absurd rumors spread about the PT were that it would take away all individually owned land, it would appropriate all production, and it would rape women. Many landowners put increased pressure on fregueses to break with the party.

The Struggle for the Rural Union

Following the elections of 1982 members of the PT, and more generally of the camponês movement, understood the dominant class' weakened position and thus intensified their drive for reform. The next step was to gain control of the Sindicato Rural, the rural workers' union. The rural union formed in 1976. It was part of the military government's efforts to co-opt rural workers into a controlled, corporate organization. Through a controlled union the government hoped to avoid the rebirth of the peasant leagues that had effectively mobilized workers in the northeast just before the 1964 revolution.

The rural union formed in Gurupá was a small and decidedly pro–status quo organization, as its function favored the dominant class' interests. Active membership in the union accounted for less than 8 percent of eligible rural workers in the municipality. During this time the union allied itself on the national level with the somewhat conservative CONCLAT (Conferência Nacional das Classes Trabalhadores, or National Conference of the Working Classes), now renamed the CGT (Confederação Geral do Trabalho, or General Labor Confederation). The union functioned as a beneficiary organization, providing sick members access to specific hospital facilities in Belém, and as a referral service for individuals with landownership problems. As such members were directed to land titling agencies (INCRA and Instituto da Terra do Pará [ITERPA], or Pará Land Institute) in Breves and Belém. The union, however, offered little counseling on legal matters, offered no financial aid for legal fees, and took no active stance on questions of occupant land rights. Because of the lack of services provided by the union and the high cost of monthly dues (approximately U.S.$1 per month), only 1,058 workers were paying members by 1983.

For several years individuals within the camponês movement had been interested in controlling the union and redirecting its functions. They had learned that the union could be an important tool in combating dominant-class hegemony and promoting camponês prosperity. They had witnessed examples of rural unions along the Transamazon Highway, in the Bragatine area east of Belém, and in Santarém. These unions actively pursued working-class interests through legal defense of occupant land rights, through organization of market cooperatives, and through technical advice for small-farmer production. These Gurupá union members wanted the union to work actively to secure occupant land rights and indemnification rights; to form a farmer/extractor-controlled cooperative to buy and sell goods directly in Belém, bypassing the trading posts; to contract an agricultural extension agent for technical advice on farming; and to find a financial institution to provide small-farmer loans. This faction within the union aligned itself to the more progressive and PT/church-aligned Central Única do Trabalho (CUT), or Unified Labor Center.

The first attempt by the camponês movement to wrest control of the rural union from the state apparatus occurred in 1982. They lost the elections, as a union slate (*Chapa Uma*) aligned with the dominant class won. The camponês movement charged the elections were unfair because of illegal activities by members of the dominant class: patrões pressuring fregueses to vote against the camponês movement, patrões buying votes, and the mayor calling in federal police to intimidate union voters.

Despite the defeat, the leaders of the camponês movement learned a valuable lesson on political tactics. In preparation for the next union elections they conducted a registration drive to recruit more rural workers. Once registered, the camponês movement regularly kept after members to pay their dues to retain voter eligibility. By early 1986 the leaders of the camponês movement estimated they had 1,700 registered voters, while the conservative faction could claim only 700. The camponês movement presented its slate for elections (Slate Two) and circulated its views on how the union should function.

At this point several political leaders from the dominant class realized the imminence of defeat in the upcoming elections. This defeat, they felt, would be an unacceptable blow to their already faltering influence. The dominant class was also receiving warnings from outside political sources (state senators, PDS and PMDB party headquarters) not to let Slate Two of the camponês movement win. The battle lines had to be drawn immediately. But the dominant class had few legal methods to stop the slate. The deadline for registration and eligibility to vote in the upcoming elections had already passed. Union rules specified that individuals must join and pay their dues for six months prior to elections to be eligible to vote.

Since the elections were less than six months away, dominant-class members could not legally recruit any new members. Instead, they had to rely on pressuring or bribing current members. In the past they accomplished this by relying on patron-client ties to produce votes. However, as shown earlier, inflation, depression, and the camponês resistance had weakened many patron-client ties. As a result the dominant class could not muster enough votes through traditional methods. Facing certain defeat, some members of the dominant class turned to a poorly planned, poorly executed, and poorly concealed attempt to falsify the voter register.

The outgoing president of the rural union, Antônio Pinto, performed the voter registration fraud. He was a confidant of one faction of the local elite that had helped him get elected in 1982. Politically, he was a member of the PMDB. In March 1986 Antônio began to systematically alter voter registration forms (fichas). He had much work to do since Slate Two had nearly a three-to-one lead on Slate One. Antônio used several methods to falsify fichas. For example, he failed to record dues paid, he failed to process fichas, he falsified information, and he simply lost fichas. To increase conservative voters' membership supporting Slate One, he kept registering workers to vote past the voting deadline.

Antônio was not adept at secretly falsifying forms. He openly changed records during working hours in the rural union headquarters. This callousness allowed others to discover his actions. A member of the camponês movement was in the union headquarters and noticed Antônio processing fichas for voting status after the voter deadline. This individual immediately reported his observation to several leaders of the movement. Among these leaders were several union delegados, or delegates. A group of twenty men, all members of the union, decided to investigate. They sent a message to the judge informing her of their activities. The judge was out of town, so they forwarded the message to the mayor and then went to the union head-quarters to ask about the alleged improprieties.

One of the men who went to the union recounted the following sequence of events to me. He said that upon entering the building the twenty men demanded a meeting with the union president. Antônio refused, saying he was busy. Nevertheless, the men pressed Antônio to answer questions about late registration. Antônio panicked and grabbed a stack of thirty-three voter fichas and attempted to tear them up. The stack was too thick to tear and the group of men restrained Antônio and saved the fichas. The fichas were all irregular and were being processed after the deadline. Antônio fled the union unharmed.

Upon searching the building the twenty men found numerous improprieties that clearly exposed the registration scandal, along with several other irregularities. For example, registration books (as opposed to fichas) were either out of date or destroyed by termites. The union staff had not maintained records of dues paid or of expenditures. More critical for the elections, voter fichas were in complete disarray. They found only 1,280 fichas out of an estimated total 2,400. Of these, only 225 were appropriately processed. Nearly all of the 225 were of supporters of Slate One.

Francisco Teixeira, a farmer/extractor of the rural hamlet of Camutá, was one of the men examining the union records. From Francisco's neighborhood chapter alone he found forty members inexplicably taken off the voting list. The union disqualified Francisco because it classified him as a truck driver and therefore belonging to another union. Francisco knew how to drive a logging truck his hamlet possessed, but he claimed this hardly disqualified him from the rural workers' union. The men also found that names, photos, and signatures on forms did not match.

Immediately following the search of the union the news spread through town, and people began to amass around the union building. The crowd exchanged accusations, and arguments grew more intense. Slate Two representatives declared Slate One to be in violation of election rules and claimed the union. Members of Slate One alleged the Slate Two people had illegally entered the building and seized material. Slate One also charged that Slate Two was behind the fraud, that Antônio had been roughed up, and that Slate Two had stolen money from the union during the intrusion.

The police arrived to restore order at the union. They arrested members of Slate Two and even arrested the local priest who had come to support the camponês movement and Slate Two. These arrests and the apparently trumped up charges infuriated the Slate Two followers. A few of the members talked of taking radical action such as taking over the town hall and the meat market. The majority restrained these individuals. Once the police released the padre, he too called for calmness.

After the turmoil of arrests had settled down, the Slate Two leaders became suspicious that someone might destroy evidence of the fraud if they did not protect it. As a precaution they photographed all the evidence and then sealed it in a bag held under their protection. Still fears remained that the conservative faction might attempt to take over the union organization. As a second precaution members of the camponês movement decided to occupy the union building and make sure the conservative faction did not take control. What followed from this point on was an impressive show of strength and organization by the movement. Leaders of the camponês movement called upon their members to send volunteers, food, and money to support the union occupation. The rural union in Santarém, unions from São Paulo, CUT, and the Catholic Church also sent aid. For the next fifty-four days—March 25 to May 17, 1986—a hundred or more women and men kept a constant vigil on the union building. They camped inside or around the union building, forming a human barrier to protect it and its records.

The union occupation shocked and polarized the town of Gurupá. The mayor reacted and called for the federal police. In response, only six soldiers flew in from Santarém. It appears that the military did not take Gurupá's disturbance too seriously, although they did come prepared with tear gas. Once in town the soldiers kept clear of the union. They did not wish to incite violence since the union protesters clearly outnumbered them.

As the union occupation progressed, counterdemonstrations by supporters of the conservative forces occurred. These consisted of shouting insults and throwing rocks and bottles at the union building. Many attacks occurred late at night after dances by drunken men. Other forms of harassment included tearing down a wooden fence surrounding the union building, putting up banners with anti-PT and anti–Slate Two slogans, making death threats to Slate Two candidates and the padre, and the sinking of the padre's boat, which had become a symbol of the camponês movement. The boat, named *Livramento* (Deliverance), was the padre's principal means of communicating with the scattered rural workers. The boat disappeared one night. Upon inspection it was found that someone had cut one of the mooring ropes. The local police conducted an investigation, but predictably, it yielded no information. The local people later hailed the boat's recovery and restoration as a miracle effected by Saint Benedict, the community's most revered and popular saint. The priest's already strong appeal to the masses grew even greater.

The leaders of the camponês movement told their members not to respond to provocation or harassment. They intended the union occupation to be a form of passive, nonviolent resistance. However, the movement members were minimally prepared to defend themselves if violence occurred. But as it turned out the union occupation was indeed a nonviolent affair.

From the outset of the conflict Slate Two had tried to use political channels within the union to settle the matter. They immediately informed the regional union representative located in Breves of the fraud. The representative, however, was a member of CONCLAT and the PMDB and thus opposed to the Slate Two workers who were members of CUT and the PT. The representative at first refused to review the matter. The Slate Two leaders then decided to take the fraud evidence directly to the union headquarters in Belém. In Belém the upper-level union officials refused to meet with the leaders, so they decided to returned to Gurupá. At this point Slate Two resolved to continue the union occupation until the Belém representatives took action. This persistence, plus media exposure of the problem in a Belém newspaper, finally forced the regional union representative in Breves to send an investigating team. Upon reviewing the evidence the team concluded there was definite election fraud and that Slate One's allegations were unfounded. They sent these conclusions to Breves where they disappeared, probably because the conclusions were very embarrassing for the union hierarchy, who were CONCLAT/CGT aligned and therefore hesitant to aid CUT-aligned protesters in Gurupá. The Breves union representatives took no legal action.

Before leaving Gurupá the investigating team suggested that Slate Two proceed to organize a union convention to elect members. In this way they could have a functioning union while the union hierarchy decided legal matters. Slate Two took the advice of the investigators and held a convention. Several thousand people attended. They held a massive march that flooded Gurupá's streets with an estimated 4,000 protestors, a number that further shocked the dominant class, as it underlined the strength of the movement. At the convention Slate Two candidates were elected to office. They sent the results to Breves. The Breves representative, however, refused to accept the results. Instead, the representative asked both union factions to send her a list of candidates. From this list she would choose an interim union board until the union could rectify registration problems and hold sanctioned elections. Predictably, the representative chose two Slate One candidates for president and secretary. One Slate Two candidate was chosen for treasurer.

After the selection Slate Two ended its union occupation. Yet it kept a strong presence in the union to monitor voter reregistration. This presence intimidated the two Slate One appointees, who then refused to take office. Both men were inexperienced with union matters. Slate One had nominated them since they were closely aligned with the dominant class. The union, however, continued to function with only the lone Slate Two treasurer working. When elections finally took place in 1988, Slate Two easily won and has been in control of the union ever since.

The Future

At the end of my research period the camponês movement had successfully captured the rural union and a variety of political posts. Although it had not won the mayorship, it did have a strong influence on the town council. One local politician estimated that the PT had the largest backing of voters in Gurupá at 40 percent, followed by the PMDB at 35 percent, and the PDS at 25 percent.

Continued success for the camponês movement will depend on its effectiveness in governing once in power. As an opposition movement much of its energy has been spent on consciousness-raising and on criticizing the dominant class. The movement has made many promises that life will be better, landownership secure, and food more plentiful if it is in power. If the leaders of the movement do not fulfill these promises, if expectations are too high, the movement will lose credibility and be greatly weakened.

To fulfill its promises the camponês movement has to overcome a wide range of obstacles. With election to office the PT will likely be an opposition party to the state and federal governments. This means funds and political favors from the federal or state governments will be minimal. Hostile politicians may ignore or indefinitely postpone petitions for doctors, for agricultural agents, for banks offering small-farmer loans, and so forth. Cecília Alburquerque's administration experienced this problem: It asked for many of the same items listed above, but a hostile state government, the PMDB, did not deliver this aid to the PDS mayor. Beyond the political problems there are long-standing social, economic, and ecological obstacles to improved living standards. As discussed previously, predatory extraction resulting in depletion of natural resources, transfer of wealth to the south and overseas, and exploitative patron-client and credit-debt relations have been actively impoverishing the community for four centuries. Reversing these trends will take a radical effort.

Despite these Herculean obstacles, the question still remains, Who will best govern in favor of the camponeses' interests if not the camponês movement? Thus far it has been clear to many Gurupaenses that the dominant class, the state government, and the federal government are unwilling or incapable to so govern. To these people of Gurupá, then, the camponês movement, even with all its faults, seems their best choice.

Carugna's Catholic Church

9

THE POLITICS OF RELIGION

I was very fortunate to be in Brazil during the transition from military rule to civilian government. As the transition neared, all of Brazil rejoiced the end of authoritarian rule. Hopes ran high as the country buzzed with talk of freedom, democracy, and justice. Although future events proved to be more compromising and change painfully slow, if occurring at all, for the moment the country was aglow.

I was in Gurupá on the day the civilian government regained control over the state. There was jubilation in the air, but there was also caution. At the time Gurupá was in the midst of its own tense transition. The political status quo was disintegrating, and new political groups openly vied for control of the municipality. People were not quite sure how the national events would affect local ones or if they would make any difference at all. I remember sitting on the municipal dock with several others listening intensely to the radio. No one spoke, and all appeared to be deep in thought about their immediate future.

The hopes and apprehensions on that day had been building for a long time. In Gurupá, as in all of Brazil, these feelings were rooted in a decades-old struggle to end dictatorship that involved opposition political parties, unions, and the Catholic Church. The church in particular was a key steward of protest when the military government had eliminated all other avenues of resistance. The church's struggle, however, went far beyond a simple desire to end military rule and reestablish the prerevolution political status quo. It called for a new social order. People in Gurupá heeded this call. They initiated an acute redefinition of the political landscape that led to the political and union struggles described in the previous chapter. In this chapter I examine the role of the church in the camponês movement.

Chapter 9 is based on work previously described in *American Ethnologist* 1992.

The Catholic Church as an Opposition Force

The military regime was brutally efficient in eliminating political protest to its rule. By the mid-1970s the only outside challenge to its, and ARENA's, power came from the Catholic Church. Historically, the church aligned itself with the state and dominant classes in both the Amazon and the rest of Brazil. However, following the miliary coup of 1964 several events pushed the church toward active opposition to the military regime. A progressive faction within the church began to dominate the institution's discourse. This faction was highly critical of Brazil's authoritarian capitalism, especially the growing poverty, exploitation, and repression of the working classes.

Led by the progressive faction, the church has pursued a social policy that favors the poor and the working poor. This policy is an inversion of the traditional role of the church—one of defense of the dominant class' interests and privileges in exchange for political power (Follmann 1985:67–68; Salem 1981:21–22). Abandoning its traditional role has been a difficult endeavor met with much resistance outside and inside the church. However, several events occurring in the 1960s and 1970s strengthened the progressive faction's influence over the Brazilian church of today.

First, between 1962 and 1965 Vatican II linked the global Catholic Church's concerns and activities to the plight of the poor. Following Vatican II there has been a new emphasis on lay participation in church activities, a heightened attention to social justice, and an increase in evangelization among the lower classes (Levine and Mainwaring 1989:210).

A second event affecting the church was the military coup in 1964. When the military regime established its decisionmaking apparatus, it completely excluded the church from any decisionmaking role (Salem 1981:35). For the first time in Brazilian history the church had no input into state policy. Adding insult to this situation, the state legalized divorce in 1977, which infuriated even the most pro-state clergy (Bruneau 1982:74).

The final series of events that solidified state opposition was the military's use of repression and violence against the working class and other opposition forces. When progressive church members began to speak out against these abuses, the military regime attacked and slandered them through a sustained policy of demoralization (Martins 1985:24; Branford and Glock 1985:140). Church members, particularly in the Amazon region, suffered intimidation, imprisonment, beatings, torture, deportation, and even murder in numbers unprecedented in Brazilian history (Martins 1985:58). With these attacks the remaining pro-state clergy withdrew their support for the military regime. They allowed the progressive faction to become the principal speaker for the church through such organizations as the Comissão Nacional de Bispos do Brasil (National Council of Brazilian Bishops), or CNBB. What next occurred was a direct church/state standoff.

The church in Pará followed the lead of the national church during the 1960s. By the 1970s there were several local events that further radicalized the progressive clergy. Among these was a series of violent acts to expel occupants from land being turned into cattle ranches near Conceição do Araguaia in the south of Pará. Measures used to expel occupants included beatings, shootings, poisoning of streams, and burning of fields and houses. There were some 200 murders, most unrecorded by the state, between 1969 and 1981 (Foweraker 1981:20). In addition, there was a small guerilla movement in southeastern Pará (São Geraldo, Xambioá, Perdidos, and Boa Vista). Approximately seventy armed individuals operated for three years until a massive military force hunted them down in 1974. A generalized repression against the local population followed the military action. It was carried out by 10,000 to 20,000 military troops occupying the area (Martins 1985:144).

In 1981 another violent event occurred that directly involved the Pará church. In São Geraldo de Araguaia conflict erupted between cattle compa- nies—supported by the local judge, police, and hired guns (*jugunços*)—and camponeses occupying land. Between 1979 and 1981 hired guns and others assassinated forty-five camponeses and made 916 attempts to expel people from land (Movimento Para Libertar os Padres da Amazônia, Movement to Free the Priests of the Amazon, 1981). In August 1981 thirteen rural work- ers assassinated two military police accompanying land surveyors in the area. The workers feared that the land surveying marked the onset of a land invasion. The assassinations sparked massive government retaliation. The military arrested hundreds of people. Among those imprisoned were two French priests working in the area. The government charged the priests with inciting the assassinations through their teachings.

Following the arrests two bishops attempted to intervene in the dispute. The government interrogated the bishops in Belém with the intention of implicating the church in the conflict and condemning it for subversive activity (Foweraker 1981:24). After these events the government denounced the progressive faction of the church as a communist organiza- tion. Many priests throughout the state received threats from right-wing hate groups such as the Comando de Caça aos Comunistas (Communist Hunt Command) and the Comitê do Apoio a Democracia (Committee in Support of Democracy).

In 1983 another event added to the tensions between church and state, an event that had particular significance for the people of Gurupá since it involved their bishop. The incident began when the Abraham Lincoln Sugar Mill, located along the Transamazon Highway, did not pay its sugar- cane cutters for seven months. To force the company to pay, the workers decided to blockade the Transamazon Highway. The bishop of the Xingu attended the blockade. After ten days the military police broke up the blockade. The police singled out and beat the bishop in full view of the workers. There were photographs taken detailing the incident. The military then briefly imprisoned the bishop.

On a national level the church remained the major outspoken opponent of the military regime into the 1980s. The church served as a protective umbrella under which the opposition could organize without excessive government repression. During Mass and during meetings held in churches, participants created a forum for the discussion of politics and resistance to the military regime. In addition, the church actively encouraged popular participation in resistance to the military. It accomplished this by political consciousness-raising (*conscientização*), often through the teaching of liberation theology, which helped develop a class consciousness.

Liberation theology may be characterized as an interpretation of Christian faith from the point of view of the disenfranchised sectors of society (Berryman 1987:4). The disenfranchised include the poor, urban workers, small farmers, ethnic minorities, and other groups suffering from inequality. They are singled out not only because of Christian views on social justice and compassion, but also because many in the church see them as retaining spiritual "richness" that more affluent groups have lost (Azevedo 1986:384). The focus on members of this group has led to the intertwining of traditional goals of spiritual salvation with problems of material suffering because proponents of this view reason that religious influence makes sense only when people have the appropriate living conditions to "feel fully human" (Bruneau 1982:50). Liberation theology, therefore, encompasses a critique of contemporary political and economic structures and calls for social and political enfranchisement of the excluded sectors of society. These sectors will actively work toward enfranchisement, which will require a basic alteration of Brazil's dependent authoritarian capitalism (Follmann 1985:79).

To legitimate the struggle for enfranchisement, proponents of liberation theology interpret passages in the Bible as anti-imperialistic and supportive of struggles against exploitation. For example, in Exodus they view God as the liberator who willed his people to be freed from slavery. In Matthew and Luke they see Jesus Christ as a liberator too. He preached the kingdom of God as spiritual, as well as material, liberation from "hunger, grief, contempt, and so on" (Boff and Boff 1986:26–27). He also led the poor, oppressed, and exploited while denouncing the rich, oppressors, and exploiters (Follmann 1985:41). Followers of liberation theology use these interpretations to educate and motivate the laity to pursue their fundamental human rights. They challenge existing views on social justice, as well as institutional structures of power and authority.

Another important way the church has promoted resistance to military rule is through the formation of ecclesiastical base communities called *comunidades eclesiais de base* (CEBs). CEBs are small, grassroots lay religious groups. Members organize them in many forms ranging from groups specializing in visitation, reflection, and prayer to mothers' clubs, youth clubs, and neighborhood clubs. Catholic theologian Clodovis Boff (1978:51) defines CEBs as small groups wherein the laity develop primary relations within a religious context. CEBs are base communities in the sense that they congregate the poor working class (the base of society). They are also base communities in the sense that they construct a grass-roots Christianity. This form of Christianity is relevant to the context of the local environment and is not imposed upon the masses by the elite church hierarchy. In many, but not all, CEBs, this grassroots Christianity (liberation theology) is critical of contemporary Brazilian society and seeks to demystify exploitation. As Leonardo Boff (Clodovis Boff's brother) wrote, in many CEBs

> one learns there to live with the truth. It is impossible to continue hiding the true social reality. There one calls things by their names. Exploitation is exploitation. Torture is torture. Dictatorship is dictatorship. (Boff 1981:201)

In these progressive CEBs people seek fulfillment of material as well as spiritual needs. Members of the CEBs deal with all the problems the poor suffer: unemployment, low salaries, bad working conditions, lack of basic services, access to land (Boff 1981:201). The CEBs develop various methods to meet some material needs. Among these are mutual aid, mutirão (labor exchanges), collective consumption, health posts, information exchange, communal gardens, cooperatives, and basic education (Follmann 1985:89). The CEBs also promote activism in the form of petitioning the government for such basic services as water and sewage systems, electricity, and health care. Some groups may organize occupation of unused land for the rural and urban landless as well as block eviction of fellows from land (Hewitt 1986:17; Levine and Mainwaring 1989:213; also see Boff 1978:51). At the same time the CEBs direct their members to other groups, including unions and political parties, that participate in promoting workers' rights. Throughout Brazil in the 1980s there were an estimated 80,000 to 100,000 CEBs of which a majority followed the pastoral line of liberation theology.

Regardless of whether individual CEBs are politically conservative or progressive, a long-term political impact results from each, as "the normal practice of CEBs encourages critical discourse, egalitarianism, and experiments in self-governance . . . [thereby] stimulating and legitimating new kinds of leadership and commitment in the larger society" (Levine and Mainwaring 1989:214). The church further aids activism through national organizations such as the Comissão Pastoral da Terra (Pastoral Land Commission), or CPT. This commission helps inform and coordinate CEB actions, give legal advice, and publicize cases of rural violence.

In response to the church's ideology of resistance and political activism (which has resulted in many minor successes), the military regime has repressed the church clergy and laity. The government has imprisoned priests as subversives and has called liberation theology a form of communist propaganda. Even within the church there has been a reactionary movement called "Tradition-Family-Property" (Follmann 1985:76). This movement, part of the Catholic right wing, believes that Marxists have penetrated the church and are trying to destroy it from the inside (Follmann 1985:98).

During the abertura of the 1980s the popular sectors influenced by the Catholic Church and liberation theology became very active in public demands for the end of dictatorship. Many individuals joined opposition political parties. Some joined the major opposition party, the PMDB, while many others joined the Workers' Party (the PT) and pushed for social justice. As mentioned in the previous chapter, industrial workers in São Paulo founded the PT. Its leadership has maintained close ties to both urban labor unions and the progressive sector of the Catholic Church. Because of these ties with the clergy, opponents of the PT have labeled it the "Church's Party."

The Politics of the Camponês Class: Church and CEBs in Gurupá

Gurupá's deteriorating economy, the weakened position of the dominant social class, the increased threat to camponês subsistence from resource depletion, the rising feelings of relative deprivation and frustration, and the abertura set the stage for the rise of the camponês movement. The final ingredient needed for the movement to develop was an organized, structured ideology of activism. Gurupá's Catholic priest, Padre Chico, introduced this ideology. Since the late 1970s Padre Chico has preached the evolving tenets of liberation theology as discussed above. He is highly critical of unjust national and local political economic structures, and he takes an active stand against oppression and class exploitation, organizing workers to fend for themselves. These activities have led him into open confrontation with Gurupá's dominant class.

In my conversations with Padre Chico he told me some of his personal history. He is an Italian-born permanent resident of Brazil who first traveled to Brazil in 1970 and worked near Macapá with poor timber extractors. In 1972 he and a colleague came to Gurupá. A U.S. priest working in Almerim introduced them to the parishioners of the municipality. Padre Chico decided to stay, while his colleague left. He began his work by concentrating on the population in the interior. Using a system developed by the Almerim priest, Padre Chico visited the communities with chapels and brotherhoods and began to reorganize and strengthen them. Also, he encouraged the gradual creation of additional religious communities where none had previously existed.

Over the years Padre Chico worked steadily to raise the politico-religious consciousness of his parishioners. He has used a variety of settings to do this including Masses, CEB services and meetings, religious festivals, and many encounters sponsored by the church: Catechism Week, Catechists Triduum, Worker's Week, Assembly of the People of God, Women's Week, Bible studies, and visits from the bishop, padres, nuns, and lay members of the church. Padre Chico continues to be particularly active in the vast interior. He often spends three weeks of each month traveling and meeting with the people there. Padre Chico also cultivates politico-religious consciousness by sending people to a variety of church-sponsored seminars in Altamira, Santarém, and Belém. The subject of the seminars ranges from land rights to community leadership. During these trips people also contact members of national and regional movements, which serves to further strengthen their understanding and commitment to the cause of social justice.

While in Gurupá I often heard Padre Chico criticize local inequalities during sermons and various discussions. For example, he points out the unfair exchange rates patrões charge their fregueses—rates only a fraction of the market value of the product. He encourages people to form independent cooperatives to bypass trading posts for the sale of produce and purchase of basic necessities. He expounds on land rights abuses of the dominant class and brings in experts from Belém to explain occupants' rights to land. He implores families threatened with expulsion to demand their rights to the land or at least indemnification. He often repeats, "Land belongs to those who make it produce." He attacks political corruption and suppression of human rights, asking people to organize and make politicians accountable for their actions. He also urges rural workers to vote in union elections. He speaks of the rural union as an important tool to resist the dominant class' economic power.

I recall one poignant Mass in 1983 during which the priest's beliefs on religion and politics were forcefully expressed. This sermon was given just after the beating of the local bishop, mentioned earlier. On that day parishioners had posted newspaper reports of the incident on the church. In large cutout letters were the words *violência* (violence) and *ambição* (ambition). As Mass started two men read articles from the regional newspapers and then condemned the violence. During the sermon Padre Chico retold the story of the nonpayment of wages to the sugarcane workers, the blockade of the Transamazon Highway, and the deliberate attack on the bishop. This happened, he reminded everyone, after the governor promised no violence. The priest asked the congregation to pray for all those involved. He then preached emotionally that Jesus Christ stood opposed to such harassment and intimidation during his lifetime. Padre Chico said that to be a good Christian one must fight against this type of oppression. Later, during the intentions, several people offered prayers to support those imprisoned and the workers in their struggle.

During the late 1970s and into the 1980s Padre Chico's words and activism led him into direct confrontation with the local dominant class. Increasingly, church attendance and participation by the dominant class and its associates declined. Dominant-class participation in and financial offerings for religious festivals also declined. Members of the dominant class often complained to me that the padre wished to divide the community between the haves and the have-nots. They accused the padre of preaching communism and of plotting to destroy the wealthier members of Gurupá. They blamed him for inciting workers to take land and resources, particularly açaí and timber, from the "rich." A few outspoken individuals flatly blamed the padre for all of Gurupá's land problems. An article from a regional right-wing newsletter even attacked the padre's activism and labeled him a communist.

An open feud developed between Padre Chico and Alberto Viana, the mayor at that time. Alberto began ridiculing the priest and calling him a communist on the loudspeaker system that broadcasts to the town from his house. During my initial interview with Alberto in 1983 I remember asking him to comment on Padre Chico. He turned red in the face and pounded the table as he repeated several times that it was wrong to mix politics and religion. He quickly changed his mood and laughed heartily when describing how he had given land located directly behind the Catholic Church to the Pentecostal Church. This forced the priest, nuns, and lay church workers to suffer through the Pentecostal's lively and loud services, replete with references to Catholics as idol worshipers and communists.

Twice Alberto called in the federal police to arrest Padre Chico. Alberto charged the padre with breaking national security laws, interfering in politics (which was outlawed for foreigners), and inciting class conflict. The padre responded to the accusations and brought in the bishop of the Xingu to support him. None of the charges stood up, and the padre has continued to preach. However, the embitterment grew. Another round of confrontation occurred in 1986 during rural union elections (described in the previous chapter). Members of the dominant class accused the padre of inciting the occupation. He received death threats from local thugs, and the police briefly imprisoned him. Also during the turmoil someone stole and sank Padre Chico's boat.

Despite the antagonism with the dominant class (or maybe because of it) the padre's popularity has grown among the camponeses. Initially, the Padre was welcome by all rural and many urban poor, who were grateful for the religious services and personalized attention given in their hamlets and neighborhoods. Building upon this positive response the padre encouraged people to form CEBs, also called comunidades by the people of Gurupá.

With the padre's encouragement, parishioners organized sixty-six comunidades by the 1980s; many in the interior were based upon the old religious irmandades (brotherhoods) that have existed for decades (see Galvão 1955:48–58ff.; Wagley 1976:188–190). The padre has expanded the irmandades' membership and functions. The irmandades maintain their patron saint and their community festival in the name of the saint. The padre does insist, however, that dancing and drinking be completely separated spatially and temporally from religious ceremonies. The comunidades are also encouraged to construct chapels and to hold weekly religious services (*culto*) on their own. Women, men, and older children participate.

Throughout the formation of the comunidades the padre has endeavored to spread progressive social Catholicism. In general the indigenous camponês class has welcomed liberation theology. Its message is appealing in that it helps explain their suffering in spiritual and political-economic terms. However, the padre's success in stimulating political-economic action within this class hinges on several factors. One involves the particular production/exchange relationships workers have with their patrões. For example, the small landowners and autonomous terra firme farming divisions of the working class have the most freedom to incorporate and act on the political messages of progressive social Catholicism. By contrast, the urban poor and landless freguês divisions are less capable of political involvement, lest they suffer retaliation by their patrões. Not surprisingly, the padre has had the most success, and has spent a large portion of his time, among small landowners and terra firme farmers on unowned land.

A second factor in raising the political consciousness of the working class is the ability to recruit brokers into the CEB movement. In many hamlets and neighborhoods the success of the comunidade is assured if the brokers/leaders agree to participate. Depending on the personal skill and following of the brokers, they can motivate a large part of the group to actively support the comunidade. Conversely, weak, undecided, or anticomunidade brokers can destroy support for the comunidade's efforts. Because of their importance, the church frequently recruits brokers as comunidade catechists. The catechists are usually the spiritual, as well as political, leaders of the comunidade. By the 1980s they numbered several hundred in the municipality. The padre gives special attention to their education, inviting them to many church meetings in town and even sending them to other cities for meetings. Through this training the church educates them to present the tenets of liberation theology. The catechists also receive instruction on land rights through contacts with the CPT and CUT.

The comunidades pursue an atmosphere of cooperation and mutual aid. They encourage an expanded use of the traditional labor exchanges (convite, troca dias, puxirão), now more generally known as mutirão. People use mutirão for agriculture, house building, and for various community projects (building chapels, maintaining a clear waterway or road, planting a communal garden, or extracting timber). Mutual aid groups run small health posts to provide minimal access to medicine, as well as small *cantinas* (canteens) that bypass local trading posts and provide cheaper goods. Some comunidades have managed to form cooperatives to sell rubber and timber in bulk quantity directly to extraction companies, again bypassing trading posts. Mutual aid is particularly important to the comunidades when individuals confront landowners over land use and ownership problems. Through strength in numbers members of the comunidades can resist abuses by patrões.

Each of the sixty-six comunidades organizes itself for maximum lay participation. During services and especially at meetings individuals offer personal interpretations of religious messages and discuss material problems of daily life. Because of the high degree of lay control, the comunidades display a wide range of behavior, from politically active and internally cohesive to politically inactive and internally fragmented.

The comunidade's behavior depends on several criteria. Among these are the strength of local brokers/leaders (mentioned above), the degree of autonomy of workers (also mentioned above), and external pressure brought to bear on the community. Examples of external pressures include threats of land invasion by timber companies or palmito companies, threats of resource depletion by excessive extractive activities or overhunting, and threats of excessive patrão repression, including expulsion of fregueses. These threats either radicalize the comunidade into action or weaken it greatly.

Although the church has designed the comunidades to be accessible to all members of the local community, there are some problems with personality clashes, ideological conflicts, and even power abuses; as a result some comunidades practice exclusion. The church recognizes this problem and labels these communities "*fechado*" or "closed." Most frequently, this problem fragments comunidades along class or segment lines. Large landowners, merchants, and professionals react to the progressive view of Catholicism and choose not to attend. They view liberation theology, and especially worker organization, as a threat to their privileged position. Usually, these people also persuade others not to attend. People most often manipulated in this way are the urban poor, the landless fregueses, and sometimes the terra firme farmers. Most closed comunidades exist in town. The dominant class is strongest in town and better able to pressure people not to join.

Closed communities form when a few overzealous progressive members decide that comunidade members are not participating sufficiently in group activities or have not developed proper attitudes (particularly class consciousness). The overzealous members pressure the nonconforming members to change, and conflict increases to the point where the noncon-forming members abandon the comunidade.

Exclusion from the comunidade carries certain penalties that strength-en the ability of leaders to impose conformity. The comunidade decides who can baptize their children and who can marry in the church. In most comunidades there are prerequisites for these services, usually consisting of attendance at meetings and participation in comunidade activities. Some people have complained to me that the church uses the threat of refusal to baptize or marry people in order to force them into participating in the comunidade. This also forces people to accept the progressive view of Catholicism. In retaliation people with sufficient money travel to a neigh-boring town controlled by conservative priests from Spain who require no prerequisites for baptism and marriage.

As suggested above, the range of behavior exhibited by comunidades varies greatly. To better show this diversity, particularly in terms of organi-zation, economic behavior, and political practices, I present four case stud-ies of comunidades. The first two examples are of comunidades that have been resistant or hesitant toward the progressive movement. The last two examples are of active comunidades. These examples do not exhaust the diversity exhibited in Gurupá, but they do sample the range of behavior. They also demonstrate the conflictual existence of camponês organizations in relation to the dominant class and the degree of external pressure brought to bear upon them.

São Pedro

The first example of a comunidade is São Pedro (Saint Peter) located on Ilha de Macaco (Monkey Island), a small island just off the main channel of the Amazon River, 10 kilometers upstream from Gurupá. Several cattle-ranching families own most of the island. Of these, Benedito Santos is the largest landholder. All of the members of São Pedro (fifteen families) have family members working for Benedito as ranch hands. They also maintain small subsistence gardens. Despite working in cattle ranching, I classified the people of São Pedro as landless fregueses. Before Padre Chico arrived, patron-client and debt ties to Benedito constituted the principal form of community organization. There was little freguês activity that did not involve Benedito, except for an occasional labor exchange to clear a gar-den.

When the padre began visiting the community, Benedito paternalisti-cally arranged for his workers to form a comunidade. Although Benedito did not attend comunidade functions, he kept himself informed of the group's activities. The comunidade began functioning without incident. The padre would come by and visit every other month, and the comunidade would send individuals to church meetings several times a year. Slowly, several comunidade members became interested in progressive social Catholicism. They began discussing problems of exploitation and expressing a desire to form a cantina to bypass Benedito's trading post.

The suggestions made by progressive members of the comunidade, however, were not accepted by most members. Many comunidade members considered Benedito a good patrão who diligently looked after their needs. They considered a cantina an immoral affront to their patrão. It was also considered a dangerous activity since many comunidade members lived on Benedito's land and feared expulsion if they offended him. Assurances by the progressive members that there was safety in united resistance and that expulsion was unlikely since all individuals had occupant land rights to their houses and gardens did not lessen this fear. They knew Benedito was a strong patrão and that he would not be easily deterred.

With the encouragement of the church, the progressive comunidade members continued their battle. They decided to take attendance at meetings and services and use this as a criterion to judge whether a family was eligible for baptisms or weddings. In this manner they hoped to pressure people to unite in the comunidade and to listen to the messages of political-religious consciousness-raising. The recording of attendance caused unrest among some families who did not care to participate regularly but wished to have their children baptized. Other families were upset since they lived far away and traveling to the chapel was a hardship. People began complaining. Several individuals took the matter to Benedito, still considered the final arbiter for conflict on the island.

Benedito listened carefully to his fregueses. He explained he was not unsympathetic to the progressive view of the church. He understood the problems of exploitation and had worked to minimize them on his land. He explained that his trading post prices were lower than most, his wages were higher than most, and working conditions on his land were better than most. However, he was wary of workers organizing against him. He was also particularly critical of the progressives and the padre inciting the unrest. He explained that the fregueses should work with him, instead of against him.

Benedito suggested to the more conservative fregueses that they should take control of the comunidade. Since they were in the majority, and since the comunidade was theoretically democratic, they should vote on the matter of recording attendance. The conservative members acted on Benedito's advice and succeeded in changing the comunidade's rules. This victory effectively mitigated the progressive members' influence and they were essentially silenced. The conflict also created a distrust among comunidade members toward the progressive church. Today most members of the São Pedro comunidade feel resentful toward the padre. Benedito's dislike for the padre has added to their resentment. The padre understands this and has gradually reduced his visits to the island to one a year. Meanwhile, the comunidade continues to function, but only to give spiritual consultation to its members. The members do not discuss the progressive social Catholic agenda.

Jocojó

The second comunidade is the hamlet of Jocojó. It is situated on unowned terra firme several kilometers upstream from Gurupá. The official name of the comunidade is São João (Saint John); however, people call it Jocojó. The hamlet is an old settlement, dating back over 100 years. Some people in Gurupá maintain that it was founded as a *quilombo,* or slave refuge. As stated earlier, Jocojó is principally a manioc farming settlement, although residents frequently migrate to extract timber and rubber and work at the Jarí tree plantation. The hamlet contains sixteen families tied together by real and fictive kinship ties.

Before the padre began visiting Jocojó, the community had organized itself to perform a variety of functions. For example, in the 1970s the hamlet had a small chapel, its own graveyard, and a religious brotherhood. There were frequent labor exchanges to clear gardens and to build or repair houses (see Wagley 1976:69). The people of the community built a small dock on the Amazon River to service the hamlet. They regularly cleaned the path and igarapé (stream) leading to the hamlet. Until recently, there was also a strong leader and broker of the hamlet, João Povo (see Wagley 1976:149, 158). People in Gurupá humorously called him the baron of Jocojó. By the 1980s, however, João was too old to continue working, so he moved to Gurupá to live with some relatives. No one has successfully filled the leadership position since João's departure.

When the padre arrived in the early 1970s he easily persuaded the people in Jocojó to develop a comunidade. Essentially, the comunidade duplicated preexisting organization in the hamlet. The only new organizational element introduced was a small cantina established in the mid-1980s. From the beginning the comunidade functioned smoothly with little internal dissension. The padre and other lay church members taught and discussed the messages of worker liberation. However, the Jocojoenses (people from Jocojó) did not develop a high level of political awareness or drive for activism for several reasons.

First, until the mid-1980s Jocojoenses had few external threats to their livelihood—there was no attempted land invasion or abusive patrão control. As a result there was little motivation to radicalize their political view and challenge the status quo. Second, with the opening of the Jarí plantation in 1978 over half the comunidade left. This migration deprived the comunidade of many of its more active members who believed in liberation theology. And third, there was a leadership void following the Jarí migration and the "retirement" of João Povo. The individuals that have succeeded João do not hold the hamlet together as in the past. They are also unsure about the validity of progressive social Catholicism. This uncertainty pervades even the catechists, who on several occasions have asked visitors if they think the padre is a communist.

Because of these events, today Jocojó is not a politically cohesive comunidade. One indication of this lack of cohesion is the recent rise of land conflict within the group. This conflict began when one family decided to obtain legal title to its land. The family indeed received titles for three 100-hectare plots (one for the father and two for the adult sons) and is now considering titling a fourth. The legalization of landholding has sent a wave of anxiety through the hamlet. The comunidade exists in a constricted area, bordered by várzea and river to the south and igapó (swamp) in all other directions. The Jocojoenses fear that if every family legalizes 100-hectare plots there will not be enough farmable land to parcel out to all members of the comunidade. In addition, landholdings consist of irregular patches of land scattered among swampy areas. Legalization of land will not recognize the patchwork nature of landholdings. As a result people will be forced to include a large percentage of nonfarmable swampland in their 100-hectare plot. Comunidade members frequently discuss these fears, but without reaching any consensus on a future course of action.

A second event has further complicated the problem of landownership. A recent migrant living on the várzea below Jocojó, Antônio Rosado, has taken out a land claim and is planning to extract timber. He has obtained assurances of financing from a local comprador. Antônio's plan is to extract from his land, which overlaps land claimed by families in Jocojó. He also plans to build a logging road and extract timber from land around the hamlet of Jocojó. Antônio has asked the people of Jocojó if they wish to extract for him. Some have agreed, while most are hesitant, especially those with overlapping claims. A debate has developed within the comunidade. The Jocojoenses have held several meetings to discuss the matter. The meetings often end in argument, sometimes with individuals storming away in anger. A few people have consulted with the church's CPT representatives in town. The CPT has warned them that a logging road could lead to land invasion by other timber firms, or even by migrants looking for land. These Jocojoenses also realize that they will lose much of the timber profit by extracting for a second party instead of for themselves. And finally, timber extraction will disrupt hunting activities by scattering game. The CPT advised the comunidade that the best way to avoid an invasion is to title their land.

Again the community of Jocojó faces the dilemma of legalizing landholdings. If Antônio proceeds with his plan to extract with the aid of some Jocojoenses, then the comunidade will be forced to title their land to protect themselves. However, if they title their land, existing divisions of land use will be disrupted and farmable land will be scarce, as some families will get more usable land than others. As a result some families will be forced to leave. The comunidade remains divided and has no joint plan for action. As of 1991, Antônio had not begun to extract, and there is some hope in Jocojó that he lacks adequate capital to do so. Nevertheless, the lack of internal cohesion against an outside threat leaves the comunidade open to abuse and possible disintegration.

Camutá

The third comunidade is Camutá, a terra firme farming settlement of twenty-four families located on the Pucuruí River. It lies on unowned state land (*terra devoluta*) far into the interior. The comunidade's official name is Nossa Senhora de Fátima (Our Lady of Fatima), but people usually refer to it simply as Camutá. From my observations and from my consultants' statements, I concluded that Camutá is probably the strongest, most cohesive comunidade in the municipality. A group of families wishing to create an agricultural colony founded the comunidade. The families were all tied by real and fictive kinship. Before the padre arrived, they were an active, united community led by the broker Francisco Teixeira. They had undertaken several joint projects including building and maintaining a dirt street through the center of their hamlet and building a small port on the Pucuruí River.

After Padre Chico arrived and began preaching about spiritual and material liberation, community unity, and the formation of CEBs, the people of Camutá intensified their pursuit of an agricultural colony. They formed a unique comunidade based on communal ownership of land and communal work. Camutá became the only comunidade in Gurupá employing these extensive communal arrangements.

By the mid-1970s Camutá's commune was fully functional. Members structured it so that participants worked on projects for the comunidade several days a week according to their time constraints or personal preferences. These projects included maintaining a communal garden (people also maintained private gardens), extracting timber, sawing lumber, running a small cantina stocking food and medicine, and routine custodial work in the hamlet (particularly, weeding paths and clearing waterways). Comunidade leaders kept records of days given to comunidade service—a practice also unique to Camutá. The comunidade divided profits and surplus produce from the communal garden and from timber and lumber sales among participants according to their labor input.

On Mondays and Thursdays, however, the people of Camutá volunteered free labor to the comunidade. They allocated the profits from the various projects performed on these days to a general fund, which has paid for community festivals, the purchase of tools and spare parts, the financing of the cantina, emergency health needs, and many other necessities. People in the hamlet were free to join and quit the comunidade's commune. Two families of Camutá never joined, while eight others migrated in, joined, quit, and then moved away. When leaving the commune, members received compensation for their labor. While the commune always gave compensation, this did put severe financial strains on the group that remained.

Francisco Teixeira is the charismatic leader and catechist of the comunidade. Francisco, a manioc farmer and timber extractor introduced in Chapter 8, is also a broker who had formerly run a small trading post in Camutá until the church politicized him about worker exploitation. He promptly discontinued his business. Francisco is very active in the comunidade, working diligently on communal projects. He is also a superb motivator. Besides Francisco, the comunidade has several other articulate catechists who are well versed in liberation theology. Through their combined leadership Camutá has solidified into a particularly cohesive and politically active comunidade.

Camutá's cohesiveness has been an important asset to the survival and prosperity of the comunidade. Through joint effort in the 1970s the community cut a logging road into the interior and began extracting timber to finance their agricultural colony. Since they lacked a truck, they hauled logs out on a hand-pulled cart. At this point Padre Chico aided the comunidade by obtaining a forty-year-old logging truck donated by a Swiss mission in Goiás. With the truck, they increased the rate of extraction. Over the next several years they used the profits and a bank loan to buy two chain saws and a second, newer truck, and to install a small sawmill (the padre provided the motor). The comunidade also expanded agricultural production, planting rice, beans, corn, and fruit trees in addition to their manioc gardens. The profits from lumber and agricultural crops allowed the comunidade to greatly improve the standard of living. They built new houses with tile roofs; they purchased radios, bicycles, home furnishings, and kitchen utensils; they even acquired a motored canoe.

Camutá's success in timber extraction did not come without external challenges. Soon after the comunidade began extracting and hauling logs out on the hand-pulled cart, commercial loggers became interested in the area. Twice in the early 1980s timber firms attempted to invade the land. The first occasion involved a company named Banicoba. This company had been scouting in Gurupá for various hardwoods to export to Breves. They learned from local timber compradores that there was high-quality timber near Camutá, that there was an adequate port in the area, and that there were several kilometers of logging road already built. Company representatives next met a man who claimed to own the land where the port was located. The company obtained a verbal agreement to use the port from him. Several days later a barge loaded with equipment and workers arrived at the port near Camutá. Upon anchoring the supervisor of the extracting crew asked a nearby resident if they could unload their equipment. The woman in the house told the supervisor her husband was not home and asked him to wait a day until her husband returned. As the company waited the word that Banicoba wanted to extract timber reached the Camutá comunidade.

The people of Camutá immediately recognized Banicoba as a threat to the future of their group. They knew that competition for the area's timber would rob them of their opportunity to develop an agricultural colony. The comunidade was well aware of the practice of outsiders coming to Gurupá, removing resources and wealth, and then leaving nothing behind. Comunidade members felt that they had first rights to the timber since they arrived first in the area. They also felt they had first rights since they intended to use the profits to develop their colony, not to transfer profits to some wealthy family in Belém, São Paulo, or overseas. The comunidade was also aware that Camutá had as much legal right to the land and timber as did any timber firm.

The comunidade called a meeting in the chapel. Comunidade members encouraged people living near Camutá, who were affected by the timber extraction, to attend. They also invited representatives from Banicoba. People from Camutá told me that the representatives were shocked when they saw over a hundred women and men attending the meeting. The comunidade started the meeting by informing the company that the verbal agreement they received to use the port was insufficient. The comunidade had built the port and had rights to it, although their ownership of the port was questionable. In addition, the logging road was the property of Camutá. Following these statements the comunidade questioned the company for several hours about labor arrangements and profit sharing. The comunidade learned the firm planned to quickly cut through the area using chain saws and imported labor. The firm also did not intend to pay any fees for using Camutá's port or road. In the debate that followed the firm offered to let Camutá's men extract alongside their workers. However, the company agreed to pay only a low fee per tree extracted.

After the meeting had ended the comunidade members decided that allowing the firm access to the timber would not serve their interests. The comunidade realized that profits would be much higher and timber reserves would last much longer if they controlled extraction instead of working for Banicoba. In addition, many members had fears that Banicoba might opt to buy the land and expel the people presently living there. They figured it was better to keep the company as far away from their land as possible.

When the comunidade informed the Banicoba representatives of the decision, the representatives were furious. They refused to let simple "caboclos" impede their access to "free" timber. The representatives of Banicoba went to Mayor Alberto Viani and demanded that he secure access. Alberto wrote a letter to the people of Camutá telling them to allow Banicoba entrance. He said that Camutá had no right to the timber or the

land and that retaliations would follow if they did not submit. The comunidade met again and discussed the threats. They took solace in the teachings of liberation theology and realized they could overcome their predica-
ment only if they held fast to their resistance and stayed united. In the
following days more threats were received, but the comunidade remained
united. They invited Banicoba back for a second meeting. But before the
meeting took place, the main office of Banicoba decided to avoid the
potential conflict and moved their operation to another municipality. The
comunidade had resisted and won.

A few years following the Banicoba incident, a second, indirect invasion occurred. This incident began when a group of eight migrant families
from the municipality of Breves asked to join the comunidade of Camutá.
The comunidade accepted the families and integrated them into the commune. The families from Breves worked in the commune for a year without
mishap. By the second year, however, a local timber comprador desirous of
Camutá's timber persuaded the eight Brevenese (from Breves) families to
break from Camutá and extract timber for him. The comprador, José Paiva,
promised to finance the Breveneses and assured them of higher returns than
they earned in the commune. The Breveneses divested from the commune
and with their capital built a new hamlet called Serraria (sawmill). José
provided them with a truck, chain saws, and a sawmill. He told the
Breveneses that they could buy this equipment with profits from extraction.
José also supplied the hamlet with food while their gardens matured.

The departure of the Brevenese families marked the second attempt to
invade and extract timber from the land behind Camutá. José Paiva pushed
the Breveneses to extract large quantities of timber. At first the Camutá
comunidade accepted Serraria's logging. They expected the Breveneses to
apply their profits and develop an agricultural colony as Camutá had.
However, within a year it became obvious that the Serraria settlement existed only to extract timber for their patrão. The Breveneses put little effort
into planting gardens. They were várzea people who previously subsisted
by fishing and extracting and were not accustomed to full-time farming.
Because of not planting, the Breveneses relied heavily on importing food
and hunting game. They sent individuals out to hunt daily, which began to
deplete the game upon which Camutá also depended.

To make matters worse, José Paiva exploited the Breveneses to the
point that they were hopelessly in debt. José paid the workers only a fraction of the value of the wood, prohibited them from selling to other companies paying higher prices, and charged dearly for importing food. He was
also tardy in repairing the truck and chain saws when they broke down.
This impeded the hamlet's ability to produce while it was importing expensive food. As a result the Breveneses' standard of living fell substantially,
especially in comparison to that of Camutá's. When I visited the hamlet in

1985 I saw firsthand how the Breveneses subsisted on poor diets, especially when game could not be found, lived in palm-covered shacks with few furnishings, and, despite a year's worth of work, were nowhere near paying off their debts for the truck, chain saws, and food.

Nearly a year after the Breveneses had departed, the comunidade of Camutá reached its breaking point with Serraria's predatory use of the area's resources. The comunidade decided to stop the Serraria residents from excessive extraction by prohibiting use of Camutá's logging road. Once they relayed this decision to Serraria, a squabble erupted. The Breveneses were forced to begin the arduous task of cutting a second logging road parallel to Camutá's. Still upset, the Camutaenses (people from Camutá) blocked all roads with downed trees and brought all logging to a standstill.

This action greatly angered José Paiva, who was enjoying heady profits from Serraria's extraction. José took the matter up with his brother, an ex-mayor of Gurupá and an official in the PMDB—by now the majority party in Pará. He used his brother's influence to call in an agent from ITERPA to settle the matter. I met this agent while staying at Seu Bena's boarding house. The agent told me it was unusual for ITERPA to directly intervene in such a small dispute. He was slightly amused over the entire case. Nevertheless, the ITERPA agent, a topographer by training, reviewed the problem and suggested the two hamlets divide the land between them. He next surveyed a boundary along the logging road, giving the west to Camutá and the east to Serraria.

Both sides initially agreed to the land partition, and the ITERPA agent left. However, within six months the dispute arose again as each hamlet accused the other of violating the boundary line. Camutá also maintained that a logging road extension constructed by the people of Serraria curved to the west onto its land. The ITERPA agent returned and resurveyed the line to settle this dispute. He warned the two groups that technically neither was extracting timber legally and they should be more careful about publicizing the conflict.

At this point it appeared the people of Camutá had resigned themselves to allow the land invasion and the harvesting of timber. However, another conflict arose that completely changed this scenario. This conflict was between the Serraria residents and their patrão. After several years of extracting timber and sawing lumber with next to nothing to show for their labor, the hamlet of Serraria turned against José. The Breveneses refused to extract exclusively for him and demanded their rights to the truck, which they figured they had paid for several times over. José retaliated and threatened to remove the truck, chain saws, and sawmill. He also threatened to import another group of loggers to replace the Breveneses. However, the Breveneses held fast to their demands. They threatened to take the dispute to court. At this point José backed down. He gave up his claims to the truck and chain saws and his exclusive rights to buy Serraria's timber. He did retain control of the sawmill.

Two factors undoubtedly influenced the Breveneses' willingness to confront their patrão. First, José did not own the land on which they extracted timber. He therefore could not invoke the ultimate form of retaliation, expulsion from the land. This factor gave the Breveneses the opportunity to resist. Second, in my opinion, the ideology, actions, and successes of Camutá motivated the Breveneses to take action. The Breveneses had lived in Camutá and had heard about workers' rights and resistance. They knew that Camutá had resisted the previous attempt at land invasion through community unity. They also saw the disparity of their exploited existence and the relative prosperity of Camutá. The combination of these factors motivated the residents of Serraria to renegotiate their dependence on their patrão. With new arrangements the Breveneses were free to extract at their own pace and to invest the higher returns as they saw fit. Consequently, their standard of living increased substantially.

Despite these victories, the Breveneses decided in the early 1990s to give up their community and move to where they could extract more wood. Although they were living better than before, the limitations of extraction and subsistence farming frustrated them. The people in Camutá commented to me on the move, saying that the Breveneses were várzea people who never really had their heart in farming.

At present the comunidade of Camutá has survived the two attempted land invasions and has remained intact. However, since external pressure has dissipated, internal pressure in the comunidade has begun to weaken its unity. The main problem revolves around the functioning of the commune. The commune does not operate as members had envisioned. First, profits made from communal labor do not meet expectations. Francisco commented that once participants assembled profits and paid comunidade debts, often there is little left to distribute. There is also a problem with individuals participating unequally in projects, yet expecting equal compensation.

The problem became so irritating to several members that they decided to reduce communal participation and increase individual work. Soon others followed their lead. By the late 1980s comunidade members had reduced all communal labor to joint work parties on Thursdays only. This limiting of communal work has resulted in the termination of the communal garden and a decline in the cantina. People also are extracting timber individually and exchanging labor (mutirão) in small groups. The truck is still used communally, however.

Another problem affecting Camutá's commune system is the continuous threat of land invasion. The comunidade realizes that to preserve its rights to land it has to obtain land titles. However, neither INCRA nor ITERPA would register land in the name of the comunidade during the

1980s. In the 1990s, even with legal precedents for extractive reserves (communal land grants) set in other parts of Amazonia, government officials in the Gurupá area do not accept the practice. Land agencies still insist on individual titles to land. The people of Camutá have been forced to comply to ensure possession of land. Once individuals establish land titles, however, they are careful to protect their private resources. This results in a sharp decline in communal use of land.

Despite internal disruptions, Camutá has readjusted. The people have gradually replaced the communal system with an individualistic system, although they still stress mutual aid and comunidade unity. This continued cohesion of the group is all important to its survival, since more timber firms are active in the terra firme surrounding Camutá. The threat of a land invasion is growing steadily. Whether the comunidade can resist invasion depends heavily on the unity of workers, as well as on aid from workers' organizations such as the rural union and the PT.

Nazaré

The last comunidade is Nossa Senhora de Nazaré (Our Lady of Nazareth), or simply Nazaré, which is located on the Mojú River of the Great Island of Gurupá. The community is a rubber and timber extracting "neighborhood" of twenty-one families spread out along the river. The community consists of two groups. One group is the small landowners (several brokers are among them), and the second is the landless fregueses working for Lourenço Braga, the major landowner/trading post owner in the vicinity. When Padre Chico arrived in Nazaré in the early 1970s he succeeded in congregating all of the residents, including Lourenço Braga. They built a chapel on Lourenço's property and formed the comunidade. During the first few years of existence the comunidade functioned smoothly. Members met weekly for lay religious services and to discuss common problems. They openly discussed topics of human rights, land rights, exploitation, and worker liberation, although without much fervor. The comunidade also increased its use of labor exchanges, although not greatly.

By the late 1970s the tranquility and general passivity of the comunidade began to change. The repeated messages of progressive social Catholicism eventually led some fregueses to question Lourenço's business practices. They became critical of the extraordinary land tax he charged (deducting 30 percent of the value of all commodities produced or extracted by his fregueses), the inflated prices of goods in his trading post (which only operated sporadically), and the very low prices paid for extracted rubber and timber.

The fregueses' view of Lourenço's dealings steadily worsened after the small landowning members of the comunidade formed a cooperative to sell their rubber directly to a rubber firm. By selling in bulk, and thereby bypassing Lourenço's trading post, they received a price several times higher than that Lourenço paid his fregueses. Next, the small landowning members opened a cantina that undersold Lourenço's post by a substantial amount. Upon seeing the difference in prices, Lourenço's fregueses became resentful of the price gouging they suffered. Some began protesting to Lourenço about exploitation. Other comunidade members, most of whom were independent small landowners, supported them. The comunidade made references to liberation theology and to the immorality of Lourenço's dealings. Three other fregueses protested in a more traditional manner by selling their produce on the side to regatões for better prices. Lourenço learned of their activities and immediately ordered them off his land.

Lourenço's order to expel the fregueses sparked the comunidade into action. Part of the comunidade united behind the fregueses. They began challenging Lourenço's rights to the land, especially since the fregueses had lived on the land for generations. They threatened to invoke Brazilian law to claim either occupant rights to the land or rights to indemnifications. Since Lourenço did not want to forfeit his land and lacked funds to pay for indemnifications, a stalemate ensued. The legal threat, plus the backing of part of the comunidade, shielded the fregueses from Lourenço's traditional rights to expel them.

The fregueses' unrest greatly angered Lourenço. He blamed Padre Chico for inciting the resistance and promptly broke with the comunidade. He had the chapel torn down. Lourenço's break with the comunidade divided the workers, for he was patrão to many members who felt they owed him loyalty as part of the patron-client relationship. Many individuals also had real and fictive kinship ties to Lourenço, which complicated any decision to side with the comunidade. In addition, Lourenço put pressure on his fregueses to break with the comunidade, promising he would succeed in expelling them from his land if they did not. Because of this schism, Nazaré, unlike Camutá, did not develop into a closely knit solidarity. Instead, it developed into a neighborhood with several opposing factions.

The group that supported the comunidade's efforts consisted mainly of small landowners. They had the economic independence, through rubber and timber extraction, to resist dominant-class pressure and become politically active if they chose. But the comunidade did include some fregueses from Lourenço's land, though their number was small due to Lourenço's pressures and threats. Nevertheless, a few participated in the comunidade and used the comunidade's backing to resist Lourenço's intimidations.

Despite the schism between the comunidade and Lourenço, part of the comunidade reunited and remained active. They built another chapel on the property of one of the small landowners. Several strong leaders/brokers emerged who worked hard to maintain the comunidade's integrity. The leaders had been well trained by the church. A few leaders had traveled to other cities, even to other states, to attend meetings on land problems and labor organization. They brought all their insights back to the comunidade and educated their co-workers. As a result of their activity the comunidade remained intact and committed to social reform.

By the 1980s the relations between Lourenço and the comunidade reached a new low. Lourenço was in need of cash to pay back taxes on his land and had decided to cut palmito. Without informing his fregueses, Lourenço signed a three-year contract with Gigante's extracting firm to cut and process the palmito. Lourenço was to receive $0.05 per tree processed. When Gigante arrived with his workers and started extracting, the fregueses were startled. Upon inquiring, they learned of the deal. A few fregueses quickly called a meeting of the comunidade to discuss the events. They invited several comunidades neighboring Nazaré that were also affected by Lourenço's palmito-extraction contract.

The comunidade's members protested Lourenço's deal because traditionally açaí (one type of tree used for palmito) was under the control of the fregueses. This is part of a historic pattern in Amazonia wherein extractors control the fruit of their labor (i.e., rubber, açaí, oleaginous seeds, and so forth) independent of tree or landownership (Barham and Coomes 1994a:54). The fregueses had been free to extract, consume, and sell açaí to regatões if they chose. In addition, most small landowners bordering Lourenço's land had enjoyed de facto rights to collect the açaí. Lourenço was breaking these traditions by destroying the açaí to extract palmito.

During the meeting the comunidades raised three objections to the extraction of palmito. First, açaí was very important to the fregueses and the small landowners as a dietary supplement. The drink made from açaí is a major part of the várzea people's diet and supplements the monotonous manioc and fish menu. People often comment that their stomachs never feel full without their bowl of açaí. The Nazarenses (people from Nazaré) were sure that if they lost their supply of açaí they would suffer nutritionally (researchers have shown that açaí contains high amounts of vitamin A [Moran 1981:105]) and would eventually be forced to abandon their land.

In addition to açaí's dietary value, the sale of the product by the 1980s had become a valuable source of cash income. Regatões from as far away as Breves, Macapá, and Almerim come to the Mojú River region to buy açaí since palmito extraction has virtually eliminated the fruit from those municipalities. The profit from açaí is fair. In a year a tree can produce about 15 liters of seeds with a value of U.S.$5. The tree will produce for up to ten years, and there are literally hundreds of thousands of them growing on the island. By contrast, felling the tree for palmito generates only $0.05 and ends all subsequent profits from the tree. Making matters worse, profit from palmito extraction goes entirely to the landowner, leaving only a depleted environment for the fregueses. Since people on the island have already lost the oleaginous seeds as a source of needed cash income, the preservation of açaí is even more important.

The second objection was that the fregueses had planted many açaí trees, especially around their houses. By local tradition and by Brazilian law the fregueses had rights to these trees that Lourenço was ignoring. Upon questioning, Lourenço maintained that the cutters would not cut açaí within 100 meters of his fregueses' houses. However, this buffer zone did not protect all the planted açaí. Furthermore, Gigante's crew had previously violated this zone. The fregueses were sure the violation would occur again.

The third objection was over the ownership status of the land where Lourenço was extracting. The comunidades challenged Lourenço to produce land titles proving he was the legal owner, but Lourenço produced no such documents. The comunidades examined Lourenço's land tax status and found he was severely delinquent (as are 90 percent of landowners in Gurupá [INCRA 1985]). The comunidades next arranged for a lawyer from the PT to search for a land title in Belém. None was found. Based on these results, the comunidades contended that the land had no legal owner. The lack of a legal owner meant that Lourenço had no right to extract palmito and that the fregueses who had lived on the land for generations could claim the land.

Lourenço rejected all these objections. He told Gigante to continue extracting. The comunidades decided that unless they acted immediately they would become victims of Lourenço's greed, thereby losing a valuable resource and suffering a drop in their standard of living. So early one morning all the members of the Nazaré comunidade—fregueses and small landowners, men, women, and children—joined with members of neighboring comunidades to surround the palmito extractors' camp, refusing to let them work. The extractors, who were poor workers from Breves, accepted the empate or stalemate. They waited for the company to make the next move. Lourenço and Gigante approached the judge and demanded that she take action. The judge held a hearing and ruled that the comunidades had no right to impede extraction. The comunidades, however, did not accept this ruling. They contended the judge had no documents to reinforce Lourenço's claim and, therefore, had no grounds to make such a decision. Apparently, the comunidades were correct since the judge did not try to have the decision enforced. The comunidades' stalemate had worked. Gigante withdrew his workers from the area.

Nazaré's victory strengthened the internal cohesion of the comunidade. A common threat, the depletion of açaí, had overridden much of the segmentation between the landless fregueses and small landowners and allowed them to act in unison. While the comunidade savored its victory and the preservation of its fruit, it was well aware that threats from the dominant class had not ended. At present palmito extraction in Gurupá is on the increase, and other extraction firms are active in the Mojú area. The possibility of another attempt to cut palmito sometime soon in the future seems likely. Nazaré's ability to resist these intrusions will again depend on the comunidade's unity.

The Future

Despite setbacks in some comunidades and persistent resistance from the dominant class, Gurupá's CEBs have continued to grow and solidify support for an alternative future. The political landscape of the municipality has been fundamentally changed and, at least in my view, will not soon revert to the status quo of past decades.

An important criterion for the camponês movement to maintain its power and continue to grow is the movement's ability to resist outside pressures to disrupt it. While the local dominant class is not too powerful, regional interest groups with access to the government and the military police are wary of Gurupá's activities. The timber companies, in particular, have a growing interest in terra firme timber and might easily react to organized resistance to exploitation of that timber. This problem is not lost upon the local members of the camponês movement. Many understand that government repression and violence are the prices they will pay for success. They also realize that they might become targets for political assassinations, as has frequently occurred in the south of Pará. So far, to my knowledge, this has not happened in Gurupá.

Renato Fonseca, the former PT candidate for mayor, put this threat of repression and assassination in perspective. According to Renato all people live with fear. If you are comfortable, if you possess many material things and freedom, you have a lot of fear. If you are less well off, fear diminishes, as necessity is more pressing. And if you are in very bad straits, landless and hungry, then fear no longer stands in the way. You are frightened, but your need to survive overcomes your fear and you act. Renato continued with an old saying: When you meet a *bicho* (beast) in the jungle, if you run it will kill you; if you freeze it will eat you. So you must confront it if you are to survive. Confronting the bicho is what the camponês movement is all about.

10

CONCLUSION:
CONFRONTING THE BICHO

The popular image of the Brazilian Amazon presented by the world press and academia in the 1980s was a disheartening one. Environmental destruction and social conflict fostered by the military government's errant development plans were rapidly destroying the world's last great rain forest and the people in it. An area estimated to be about the size of France had been deforested. What was left behind was a devastated landscape, disrupted rain cycles, release of greenhouse gases from burning forests, and countless destroyed species. Native Americans were victims of genocide, and camponeses were victims of expulsions and assassinations. The human condition in Amazonia was deplorable with excessive landlessness, joblessness, undernutrition, disease, lack of health care, economic exploitation, and political repression. As I have shown in the previous chapters, Gurupá suffered many of these maladies.

Despite the bleak 1980s, the 1990s began with guarded optimism about the future of Amazonia. Why optimism? Several recent developments hold the promise of altering Amazonia's dire circumstances, among these, the end of military rule and several successes of emergent camponês movements. The local inhabitants are organizing and defending themselves and their livelihoods in innovative ways. In places like Gurupá, when the disenfranchised empower themselves they are better able to take advantage of economic opportunities and raise their standard of living. The cases of the CEBs in Camutá and the Mojú River region are good examples. Of course, these improvements are incremental, and dominant-class interests challenge them. However, they prove to the people involved that change is possible.

Optimism for Amazonia's future also stems from recent studies on alternative development. Researchers have documented the productive and sustainable economic activities of Native American and indigenous camponês groups (see Posey and Baleé 1989; Moran 1993; Anderson 1990). If people have the freedom to pursue these activities, unfettered by exploitative or repressive control, then they can usually achieve higher standards of living. Much of this information surfaced during the debates on the effectiveness of cattle ranching versus a combination of extraction and small-scale farming. Repeatedly, studies have shown that almost any type of extraction/farming activity is more cost effective and far less destructive then ranching. Ranching is only profitable if heavily subsidized by the government.

Another source of optimism comes from the creation of new ties between indigenous groups (Native American and camponês) and national and international nongovernmental organizations (NGOs) that monitor human rights abuses and environmental destruction. The environmental ties have evolved as such groups as the Environmental Defense Fund, Conservation International, the Nature Conservancy, and the World Wildlife Fund have modified extreme ecocentric views of Amazonian nature to acknowledge not only the role of the local population in the sustainable use of the forest, but also its actual role in shaping the forest over the millennia.

Through ties to national and international NGOs some Native Americans and indigenous camponeses have publicized their plight as never before. Armed with newsletters, telephones, camcorders, and even fax machines, the world can learn almost instantaneously of threats to these peoples. NGOs then use their lobbying power to encourage governmental agencies to mitigate the threats. While many efforts to resolve conflicts have been ineffective, there have been a few successes. For example, NGOs played a role in the suspension of many subsidies to cattle ranchers during the Collar presidency and the cancellation of large projects like the damming of the Xingu River to produce hydroelectric power. Of course, global economic recession, failure rates of such programs, and their general impracticality also weighed heavily against them. Nonetheless, access to the NGOs is clearly a new and important tool being employed in the Amazon region by indigenous peoples.

At the end of my research period Gurupá was beginning to feel the effects of these new trends. I remember asking my consultants about extractive reserves, the Rubber Tappers' Union originating in Acre, and the union leader Chico Mendes, who was assassinated while defending the rubber tappers' way of life. In the 1980s no one I talked to was aware of any of these. By the 1990s, however, union leaders were discussing joining the Rubber Tappers' Union and setting aside land for a biological reserve. They are actively pursuing information on replanting strategies for many hardwoods and palms depleted in the area. They are also trying hard to form a fishers' cooperative and to limit commercial fishing in the municipality. The idea of extractive reserves, however, is less well received. Communal use of resources as envisioned in extractive reserves runs counter to Gurupá's long history of small- and medium-sized landowning patterns.

When I asked rural union officials about extractive reserves in 1991, they were indecisive, if not distrustful, about their benefits.

Ties to NGOs are also evident. Through the aid of Paulo H. B. Oliveira and others, Gurupá's rural union has secured a grant from a Canadian NGO development agency to build several manioc processors (*casas de farinha*, or manioc flour houses). The idea is to increase local production and distribution of the basic staple and thereby begin to resolve the centuries-old problem of importing food.

Continued work in grassroots organizations, empowerment, alternative and sustainable development, and international ties offer new hope for Amazonia in the 1990s. Of course, one very important question remains: If these new trends are really productive and sustainable—not simply old patterns cleverly disguised in new jargon—how will the historic limitations of the political economy shape their implementation? Will the new environmental/sustainability discourses actually guide policies and programs that will benefit Amazonian peoples? Or will history repeat itself again, leaving behind a depleted environment and an impoverished population?

The cynic in me fears the worst. As shown in this work, there is little precedent in 400 years of Amazon history upon which to found hopes for long-term equitable improvement. From the beginning of European contact until the 1800s the colonial system functioned to impoverish the region. The three prominent patterns of depopulation, environmental destruction, and the creation of commodity production for export ensured the region's underdevelopment.

Over the following 200 years the patterns of underdevelopment and poverty continued. The indigenous campesinato emerged, eking out a living under an extractive economy with a history of resource depletion and food shortages. Exploitation persisted, structured by a class system divided between merchants/landowners and subservient camponeses. The trading post, debt-peonage, and the aviamento system were the principal institutions for labor control. With the coming of the rubber boom the aviamento system matured, holding workers and merchants alike in debt while siphoning off wealth overseas. With the rubber bust and depression, the aviamento system declined greatly, but it continued to siphon wealth away from the lowly farmer/extractor.

The massive development efforts of the 1960s and 1970s promised a radical break with the past but delivered much less. I have argued that history basically repeated itself during this period, as labor shortages, environmental destruction, and exploitative labor relations continued local impoverishment. Amazon development has meant gaining massive short-term profits for a few by using socially and environmentally destructive practices. Despite the rhetoric of development and progress offered by government planners and politicians, poverty for the majority has been the main consequence of the effort.

Gurupá's experience with development has been dismal. As in the past, extraction of commodities largely proceeds until extractors have depleted resources. Resource management is virtually nonexistent. Each boom and depletion cycle alters the environment and creates increasing limitations on future human use. By the 1990s the extraction booms and bureaucratic expansion had at best brought only temporary and superficial prosperity.

Deeper problems with "development" began to surface—or resurface—at the end of my research period. They include a very real threat to the camponês livelihood from an accumulation of factors. Among these are the continual depletion of extracted resources (timber, oleaginous seeds, palmito), continual reduction of fish, persistent limitations on agricultural production and marketing, increasing competition with timber companies and others for access to resources and land, inflation, loss of trading posts and credit opportunities, lack of wage labor jobs in the urban sector, and population growth.

Worsening life conditions have led to social tensions. When coupled with political repression and frustrations arising from a new self-awareness of local poverty and exploitation, gathered from exposure to television and opposing political viewpoints, tensions have transformed into conflict. The Catholic church, unions, and oppositional political parties have been crucial in organizing resistance to the status quo. In Gurupá the focus of resistance has been on a small faction within the dominant class that has held power for nearly eighteen years. The leader of this faction did the military's bidding by encouraging predatory extraction of resources by both national and international firms and by suppressing local dissent.

The Catholic church has been at the forefront of the resistance movement in Gurupá. Church members preach liberation theology and spend considerable energy on organizing the camponês class into comunidades. The comunidades have been active in the struggle for individual land rights, resource rights, and general improvements in standards of living. They use several strategies to pursue their goals: arranging labor exchanges, developing cooperatives to bypass trading posts, and organizing empates to block the expulsion of occupants from contested land as well as the extraction of contested resources. The comunidade movement has fed into an activist union movement and an opposition political party. The rural union and the Workers' Party have further challenged the dominant class and the status quo through public demonstrations, legal challenges, and election successes.

The best hope of an improved future for Amazonia and Gurupá, I suggest, lies with the continual growth of the grassroots movements and their capability to enact some form of sustainable use of the rain forest. In them exists the potential for equitable improvement in the standards of living for the majority of people. In them also exists the ability to preserve the rain forest. In Gurupá the cases of the Camutá and Mojú communities demonstrate some of this potential.

Despite these new promises of a better life, the old problems of environmental destruction and social inequality still loom onerously. The successful struggle for improved standards in Gurupá and Amazonia is far from certain. Yet the struggle continues, gaining momentum as incremental successes fuel the hopes for bigger future successes. Through it all, Amazonian peoples, such as those found in Gurupá, display their tenacity, fortitude, and perpetual hopes as they confront the bicho of inequality in their struggle for survival.

ACRONYMS & ABBREVIATIONS

ARENA   Aliança Renovadora Nacional (National Renovation Alliance)

BA state   Bureaucratic-authoritarian state

CEBs   *comunidades eclésiais de base* (ecclesiastical base communities)

CELPA   Centrais Elêctricas do Pará (Electrical Centers of Pará)

CGT   Confederação Geral do Trabalho (General Labor Confederation)

CNBB   Comissão Nacional de Bispos do Brasil (National Council of Brazilian Bishops)

CONCLAT   Conferência Nacional das Classes Trabalhadores (National Conference of the Working Classes)

CPT   Comissão Pastoral da Terra (Pastoral Land Commission)

CUT   Central Única do Trabalho (Unified Labor Center)

FUNRURAL   Fundo de Assistência ao Trabalhador Rural (Assistance Fund for Rural Workers)

IBAMA   Instituto Brasileiro de Recursos Naturais Renováveis e do Meio Ambiente (Brazilian Institute for Renewable Natural Resources and the Environment)

IBGE   Instituto Brasileiro de Geografia e Estatística (Brazilian Institute of Geography and Statistics)

INCRA   Instituto Nacional de Colonização e Reforma Agrária (National Institute for Colonization and Agrarian Reform)

I PDA-NA   New Republic's First Amazon Development Plan

ITERPA   Instituto da Terra do Pará (Pará Land Institute)

MOBRAL	Movimento Brasileiro de Alfabetização (Brazilian Movement for Adult Literacy)
NGOs	nongovernmental organizations
PDA	Plano de Desenvolvimento da Amazônia (Amazon Development Plan)
PDS	Partido Democrático Social (Social Democratic Party)
PIN	Programa de Integração Nacional (National Integration Plan)
PMDB	Partido do Movimento Democrático do Brasil (Democratic Movement Party of Brazil)
POLAMAZONIA	Programa de Polos Agropecuários e Agrominerais da Amazônia (Program of Agricultural and Mineral Poles in the Amazon)
PT	Partido dos Trabalhadores (Workers' Party)
SEDUC	Superintêndencia de Estado de Educação (State Secretary of Education)
SESP	Serviço Especial de Saúde Pública (Public Health Special Service)
SESPA	Secretaria de Estado de Saúde Pública (State Secretary of Public Health)
SUCAM	Superintêndencia de Campanhas (Superintendency of Campaigns)
SUDAM	Superintêndencia do Desenvolvimento da Amazônia (Superintendency for the Development of the Amazon)
SVPEA	Superintêndencia do Plano de Valorização Econômica da Amazônia (Amazon Economic Valoriation Plan Superintendency)

GLOSSARY

abertura	opening; loosening of political restrictions near the end of military rule in the 1980s
açaí	*Eutrepe oleracea,* which produces a palm seed used in a traditional drink and is also one species harvested for palmito
afilhado	god-child; fictive kin relationship
agregados	boarders; tenant farmers
água flórida	perfumed water; magic water
aguardente	liquor distilled from sugarcane
Amazônida	non-Native American Amazonian culture
ambição	ambition
amigos de fogueiro	friends of the bonfire, which is a form of fictive kinship
apinhoar	process of agglomeration or piling up
assombrar	to frighten or to steal one's soul
assustamento	fright which leads to illness
atrasado	backward, as in behind the times
aviadores	suppliers within the *aviamento* system, including riverboat merchants and import/export firms
aviamento	a pyramid trading system of credit and debt established in 18th century Amazonia
barracão	large shelter
batuque	a version of Umbanda found in Amazonia
beata	overseer of church, pious woman

benza	blessing
benzedeiros	blessers, faith healers
bicho	beast
bichos visagentos	magically malignant animals
boto	freshwater dolphin
branco	white
brasilite	corrugated asbestos material
breu	blue dye
Breveneses	people from Breves
cabanos	cover term for *mestizos,* Native Americans, and Africans who comprised the rural population of the early 19th century Amazonia
caboclos	rural inhabitants of Amazonia; pejorative term for indigenous componeses
cachaça	type of rum
Calha Norte	Northern Trench; a proposed road
campesinato	rural inhabitants whose livelihood is at least partially based on small-scale agriculture; in Amazonia usually small farmers and forest resource extractors
camponeses	small-scale farmers/extractors; plural form
Camutaenses	people from Camutá
cantinas	"canteens," exchange posts
Caramurus	a conservative monarchistic political party of the early 19th century that did not favor Brazilian independence from Portugal
cartorário	municipal archivist, notary
casa de farinha	manioc flour houses; small enterprises that produce manioc flour
Casa Gato	literally "house of the cat," a trading post
Chapa Uma	union slate number one
cobra grande	supernatural big snake
comadre	co-mother; form of fictive kinship
Comando de Caça aos Comunistas	Communist Hunt Command
comarcas	judiciary district of a state
comerciantes	merchants
Comitê do Apoio a Democracia	Committee in Support of Democracy

compadresco	fictive kin relationship, as in godparenthood
compadres	co-parents or co-fathers; form of fictive kinship
compadres de foguerio	co-parents of the bonfire
compradores	contractors; buyers of wood, palmito, rubber, etc.
comunidades eclesiais de base	ecclesiastic base communities or Christian base communities (CEBs)
conscientização	consciousness-raising
convite	cooperative work parties or labor exchange groups
coronel	town boss
Corpo de Trabalhadores	Workers' Corps
corrente branco	good magic
corrente	current of special powers as found in practitioners of Umbanda and spiritism
cortar izepla	"to cut izepla," izepla being a supernatural illness caused by the penetration of a malignant object into one's body
culto	weekly religious services
curupira	a supernatural forest creature
delegados	delegates
Dona	mistress; form of address
drogas do sertão	backland drugs
empates	human blockades
estopa	bark used for caulking
família	family
fazendas	ranches
fechado	"closed," in regards to restrictive membership in CEBs
feitiço	evil magic
fichas	voter registration forms
Filantrópico Party	a liberal political party of the early 19th century that favored independence from Portugal
filho de criação	adopted child
filhos de santo	children of the saint/Umbanda specialists or mediums
freguês	client

freguesia	total number of fregueses working for one trading post merchant
furos	literally a hole; refers to a natural river channel connecting high *várzea* to low *várzea*
garimpeiros	small-scale gold miners
gatos	literally "cats"; a type of labor recruiter
gente	people, sometimes used to designate a kindred
gente de primeira	upper-class people
gente de primeiro seleção	people of the first selection
gente de segunda	second-class or working-class people
gente de segundo seleção	people of the second selection
gente formada	educated or mannered people
grileiros	land grabbers
Gurupaenses	people from Gurupá
igapós	flooded forest/swamps
igarapés	streams navigable by canoe
Ilha de Macaco	Monkey Island
índios	Indians/Native Americans
inhambu	*tinamou,* bird thought to have supernatural power
inveja	envy/jealousy
irmã	sister
irmandades	religious brotherhoods
irmão	brother
Jocojoenses	people from Jocojó
jogo dos bichos	the animal lottery
jugunços	hired guns
latifundiário	owner of a latifundium or large landed estate, also the class of large land owners
latifúndio	latifundium; large landed estate
lavradores	manual laborers in agriculture; extractors
lingua geral	general language; a pidgin of Tupi-Guarani languages
macumba	evil magic
Mãe de bichos	mother of the bichos visagentos
mães de santo	mothers of the saint; Umbanda specialists or mediums
marreteiros	riverboat merchants

meia lua	half moon; a boat procession for Saint Benedict
minifúndio	small-scale landholding
mestizos	people of mixed European and Native American descent
movimento	movement; bustle of town life
Movimento Para Libertar Os Padres da Amazônia	Movement to Free the Priests of the Amazon
mutirão	cooperative work parties or labor exchange groups
Nazarenses	people from Nazaré
Nossa Senhora de Fátima	Our Lady of Fatima comunidade
Nossa Senhora de Nazaré	Our Lady of Nazareth comunidade
novelas	soap operas
orixás	gods of African origin, part of Umbanda religion
padrinho	godparent or sponsor
pais de santo	fathers of the saint; Umbanda specialists or mediums
pajés	shaman-type healers
palmito	palm heart; palmetto
panelança/panema	supernatural force bringing bad luck
paraná	riverside channel
Paraense	person from Pará; a dialect of the state of Pará
parentes	relatives
parteiras	midwives
passe	pass; a spiritist therapy similar to "laying on" of hands
patrão	patron
pelles	semi-processed rubber balls
posserios	land occupants, squatters
prefeito	mayor
prefeitura	county government
pretos velhos	elderly African slave spirits, part of Umbanda religion
primo/prima	cousin
promesa	religious promise
quilombo	slave refuge
puxirão	cooperative work parties of labor exchange groups
quimbanda	evil magic

regatões	itinerate riverboat merchants
resgatado	rescue mission
roças	gardens
São João	the comunidade of Saint John in Jocojó
São Pedro	the comunidade of Saint Peter
Senhora	mistress; form of address
seringais	rubber fields
seringalistas	owners of rubber estates
Serraria	"sawmill;" name of a developed hamlet
Seu	senor, mister; form of address
Seu Bena	literally "Mr. Benedito's"; name of boarding house
taipa	wattle work filled with clay, finished with a sand and lime plaster
terra devoluta	unowned state land
terra firme	highland that is never inundated by floods
terreiro	roughly, "church" or meeting place for Umbanda ceremonies
trapiche	wharf
Umbanda	an African-Brazilian religion
Umbandistas	practitioners of Umbanda
várzea	floodplain
vereador	council member
vergonha	shame
visagens	malignant forest and river spirits
violência	violence

REFERENCES

Acuña, Cristóbal de
1942   *Nuevo Descubrimiento del Gran Río de las Amazonas.* Buenos Aires: Emecé Editores.
Anderson, Anthony, ed.
1990   *Alternatives to Deforestation: Steps Toward Sustainable Use of the Amazon Rain Forest.* New York: Columbia University Press.
Anderson, Anthony, and Edviges M. Ioris
1992   "Valuing the Rain Forest: Economic Strategies by Small-Scale Forest Extractivists in the Amazon Estuary." *Human Ecology,* vol. 20, no. 3: 337–369.
Anderson, Robin
1985   "The Caboclo as Revolutionary: The Cabanagem Revolt, 1835–1836." In Eugene Parker, ed., *The Amazon Caboclo: Historical and Contemporary Perspectives* (pp. 51–87). Studies in Third World Societies, no. 32. Williamsburg, VA: College of William & Mary.
Azevedo S. J., Marcello
1986   *Comunidades Eclesiais de Base e Enculturação da Fé: A Realidade das CEBs e a sua Tematização Teórica, na Perspective de uma Evangelização Inculturada.* São Paulo: Loyola.
Barham, Bradford, and Oliver Coomes
1994a   "Wild Rubber: Industrial Organisation and the Microeconomics of Extraction During the Amazon Rubber Boom (1860–1920)." *Journal of Latin American Studies,* vol. 26: 37–72.
1994b   "Reinterpreting the Amazon Rubber Boom: Investment, the State, and Dutch Disease." *Latin American Research Review,* vol. 29, no. 2: 73–109.
Bayley, P., and M. Petrere
1989   "Amazon Fisheries: Assessment Methods, Current Status and Management Options." *Canadian Special Publications Fisheries and Aquatic Science,* vol. 106: 385–398.
Berryman, Philip
1987   *Liberation Theology: Essential Facts About the Revolutionary Movement in Latin America and Beyond.* Philadelphia: Temple University Press.

225

Bodley, John
   1990   *Victims of Progress.* Mountain View, CA: Mayfield Publishing
          Company.
Boff, Clodovis
   1978   *Teologia e Prática: Teologia do Político e suas Mediações.* Petrópolis,
          Brazil: Vozes.
Boff, Leonardo
   1981   *Igreja, Carisma, e Poder—Ensaios de Eclesiológia Militante.*
          Petrópolis, Brazil: Vozes.
Boff, Leonardo, and Clodovis Boff
   1986   *Liberation Theology: From Dialogue to Confrontation.* San Francisco:
          Harper & Row.
Branford, Sue, and Oriel Glock
   1985   *The Last Frontier: Fighting over Land in the Amazon.* London: Zed
          Books Ltd.
Browder, John
   1986   "Logging the Rainforest: A Political Economy of Timber Extraction
          and Unequal Exchange in the Brazilian Amazon." Ph.D. dissertation,
          University of Pennsylvania.
Bruneau, Thomas C.
   1982   *The Church in Brazil: The Politics of Religion.* Austin: University of
          Texas Press.
Bunker, Stephen G.
   1985   *Underdeveloping the Amazon: Extraction, Unequal Exchange, and the
          Failure of the Modern State.* Chicago: University of Illinois Press.
Carvajal, Gaspar de
   1934   *The Discovery of the Amazon, According to the Account of Friar
          Gaspar de Carvajal and Other Documents,* comp. José Toribio
          Medina, ed. H. C. Heaton. Special publication, no. 17. New York:
          American Geographical Society.
Cochrane, T. T., and P. Sánchez.
   1982   "Land Resources, Soils, and Their Management in the Amazon
          Region." In S. Hecht, ed., *Amazonia: Agriculture and Land Use
          Research.* Cali, Colombia: CIAT.
Comstock, G., S. Chaffee, N. Katzman, M. McCombs, and D. Roberts
   1978   *Television and Human Behavior.* New York: Columbia University
          Press.
Coomes, Oliver, and Bradford Barham
   1994   "The Amazon Rubber Boom: Labor Control, Resistance, and Failed
          Plantation Development Revisited." *Hispanic American Historical
          Review,* vol. 74, no. 2: 231–257.
Cota, Raymond Garcia
   1984   *Carajás: A Invasão Desarmada.* Petrópolis, Brazil: Vozes.
Emmi, Marilia Ferreira
   1985   "Estrutura Fundiária e Poder Local: O Caso de Marabá." Master's the-
          sis, Núcleo de Alto Estudos Amazônicos, Universidade Federal do
          Pará, Belém, Brazil.
Fisk, Brian
   1985   "The Jarí Project: Labor Instability in the Brazilian Amazon." Master's
          thesis, University of Florida, Gainesville.
Fittkau, Ernst Josef
   1973   "Crocodiles and the Nutrient Metabolism of Amazonian Waters."
          Amazoniana, vol. 4 (March): 103–133.

Follmann, José Ivo
  1985   *Igreja, Ideologia, e Classes Sociais.* Petrópolis, Brazil: Vozes.
Foweraker, Joe
  1981   *The Struggle for Land: A Political Economy of the Pioneer Frontier in Brazil from 1930 to the Present Day.* New York: Cambridge University Press.
Galvão, Eduardo
  1955   *Santos e Visagens: Um Estudo da Vida Religiosa da Itá, Amazonas.* São Paulo: Campanhia Editôria Nacional.
Gerbner, George
  1967   "An Institutional Approach to Mass Communication Research." In L. Thayer, ed., *Communication: Theory and Research* (pp. 429–445). Springfield, IL: Charles C. Thomas Publisher.
Goulding, Michael
  1983   "Amazonian Fisheries." In Emilio Moran, ed., *The Dilemma of Amazonian Development* (pp. 189–210). Westview Press.
Hall, Anthony
  1989   *Developing Amazonia: Deforestation and Social Conflict in Brazil's Carajás Programme.* New York: Manchester University Press.
Hecht, Susanna
  1984   "Cattle Ranching in Amazônia: Political and Economic Considerations." In Marianne Schmink and Charles Wood, eds., *Frontier Expansion in Amazonia* (pp. 366–398). Gainesville: University of Florida Press.
  1983   "Cattle Ranching in the Eastern Amazon: Environmental and Social Implications." In Emilio Moran, ed., *The Dilemma of Amazonian Development* (pp. 155–188). Boulder, CO: Westview Press.
Hecht, Susanna, and Alexander Cockburn
  1990   *The Fate of the Forest: Developers, Destroyers, and Defenders of the Amazon.* New York: HarperCollins.
Hemming, John
  1978   *Red Gold: The Conquest of the Brazilian Indians.* Cambridge, MA: Harvard University Press.
Hemming, John, ed.
  1985   *Change in the Amazon Basin, Volume 2: The Frontier After a Decade of Colonisation.* Manchester, England: Manchester University Press.
Henfrey, Colin
  1986   "Peasant Brazil and Agrarian Reform: The Making of Another Country?" Paper presented at the Liverpool Workshop on Brazilian Agrarian Change, December 19–20, 1986.
Heriarte, Maurício de
  1874   *Descrição do Estado do Maranhão, Pará, Corupá e Rio das Amazonas.* Vienna: Imprensa do Filho de C. Gerold.
Hess, David
  1994   *Samba in the Night: Spiritism in Brazil.* New York: Columbia University Press.
Hewitt, W. E.
  1986   "Strategies for Social Change Employed by Comunidades Eclesiais de Base (CEBs) in the Archdiocese of São Paulo." *Journal for the Scientific Study of Religion,* vol. 25, no. 1: 16–30.
Ianni, Octávio
  1978   *A Luta Pela Terra: História Social da Terra e da Luta Pela Terra*

numa Área da Amazônia. Petrópolis, Brazil: Vozes.
1970   *Crisis in Brazil.* New York: Columbia University Press.
IBGE (Instituto Brasileiro de Geográfia e Estatística)
1981   *Sinopse Preliminar do Censo Demográfico e Agropecuária de 1980.* Vol. 1, no. 1. Rio de Janeiro: IBGE.
1967   *Censo Demográfico e Censo Econômico de 1960.* Vol. 1, no. 1. Rio de Janeiro: IBGE.
1956   *Censo Demográfico e Censo Econômico de 1950.* Vol. 10, nos. 1 and 2. Rio de Janeiro: IBGE.
1940   *Censo Demográfico e Censo Econômico de 1940.* Vol. 10, nos. 1 and 2. Rio de Janeiro: IBGE.
IDESP (Instituto do Desenvolvimento Econômico-Social do Pará)
1989   *Anuário Estatístico do Estado do Pará,* 1986/87. Vol. 9, nos. 1–2. Belém: IDESP.
INCRA (Instituto Nacional de Colonização e Reforma Agrária)
1985   "Sistema Nacional de Cadastro Rural Relação Para Prefeitura." Unpublished report on Gurupá.
Kelly, Arlene
1984   "Family, Church, and Crown: A Social and Demographic History of the Lower Xingu River Valley and the Municipality of Gurupá, 1623–1889." Ph.D. dissertation, University of Florida, Gainesville.
Kiemen, Mathias C.
1954   *The Indian Policy of Portugal in the Amazon Basin, 1614–1693.* Washington, DC: Catholic University Press.
Kottak, Conrad
1990   *Prime Time Society: An Anthropological Analysis of Television and Culture.* Belmont, CA: Wadsworth Publishing.
Lathrap, Donald
1974   "The Moist Tropics, the Arid Lands, and the Appearance of Great Art Styles in the New World." In M. E. King and I. Taylor, eds., *Art and Environment in Native America* (pp. 115–158). Special Publications of the Museum, no. 7. Lubbock: Texas Tech University.
1970   *The Upper Amazon.* New York: Praeger Publishers.
Leacock, Seth, and Ruth Leacock
1972   *Spirits of the Deep.* Garden City, NJ: Doubleday.
Levine, Daniel, and Scott Mainwaring
1989   "Religion and Popular Protest in Latin America: Contrasting Experiences." In Susan Eckstein, ed., *Power and Popular Protest: Latin American Social Movements* (pp. 203–240). Berkeley: University of California Press.
Lopes, D. F., M. Imazio da Silveira, and M. P. Magalhães
1989   "Current Research: Pará." *American Antiquity,* vol. 54, no. 1: 186.
Loureiro, V. R.
1985   *Os Parceiros do Mar.* Belém: CNPq/Museu Paraense Emílio Goeldi.
MacLachlan, Colin
1973   "The Indian Labor Structure in the Portuguese Amazon, 1700–1800." In D. Alden, ed., *The Colonial Roots of Modern Brazil* (pp. 112–145). Berkeley: University of California Press.
1972   "The Indian Directorate: Forced Acculturation in Portuguese America (1757–1799)." *Americas,* vol. 28:3 57–387.
Magee, Penny
1986   "Plants, Medicine, and Health Care in Amazônia: A Case Study of Itá."

Master's thesis, University of Florida, Gainesville.
Mahar, Dennis J.
1979   *Frontier Development Policy in Brazil: A Study of Amazonia.* New York: Praeger Publishers.
Marcus, George, and Michael Fischer
1986   *Anthropology as Cultural Critique.* Chicago: University of Chicago Press.
Martins, José de Souza
1990   "The Political Impasses of Rural Social Movements in Amazonia." In Goodman and Hall, eds., *The Future of Amazonia* (pp. 245–263). New York: St. Martin's Press.
1985   *A Militarização da Questão Agrária no Brasil.* Petrópolis, Brazil: Vozes.
McGrath, David, Fabio de Castro, Celia Futemma, Benedito Domingues de Amaral, and Juliana Calabria
1993   "Fisheries and the Evolution of Resource Management on the Lower Amazon Floodplain." *Human Ecology,* vol. 21, no. 2: 167–195.
Meggers, Betty J.
1971   *Amazonia: Man and Culture in a Counterfeit Paradise.* Chicago: Aldine.
Miller, Darrel L.
1976   "Itá in 1974." In Charles Wagley, *Amazon Town* (pp. 296–325). New York: Oxford University Press.
Miller, Kenton, and Laura Tangley
1991   *Trees of Life: Saving Tropical Forests and Their Biological Wealth.* Boston: Beacon.
Miranda, R., and C. A. M. Pereira
1983   *Televisão: O Nacional e o Popular na Cultura Brasileira.* São Paulo:
Moran, Emilio F.
1993   *Through Amazonian Eyes: The Human Ecology of Amazonian Populations.* Iowa City: University of Iowa Press.
1983   *The Dilemma of Amazonian Development.* Boulder, CO: Westview Press.
1981   *Developing the Amazon.* Bloomington: Indiana University Press.
Movimento Para Libertar os Padres da Amazônia
1981   Boletim 2, November, Belém.
Nash, June
1981   "Ethnographic Aspects of the World Capitalist System." *Annual Review of Anthropology,* vol. 10: 393–423.
Nugent, Stephen
1993   *Amazon Caboclo Society.* Providence, RI: Berg.
O'Donnell, Guillermo
1978   "Reflections on the Patterns of Change in the Bureaucratic-Authoritarian State." *Latin American Research Review,* vol. 13, no. 1: 3–39.
Oliveira, Adélia Engrácia de
1994   "The Evidence for the Nature of the Process of Indigenous Deculturation and Destabilization in the Brazilian Amazon in the Last Three Hundred Years." In Anna Roosevelt, ed., *Amazon Indians* (pp. 95–119). Tucson: University of Arizona Press.
1983   "Ocupação Humana." In Eneas Salati, Herbert Otto, Roger Shubart, Wolfgang Junk, Adélia Engrácia de Oliveira, eds., *Amazônia:*

Desenvolvimento Integração, Ecologia (pp. 144–327). São Paulo: Editora Brasiliensa.

Oliveira, Paulo H. B.
1991 "Ribeirinhos e Roçeiros: Subordinação e Resistência Camponesa em Gurupá, Pará." Master's thesis, University of São Paulo, Campinas, Brazil.

Pace, Richard
1993 "First-Time Televiewing in Amazônia: Television Acculturation in Gurupá, Brazil." *Ethnology,* vol. 32, no. 2: 187–205.
1992 "Social Conflict and Political Activism in the Brazilian Amazon." *American Ethnologist,* vol. 19, no. 4: 710–732.
1987 "Economic and Political Change in the Amazonian Community of Itá, Brazil." Ph.D. dissertation, University of Florida, Gainesville.

Pace, Richard, and Ricardo Santos
1988 "Analysis of Nutritional Levels Among Children in Gurupá." Unpublished paper.

Parker, Eugene
1981 "Cultural Ecology and Change: A Caboclo Várzea Community in the Brazilian Amazon." Ph.D. dissertation, University of Colorado, Boulder.

Parker, Eugene, ed.
1985 *The Amazon Caboclo: Historical and Contemporary Perspectives.* Studies in Third World Societies, no. 32. Williamsburg, VA: College of William & Mary.

Pinto, Lucio Flavio
1986 *Jarí: Toda a Verdade sobre o Projecto de Ludwig.* São Paulo: Editora Marco Zero.

Posey, Darrel, and William Baleé, eds.
1989 *Resource Management in Amazônia: Indigenous and Folk Strategies.* Advances in Economic Botany, vol. 7. New York: New York Botanical Garden.

Reis, Authur Cezar Ferreira
1974 "Economic History of the Brazilian Amazon." In Charles Wagley, ed., *Man in the Amazon.* Gainesville: University of Florida Press.

Roosevelt, Anna C.
1994 "Amazonian Anthropology: Strategy for a New Synthesis." In Anna C. Roosevelt, ed., *Amazon Indians* (pp. 1–29). Tucson: University of Arizona Press.
1991 *Moundbuilders of the Amazon: Geophysical Archaeology on Marajo Island, Brazil.* San Diego, CA: Academic Press.

Ross, Eric
1978 "The Evolution of the Amazon Peasantry." *Journal of Latin American Studies,* vol. 10: 193–218.

Salem, Helena
1981 "Dos Palácios a Miséria da Períferia." In Antônio Carlos Moura, Helena Salem, Luiz Carlos Antero, Luiz Maklouf, and Sergio Buarque de Gusmão, eds., *A Igreja dos Oprimidos* (pp. 17–64). São Paulo: Editôria Brasil Debates (Brasil/Hoje 3).

Sánchez, Pedro.
1981 "Soils of the Humid Tropics." *Studies in Third World Societies,* no. 14: 347–410.

Santos, Roberto
1984 "Law and Social Change: The Problem of Land in the Brazilian

Amazon." In Marianne Schmink and Charles Wood, eds., *Frontier Expansion in Amazônia* (pp. 439–462). Gainesville: University of Florida Press.

1980   *História da Amazônia (1800–1920).* São Paulo: TAO.

Sawyer, Donald R.
1979   "Peasants and Capitalism on an Amazon Frontier." Ph.D. dissertation, Harvard University, Cambridge, Massachusetts.

Schmink, Marianne
1982   "Land Conflicts in Amazonia." *American Ethnologist,* vol. 9 (May): 341–357.

Schmink, Marianne, and Charles Wood
1992   *Contested Frontiers in Amazonia.* New York: Columbia University Press.

Schmink, Marianne, and Charles Wood, eds.
1984   *Frontier Expansion in Amazônia.* Gainesville: University of Florida Press.

SESPA (Secretaria de Estado de Saúde Pública)
1990   Unpublished annual statistics for Pará. Belém: SESPA.
1985   Unpublished annual statistics for Pará. Belém: SESPA.

Shanklin, Eugenia
1994   *Anthropology & Race.* Belmont, CA: Wadsworth Publishing.

Sternberg, H.
1975   *Amazon River of Brazil.* New York: Springer Verlag.

Sweet, David
1974   "A Rich Realm of Nature Destroyed: The Middle Amazon, 1640–1750." Ph.D. dissertation, University of Wisconsin-Madison.

Velho, Otávio
1972   *Frentes de Expansão e Estrutura Agrária.* Rio de Janeiro: Zahar Editores.

Wagley, Charles
1976   *Amazon Town: A Study of Man in the Tropics.* ed. New York: Oxford University Press. Originally published in 1953; reprinted in 1968.

Weinstein, Barbara
1983   *The Amazon Rubber Boom, 1850–1920.* Stanford, CA: Stanford University Press.

Wesche, Rolf, and Thomas Bruneau
1990   *Integration and Change in Brazil's Middle Amazon.* Ottawa, Canada: University of Ottawa Press.

Wolf, Eric
1982   *Europe and the People Without History.* Berkeley: University of California Press.
1969   *Peasant Wars of the Twentieth Century.* New York: Harper & Row.

Wood, Charles, and Marianne Schmink
1979   "Blaming the Victim: Small Farmer Production in an Amazon Colonization Project." *Studies in Third World Societies,* no. 7: 77–93.

INDEX

ABOUT THE BOOK

Massive changes have engulfed the Brazilian Amazon region in the forty years since Charles Wagley's landmark study, *Amazon Town,* was first published. In his engaging restudy, Richard Pace explores today's "Amazon Town" (Gurupá), where development efforts have left little untouched, little familiar.

Focusing on the actions of the community as it faces new opportunities and recurring adversity, Pace examines the social and cultural history of Gurupá—including such factors as regional underdevelopment, environmental degradation, and social conflict—as well as the more recent effects of political mobilization and liberation theology on human rights awareness and social justice. He richly illustrates the political and economic forces—national and international—that affect Gurupá, and explores the motivations and means of those searching for alternatives to current patterns of development.

Richard B. Pace is assistant professor of Anthropology at Middle Tennessee State University.

981
Pac

Pace, Richard,
1956-

The struggle for
Amazon Town.

DATE			